INTRODUCTION TO REFERENCE WORK

VOLUME II *Reference Services and Reference Processes*

McGRAW-HILL SERIES IN LIBRARY EDUCATION
Jean Key Gates, Consulting Editor
University of South Florida

Boll INTRODUCTION TO CATALOGING, VOL. I:
DESCRIPTIVE CATALOGING
Boll INTRODUCTION TO CATALOGING, VOL. II:
ENTRY HEADINGS
Chan CATALOGING AND CLASSIFICATION:
AN INTRODUCTION
Gardner LIBRARY COLLECTIONS:
THEIR ORIGIN, SELECTION, AND DEVELOPMENT
Gates INTRODUCTION TO LIBRARIANSHIP
Jackson LIBRARIES AND LIBRARIANSHIP IN THE WEST:
A BRIEF HISTORY
Katz INTRODUCTION TO REFERENCE WORK, VOL. I:
BASIC INFORMATION SOURCES
Katz INTRODUCTION TO REFERENCE WORK, VOL. II:
REFERENCE SERVICES AND REFERENCE PROCESSES

INTRODUCTION

TO REFERENCE WORK

Volume II **Reference Services and Reference Processes**

Fourth Edition

William A. Katz

Professor, School of Library and Information Science
State University of New York at Albany

McGraw-Hill Book Company

New York   St. Louis   San Francisco   Auckland   Bogotá
Hamburg   Johannesburg   London   Madrid   Mexico
Montreal   New Delhi   Panama   Paris   São Paulo
Singapore   Sydney   Tokyo   Toronto

For Lou, Harriet, and Linda,
the noble three

INTRODUCTION TO REFERENCE WORK, Volume II
Reference Services and Reference Processes

Copyright © 1982, 1978, 1974, 1969 by McGraw-Hill, Inc. All rights reserved. Printed in the United States of America. Except as permitted under the United States Copyright Act of 1976, no part of this publication may be reproduced or distributed in any form or by any means, or stored in a data base or retrieval system, without the prior written permission of the publisher.

1 2 3 4 5 6 7 8 9 0   D O D O   8 9 8 7 6 5 4 3 2

ISBN 0-07-033334-3

This book was set in Baskerville by Black Dot, Inc. (ECU).
The editors were Marian D. Provenzano and Scott Amerman;
the production supervisor was Dominick Petrellese.
R. R. Donnelley & Sons Company was printer and binder.

Library of Congress Cataloging in Publication Data

Katz, William A., date
    Introduction to reference work.

    (McGraw-Hill series in library education)
    Includes bibliographies and index.
    Contents: v. 1. Basic information sources—
v. 2 Reference services and reference processes.
    1. Reference services (Libraries)   2. Reference
books.   I. Title.   II. Series.
Z711.K32   1982   025.5'2   81-12432
ISBN 0-07-033333-5 (v. 1)   AACR2
ISBN 0-07-033334-3 (v. 2)

CONTENTS

PART IV EVALUATION OF REFERENCE

SERVICES

PREFACE

The purpose of this second volume is to give the reader an overview, or a broader understanding, of the possibilities of reference service. An effort is made to introduce the sophisticated, imaginative, and, I believe, really more interesting aspects of the reference process.

There are some major departures here from the third edition. The introductory chapter on the community has been shortened. The writer must apologize for not including all members of the community in this section, but space simply does not allow for the consideration of the vast numbers and types of audiences now in need of additional, not less, library service. The suggested reading section at the end of the chapter may at least point up the importance of this area and what other material is available.

The "interview and search" section (Part II) is closer to what was found in the third edition than any other part of this revised text. Still, even here there have been necessary cuts and additions. And this points up another aspect of the text: one need not read each chapter consecutively. For example, having considered the interview and search section, some readers may want to skip to the chapter on the on-line search, a chapter which considers many of the same problems, but in the context of the computer.

The most obvious departure from the third edition is found in the emphasis here on the place of online reference services. In addition to the introductory chapter, there is a more detailed chapter on bibliographic data bases. Here basic individual sources are treated separately, in the same fashion as printed works are treated in the first volume.

In discussion of the individual data bases, an effort has been made to avoid the usual emphasis on scientific sources. More space has been given to general and ready-reference works, as well as to those likely to be used in the social sciences and the humanities. This is done not to downgrade scientific sources, only to redress a lack of balance. It is the conviction of this writer, and of many experts in the field, that in the next decade the social sciences and the humanities will become increasingly important as bibliographic data bases.

Beyond this chapter there is increased emphasis on the general methods employed in searching data bases. Here "general" must be stressed because it is not the scope and purpose of this text to give detailed instruction on how to use individual data bases. Still, an effort is made to establish the general rules and principles which beginners should appreciate before taking up specific search patterns for particular systems and data bases.

Networks, and their increasing importance as the major link in on-line reference service, are given a separate chapter, which provides much more detail than in the previous edition. Also, interlibrary loan and document delivery are considered in greater depth.

The economics of the online search is given much more space than before, and the reader is asked to consider a major question: Who pays for what? The problem of fees for computer-aided reference service is one of the primary ethical questions of the decade. By implication the fee situation may change the traditional role of the library in society.

In other chapters current problems are considered in more detail than previous editions. There has been a cutback in the treatment of communications—in fact, the material is now treated as part of another chapter rather than standing alone. This revision was done at the suggestion of several teachers.

The final chapter concerns basic methods of evaluating the reference collection and reference services. Parenthetically, evaluation is a major concern of both volumes of this text, and almost every chapter has some material on evaluation of particular types of reference sources.

As in the first volume, an effort has been made to list current sources (i.e., 1979 and later) in the footnotes and in the suggested readings section. Often some excellent material is mentioned in the footnotes but not repeated in the suggested readings in order to avoid citation duplication.

I wish to conclude by expressing thanks to all those students, teachers, and librarians who made so many helpful suggestions for the improvement of this work. I again am particularly grateful to Sara D. Knapp, the skillful and intelligent librarian in charge of computer searches at the library of the State University of New York at Albany. Ms. Knapp not only read the chapters on online reference service, but made numerous suggestions which have considerably improved the section.

William A. Katz

INFORMATION AND
THE COMMUNITY

PART

I

CHAPTER ONE

Reference Service
and the Community

T HE LIBRARY is an institution obedient to the attitudes
and the whims of the community it serves. Librarians
may formulate long-range policy and make daily
decisions about service, but ultimately they must
answer to those served—or not served.

Today librarians face economic and technologi-
cal pressures which are rapidly changing many concepts of reference
service. Public libraries must consider whether to continue to try to
reach out to serve nonusers or to concentrate on serving the small,
but active, user group. Academic libraries are faced with serious
problems of rising costs for reference service and shrinking enroll-
ments and budgets. School librarians may have to decide whether
they should even try to serve reluctant students. The special libraries
appear to be in an easier position than others, although they also face
budget and technological problems.[1]

Community attitudes tend to be favorable to the idea and the
existence of the library, yet they are far from supportive of the
financial needs of the institution. Individuals who believe in free

[1]*The National Inventory of Library Needs* (Washington, D.C.: National Commission on
Libraries and Information Science, 1977). Here it is reported that in 1975 "libraries in
the United States were grossly underfunded" and that about $5 to $6 billion a year
more was needed, as well as about $12 billion for one-time catch-up expenditures. Now
several years old, the report's findings today would be even more negative, estimates of
needed funding even higher.

education and library service may still vote against state or federal measures to finance those services. The same Americans who vote down funding for libraries and education in general are often enraged when the local library suffers. *That* library deserves support. It's just the *others* that are wasting money.[2]

The information literates

The trend in library services for the last decade or so has been to give most reference service to those users whose education and background lead them to value information. As a group these people are sometimes called the "information literates," and they inevitably compose the professional strata of the middle and upper-middle classes.[3]

When one speaks of serving this group, it is usually in terms of supplying information for the persons who operate within the academic, business, scientific, government, or technological environment.

At the other extreme are the non-library users, those who, in fact, may be most in need of information, but who rarely, if ever, turn to the library. The failure of this group to make use of library services reinforces the notion that library audiences are generally limited to the more affluent and educated groups.

There are major disparities between socioeconomic groups, disparities reflected in library use. Some critics see it as an inevitable circle: education and economic security lead to exposure to information, which in turn leads to increased knowledge about self and the community. The poor and undereducated rely on interpersonal communication and organization, usually outside formal channels. If librarians are to reach these people, they must understand the methods of communications and the limited information universe of the information illiterates, who number in the many millions.

Conversely, the number of information literates may be no more than two or three million, less than one or two percent of the adult population. Probably this ratio is true not only for the population at large, but holds within the scientific, technical, and business sector as well. And the ratio seems to remain fairly stable.

Librarians are concerned with striking a balance between meet-

[2]Noel Savage, "News Report 1979," *Library Journal,* January 15, 1980, pp. 168+. Here Savage gives several examples of communities which cut aid to libraries. On the other hand, Savage notes: "Community support has in many other cases given libraries the muscle to fight off assaults on their budgets" (p. 170).

[3]Charles R. McLure, "The Information Rich Employee . . . ," *Information Processing and Management,* No. 6, 1978, pp. 381–394. An analysis of the "information literates."

ing the needs of the information literates and reaching out to the rest of the public who do not, or cannot, use a library. Librarians recognize a need as well to reach others who use the library only from time to time. As one observer puts it, "As far as information technology is concerned, the entire public is a disadvantaged group."[4] Information and Referral Services (I&R) offer one approach to balancing needs and serving more people.

INFORMATION AND REFERRAL SERVICES (I&R)[5]

Information and referral services take many forms and have numerous names—information counseling, community information, operation outreach, learning service, etc. The primary purpose of I&R centers is to bring reference services to people where they work and where they live. Information and referral service is an effort by the library to reach out to both users and nonusers rather than expecting the public to "reach out" to the library. As Jones observes:

> Perhaps we have grown too cynical to speak of libraries in terms of "irresistible" or "compelling" except when referring to confirmed readers (certainly mystery fans qualify). On the other hand, it is not ludicrous to speak of offering something at the "gut level," help that reaches people where they are. Information and referral service in public libraries merits serious consideration as a major additional tool to help people in their everyday lives. In the evolution of library practice it has emerged as a logical response to a demonstrated need.[6]

The information center adapts the library to the needs of people, instead of asking them (as was the case too often in the past) to adapt to the needs of the library and the librarian. Centers are located in urban districts previously without library service and often where the nonlibrary users are unable to reach a larger library. Hence, convenience of location is provided in the atmosphere of the area familiar to the nonuser. In cities with extensive branch libraries, information centers often operate within the libraries, as an extension of the reference function, but with special personnel and services.

[4]Colin Mick, "Specialization, Information Technology and Libraries," *The Catholic Library World,* July/August 1977, p. 25.

[5]For a listing of such services see: *Directory of Outreach Services in Public Libraries* (Chicago: American Library Association, 1980). There are many books and hundreds of articles on this subject. One of the best books: Clara S. Jones, *Public Library Information and Referral Service* (Syracuse, N.Y.: Gaylord Brothers, 1978).

[6]Clara S. Jones, "The Urban Public Library: Proving Utility," *Library Journal,* January 1, 1976, p. 84.

Types of questions and answers

I&R services might be called upon to answer such typical questions as: "I am in need of some help with my landlord, who has increased the rent beyond what I can pay. Where do I go, whom do I see?" "Where can I find information on a senior citizens' home?" "Do you have anything or anyone who can explain the raise in my taxes?" "My social security check has not arrived. Whom do I contact?" "Where can I find a speaker on gardens to talk to my group?"

Answers to the questions may be found by using regular reference sources or, more likely, by using library files of names of people and organizations to whom the librarian or the questioner may turn for information.

Even at the less personal level, the need for information is "problem-oriented." The majority of people seek data in hope of finding answers, if only partial ones, to such concerns as air pollution, energy conservation, production problems, public health matters, etc.[7]

The purpose of these I&R centers is twofold: (1) to provide current information and data on local community services, and (2) to maintain a constantly updated file of names and organizations to which a person may turn for specific information about a special or a community problem. Since the material tends to be local, and since it must be updated frequently, it is usually not available in printed form, but is maintained as a file by the librarian. The file may be in a form as simple as a card index or as complex as a computer data base.[8]

In actual practice much I&R service is limited to standard reference work, although, to be sure, it is at a level which does meet individual need. The "referral" aspect is only infrequently used by librarians.

Specifically, Childers found that 68 percent of the public libraries with I&R service provide "the inquirer with the asked-for information on outside resources, such as phone numbers, addresses, contact persons, etc., without further probing." This is really little more than ready-reference work and is closely related to such existing reference services as providing information from a telephone book or city directory. Childers also found that a more complex type of reference search is done by slightly more than one-half (54 percent)

---

[7]"Studies Probe Information Systems," *American Libraries,* May 1979, p. 251.

[8]Detailed information on the type of material in such a file and how it is collected will be found in numerous sources. See Jones, op. cit., and Catherine McKinnon, "Developing an Information Service," *Ontario Library Review,* September 1978, pp. 210–215.

of the libraries queried. Here the same information as described above is requested, but some time is spent in trying to find out precisely what is needed. Some 43 percent of the libraries in Childers' study "construct a file or directory of outside resources and make it available for the inquirer to consult." However, Childers reports that of all the libraries in the study, only 13 percent "provide a bona fide I&R service in that they actively help the client make contact with an outside resource by making an appointment, calling an agency, etc."[9]

This wide failure of librarians to accept the referral role may be explained in terms of advocacy. In referral, and in follow-through, which is implied in referral cases, the reference librarian assumes an advocate role rather than serving merely as a passive source of information. A number of librarians feel somewhat uncomfortable in the advocate role, particularly those librarians trained to be "objective" in all aspects of their work.

In some libraries the narrow line between regular reference questions and I&R queries makes it difficult to determine who is in charge of what. The result may be conflict between the I&R staff and the regular reference staff. Since the I&R center does not operate in a vacuum, but draws upon the regular reference services, any conflict or ill-feeling between the two staffs can present problems.

ADULT SERVICES

Information and referral service is one method of providing services to the adult community. However, there are other approaches. One such approach is "adult services." As with many library operations, the term "adult services" has numerous definitions and interpretations. Generally it has come to be applied to those services which give special attention to the disadvantaged, the illiterate, the aged, the various ethnic minority groups, and any other groups of people requiring special attention.[10] Adult services, together with I&R, con-

[9]Thomas Childers, "Trends in Public Library I&R Services," *Library Journal*, October 1, 1979, pp. 2036–2037. This is an excellent overview and a fine summary. See also Childers' "Profiles of Public Library I&R," p. 2038, where he outlines moderate and maximum services.

[10]Joyce Wente, "What Are Adult Services?" *RQ*, Spring 1979, p. 231. Most of this issue is given over to articles on the subject and it is a good beginning point for anyone interested in a modern interpretation and discussion of adult services. Space here does not permit treatment of all groups, e.g., service to women, service to labor, but see *Directory of Outreach Services* (Chicago: American Library Association, 1980).

stitute a trend moving libraries toward a dynamic and useful place in the community.

What follows is an abbreviated look at a few of the more reference-oriented adult services.

Adult education

Estimates vary, but a conservative judgment is that about 50 percent of the adult American population borders on being illiterate.[11] This is an astonishing figure, and one which has been a constant challenge to librarians.

While I&R represents one effort to reach many of the functionally illiterate, libraries today are also carrying on active literary training programs.[12] In that the reference librarians are invariably called upon for resources and materials for such programs, they are directly involved with the services offered in adult literary training.

The adult independent-learner program in the past few years has assumed increasing importance to universities and colleges seeking to boost enrollment. While the learner's program is supervised by an academic, the student may use either the public library or the college library for necessary materials.

Ethnic groups[13]

There are various ways of designating the groups which are composed of other than the white, middle-class, "average" users of the library. The descriptors of these groups vary because it is impossible, and unwise, to lump all of them under a single name. However they are called, they very likely represent nonusers of library services.

Primarily, there are two large groups in the category of "the

[11]*Adult Illiteracy in the United States* (New York: The Ford Foundation, 1979).

[12]The American Library Association, particularly active in literacy programs, regards the problem as a major consideration of all libraries. For an overview see Helen Lyman, *Literacy and the Nation's Libraries* (Chicago: American Library Association, 1977). The work lists "sample programs, funding sources, and kinds of materials needed for the library's literacy collection." See, too: Henry Drennan, "Libraries and Literacy Education," *Catholic Library World*, April 1981, pp. 376+.

[13]*Ethnic Groups in American Life* (New York: Arno Press, 1978) begins with a brief historical survey. This is substantially a reprint of articles from *The New York Times*. There are numerous useful articles for reference librarians, e.g., Michael Gonzalez et al., "Assessing the Library Needs of the Spanish-Speaking," *Library Journal*, April 1, 1980, pp. 786–788; David Cohen, "Ethnicity in Librarianship . . ." *Catholic Library World*, March 1980, pp. 342–346.

disadvantaged." The first is composed of the educationally disadvantaged. The second, which may be a part of the first, comprises the ethnic minorities: black, Mexican-Americans, American Indians, Asian-Americans, etc. While not all members of the minority groups are underprivileged, their numbers are sufficient to identify them with the larger, deprived group. In any case, and whatever the descriptor, the disadvantaged include both adults and youngsters, both city and country dwellers.

In providing reference service to ethnic minorities there are several factors to be considered: (1) Foreign language materials, particularly the basic reference works, e.g., encyclopedias, dictionaries, geographical sources, etc., should be part of acquisitions whenever possible. (2) Members of the reference staff should be familiar with the language(s) of the ethnic groups. (3) Community information files should be tailored for the needs of these groups. (4) Maximum effort should be made to reach these groups through I&R centers, publicity, etc. The use of television and radio and door-to-door canvassing are effective tools here.

The handicapped

Many people have limited access to library services, largely because they are "invisible," either in institutions or at home, and because they are unable to make their needs known. These are the physically and mentally handicapped.

Renewed interest in and financial aid for the disabled and the handicapped, who are estimated to number over 38 million in the United States, has brought increased interest in providing library services for this large portion of the American population. Actually, the libraries' involvement is many decades old, but until the federal government made funds available, much of the work, particularly in public libraries, had to be carried on with a minimal budget. Funds are still limited, but available monies are increasing.

Some of the services which the library might offer the handicapped include: a referral center for volunteer reader services; a space set aside where impaired patrons can work with librarians; and specialized materials and equipment. A recent study offered advice applicable to reference librarians: "Sensitivity and training programs should be undertaken for library employees and patrons. Regular and special services (e.g., homebound, bookmobile, etc.) should be expanded to include disabled people. Qualified disabled people should be used as advisors for the programs. Information about programs should be distributed through conventional as well as unconventional means such as TTY's, braille, interpreters for the hearing-impaired."[14]

STUDENTS

In almost any type of library the student population constitutes from 50 to 80 percent of the users. The attitude of reference librarians toward students is mixed. While most are anxious to help, others look upon the young people as a headache, or at best a group to put up with, and tend to treat their questions in a perfunctory manner: "Look in the index, . . . the card catalog, . . . the encyclopedia, . . . etc."

The various attitudes support a paradox: While the reference librarians feel the pressure of students' demands, the students are less than sure that the reference librarian is the beginning and end of assistance. Still, librarians are not entirely at fault. One suspects that students' attitudes reflect a failure to either appreciate or understand the importance of information in their daily lives.

Despite this dreary situation, reference librarians today are making a gallant effort to find new ways to make the library a place for students. The methods extend from elaborate user-education programs to a one-to-one effort to encourage and welcome the student's questions.[15]

SUGGESTED READING

Boss, Richard W., and Lorig Maranjian, *Fee-Based Information Services.* New York: R. R. Bowker Company, 1980. Written for the person who wants to begin an information broker business, this text includes basic data on reference work. For the average reader it offers a discussion of marketing strategies and profiles of major companies in the area.

Davis, Emmett, and Catherine Davis, *Mainstreaming: Library Service for Disabled People.* Metuchen, New Jersey: Scarecrow Press, 1980. A manual on various methods of helping the disabled in the average library; suggested sources of materials are included.

[14]"Special Services for Special People. . . .," *Minnesota Libraries,* Winter 1978/1979, p. 374. A basic guide in this area is Ruth Velleman's *Serving Physically Disabled People* (New York: R. R. Bowker, 1979). See, too: *Drexel Library Quarterly,* April 1980. The complete issue is devoted to "Information Services to Disabled Individuals."

[15]For a more detailed discussion of students and user education, see the section "Levels of Reference Service" in Chapter 3.

Espar, Sadie, "Building and Maintaining the Community Resources File for I&R Services," *Collection Building,* No. 1, 1978, pp. 7–18. This article presents a step-by-step approach, complete with forms, for building necessary files for I&R service.

"Information Seeking Patterns of Selected Professionals," *Public Library Quarterly,* Spring, 1980, pp. 27–48. A series of short articles on how various members of the community, from the lawyer to the electrician, use various reference and information services offered by the public library.

Lederman, Linda, "Fear of Talking: Which Students in the Academic Library Ask Librarians for Help?" *RQ,* Summer, 1981, pp. 382–393. While this is concerned with user education, it is more a study of what type of students are likely to use the resources available at the reference desk. Much of the material would be applicable in school and public libraries.

Mershon, Loretta, "A Model Automated Resource File for an Information and Referral Center," *Special Libraries,* August 1980, pp. 335–344. The author treats problems found in building an I&R file and suggests solutions. Various topics and areas are considered; of particular interest is the treatment of the question of subject headings.

Monroe, Margaret, and Kathleen M. Heim (eds.), "Emerging Patterns of Community Service," *Library Trends,* Fall 1979. This issue includes an introduction and nine detailed articles on serving various elements in the community. It is unusual for attention given to concerns with finance and administration. Margaret Monroe's and Kathleen Heim's independent introductions are particularly valuable for an overview of the topic.

Penland, Patric, *The Library As a Learning Center.* New York: Marcel Dekker, Inc., 1978. This is a discussion of adult learning, the public library, and the training of consultants. It should be of some assistance for those involved with adult education and I&R services.

Robertson, W. D., "A User-Oriented Approach to Setting Priorities for Library Services," *Special Libraries,* August 1980, pp. 345–353. This study matches the needs as they are expressed by users with those same user needs as they are seen by librarians. The model is useful for evaluating similar user needs in other types of libraries.

Schiller, Anita, "Shifting Boundaries in Information," *Library Journal,* April 1, 1981, pp. 705–709. An objective look at what the introduction of online databases, fees and specialized services is likely to mean to the future of reference and information services in American libraries. The author is not always pleased with what she sees in the future.

Vavrek, Bernard, "Information Services and the Rural Library," *Library Trends,* Spring 1980, pp. 563–578. "After some thirty years of neglect, American librarianship is discovering that not everyone lives in the city." And with that opening sentence, the author begins to explore the information needs of people living outside urban areas. He is the founder of *Rural Libraries,* a journal which began publishing in 1980 and is dedicated to the audience suggested in the title.

CHAPTER TWO

Information,
Communication,
and Reference Service

 I T IS ALMOST A CLICHÉ that this is the age of informa-
tion. It is estimated that by 1985 the total American
expenditure for scientific and technical communication alone will be about 6 percent of the gross
national product.[1] Some even claim that the "handling and communication of information is the most
important economic activity of the U.S. work force."[2] In a special issue
of *Library Journal*, editor John Berry comments:

> *Suddenly the stakes in America's information future are rising as fast as
> the price of Arabian crude oil. . . . Suddenly it is urgent that we have a
> national information policy . . .*[3]

There are almost as many reasons for the new interest in
information as there are commentators, but it is a byproduct more of
a new technology than of a new intellectual involvement. Communi-

---

[1]Martha Williams, "Online Retrieval—Today and Tomorrow," *Online Review,* December
1978, p. 354.

[2]Vincent E. Giuliano, "A Manifesto for Librarians," *Library Journal,* September 15,
1979, p. 1838.

[3]John Berry, "Information Ideology," *Library Journal,* September 15, 1979, p. 1731.
This complete issue of 150 pages is devoted exclusively to 18 articles on "Information in
America" and is a basic guide to the present state of affairs in reference and
information services. Also, it serves as an introduction to the much-discussed White
House Conference on Library and Information Services of November 1979.

cation with the whole world is now available in almost anyone's living room. Rapid transportation brings the world even closer and, whether by choice or by necessity, depleted resources and new centers of power link us all.

Still, information was around in one form or another for a good many years before the sudden recognition of its national and international importance. The new interest indicates several developments. First, thanks to computers and data bases it is now possible to make information commercially viable. Not only can it be produced in different formats, but it can be sold to individuals, government, and business like any other commodity. Second, as a product, information must be more accessible, and this requires sophisticated channels of communication, including national and international networks of information. Third, given this new dimension to information, there is a need for a new type of librarian or information manager who is able to secure, process, and make available data for a specialized audience.

In all of the justified excitement over new technology and new methods of assembling data for retrieval, there is little enough attention paid to the basic communication patterns of librarians and of those who use (or do not use) the library. The communication of information is a highly specialized field, and it is important to consider for a moment the communication system involved in an information-seeking situation.

COMMUNICATION PATTERNS

The communication process may be divided into given elements or constants:

1. The communicator or transmitter, i.e., the speaker, writer, artist, etc.
2. The message, or what the communicator delivers. For most library purposes the message is generally known as information.
3. The method of transmission, or the medium. The communicator may deliver the message in the form of book, journal article, dialogue, radio speech, film, etc.
   a. Here the information community, including publishers, producers, indexers, etc., enters in.
   b. Through the medium, the message is processed and recorded on any device from a printed page to a computer disk.

    c. The library then classifies and stores the message in the form given by the processors.

    d. In most reference service, the transmission of the message usually implies an intermediate agent, i.e., the librarian, who may assist in the transmission of the message by clarifying what type of information or communicator is needed, by searching the various methods of transmission, etc.

4. The receiver, i.e., the listener, reader, observer, or anyone who receives the message originated by the communicator or transmitter and sent via one of the numerous channels.

Foskett summarizes communication as "a psychosocial linguistic act or performance, in which a system of thought formed in the mind of one human being is transferred and assimilated into the mind of another. . . . A basic factor in the process of assimilation . . . is recognition."[4] For example, a complicated message using mathematical terms will mean little to a person who has no mathematical training, and the simplest Chinese expression will mean even less to a person who understands only English. To make assimilation possible, the information package must be not only presented clearly but presented in a form which the receiver will recognize.

Commonsense rules of communication can be formulated through everyday encounters. Several general principles are outlined here. First, whether the information is written down or given orally, "it is essential the sender is familiar with the subject and is prepared to answer questions."[5] Second, as noted above, the message should be clear and need no translating to be understood. Finally, to quote DeSomogyi, "The sender should make sure recipients have thoroughly grasped the message."[6]

Vavrek, a constant writer on the subject of reference librarians and communications, summarizes all of this in terms of the library environment.

> *If one were to reduce reference service to its basic elements, one would probably agree that it includes the library inquirer, the inquiry itself, and the reference librarian. To be sure these ingredients cannot operate*

[4]D. J. Foskett, "Theory and Practice in the Presentation of Information," *International Forum on Information and Documentation,* vol. 1, no. 1, 1975, p. 6.

[5]Aileen DeSomogyi, "Communication," *Canadian Library Journal,* February 1975, pp. 41–42. The article neatly categorizes the commonsense rules for successful communication.

[6]Ibid.

without an informational environment, the library, but information retrieval is a product of the interaction of the inquirer, inquiry, and librarian, not a prerequisite to their interrelationship.[7]

Communication is directed and modified by variables such as personality, education, social background, and national origin. These countless factors create a pluralism that can lead to a lack of communication, in spite of logical rules. For example, an individual may have all the data necessary to make X decision—the correct one—but, for personal reasons, makes Y decision—the wrong one. Perfect information does not make for perfect understanding or correct decisions.

It is not clear how one can scientifically describe the decision-making process.[8] It has been suggested that people tend to make wrong decisions because much of the information they receive is not understood. Any librarian who has laboriously sought out articles and books for a student, only to discover later that the material was much too advanced for the user, will certainly appreciate that suggestion.

User studies[9]

A user study is an analysis of the behavior of users (and nonusers) of information in their relationships with libraries (or information systems) and services. There have been countless studies made of various types of users and libraries, studies which are valuable in understanding how information is matched with the needs of the individual.

Several generalities have emerged from these works, and some of them are outlined here.

(1) People have different patterns of behavior when they are seeking information, at least information other than the ready-reference variety. While libraries may separate information into the classical divisions, such as the humanities and science, and their subdivisions, people do not always seek information within those specific, logical areas.

For example, the typical library is organized along subject or divisional lines. This does not mean someone in need of information

[7]Bernard Vavrek, "The Nature of Reference Librarianship," *RQ,* Spring 1974, p. 214.

[8]James D. Halloran, "Information and Communication," *Aslib Proceedings,* January 1979, pp. 21–28. This is a good discussion of failures in communication.

[9]Michael E. Roloff, "Communication at the User-System Interface: A Review of Research," *Library Research,* no. 1, 1979, pp. 1–18. The survey covers studies done primarily since 1970. It is updated from time to time in the same journal.

on Chinese pottery will necessarily confine the search to the area of art. The user may not even begin the search there but may start with the history or the science section.

(2) The average user does not contact the reference librarian. Users may talk to student assistants, other nonprofessionals, and professional librarians. Any member of the library staff may become involved with the communication process. The overall impression of the library will be one made through an encounter with any of the staff, none of whom may be directly involved with reference service, but all of whom, incidentally, the average person considers librarians. This easy confusion has numerous ramifications, and there is no better reason for properly trained staff at all levels. Signs indicating where to get the right type of help and an understanding among staff about directing an individual to a reference librarian are helpful in improving information communication.

(3) Despite the mass of material on communication and information, there is still too little known of these specialized fields. In fact, it is almost impossible even to define information.

Information is not the proprietary bailiwick of any one profession. The structure of the information world is constantly changing and there is an overall lack of comprehension of the whole scope of the so-called information world. Where does the subject begin and end? How do we talk about it? Who's involved? After all, everyone is a user of information and just about everyone provides it in one form or another.[10]

(4) The average person copes with the masses of information from radio, television, newspapers, and magazines in a simple fashion. Most often, it is neither heard, nor viewed, nor read—it is ignored. When information is "received," the receiver may:

a. Accept it, that is, use it as a means of reinforcing existing opinion or reject it because it challenges existing opinion. A characteristic verbal response would be "I know that," or else, "I don't know that."

b. Add it to memory without allowing it to make any real impression. Verbally the response would be "Yes," or "Oh, I see," or, simply, "O. K., I understand."

[10]Alice S. Warner, "Bridging the Information Flow," *Library Journal*, September 15, 1979, p. 1794. Other experts have the same definition problems. The term tends to be overused and easily loses precision and useful meaning. For a definition see J. Farradane, "The Nature of Information," *Journal of Information Science*, no. 1, 1979, pp. 13–17. He defines it as "any physical form of representation, or surrogate, of knowledge, or of a particular thought, used for communication."

c. Use it to answer a latent question, i.e., "the information may be pictured as connecting two previously isolated elements of knowledge." Here one would say, "Oh, that explains things."

d. Or in some cases, accept the new information and use it to transform an opinion or an idea. Verbally it would be expressed: "That does change matters," or "That alters my position."[11]

(5) Certain information may be graded in terms of potential value to certain users, but because there are so many relationships between information sources, there is no valid way to determine what is or is not valuable for all people at all times and in all places. For example, a finding in an otherwise undistinguished article may trip the thought processes of one researcher in such a way that she is led into a completely new approach to a problem. As Swanson puts it:

> *The number of potential relationships among the pieces grows at a much faster rate than the number of pieces. Though we do not have any way to know just how the number of meaningful or useful relationships is growing, my argument at least suggests that the growing total quantity of recorded information poses a special kind of threat to the future growth of knowledge that may be disproportionate to the increase itself.*[12]

(6) The successful decision makers are those who are able to acquire and process information quickly, no matter what type of situation they happen to be in. Such people are able to evaluate a morass of data and add or discard quickly, concentrating only on what is needed.

INFORMATION PACKAGES

The steps in the creation and packaging of information may be traced in various ways. While not everyone will agree with this or that analysis, a general overview of the different communication packages is possible. There are three phases which lead from the inception of the idea to its eventual publication in some traditional reference form such as a book or periodical article. These phases are (1) the origin of the message, (2) the informal communication of the message, and (3) the formal communication of the message.

[11]J. Farradane, "The Nature of Information," *Journal of Information Science*, no. 1, 1979, p. 15.
[12]Don Swanson, "Libraries and the Growth of Knowledge," *The Library Quarterly*, January 1979, p. 15.

Phase 1—Origin of the message

The message originates when the individual author begins to think about his or her next novel and to put some of it on paper. Or it can originate when the inventor developing a better mousetrap is working on the project with six other mousetrap experts. Each is thinking, exploring, and experimenting, but none has yet arrived at any conclusive way to catch the mouse.

In more explicit terms, Garvey and Gottfredson summarizes the beginning stages of scientific research, or the origin of the message:

> *(1) Preliminary planning (general), (2) Specific planning: theoretical/ conceptual, (3) Preparation of written proposal, (4) Preliminary experimentation/field trials or mock-ups, (5) Calibration, pretesting, etc., (6) Design and development of equipment/apparatus, (7) Formulation of experimental study design, (8) Collection of data, (9) Analysis of data, (10) Interpretation of results, and (11) Preparation of report of work.*[13]

The same process goes on when one undertakes the common task of writing a paper for a class. First there has to be an idea for the paper, even if only a suggestion from a teacher, a friend, reading, television, etc. The "idea generation" may be the most difficult phase, although the consequent efficient solving of the problem posed by the idea offers another major challenge—deciding how the idea is to be implemented by research and eventually modified for the purposes of the paper. Still, those who have struggled with the innovative process itself recognize the difficulty of phase 1 of the communication process.

Phase 2—Informal communication

Once the message is conceived, how is it passed on? Librarians are familiar with the formal method of communication, the translation into the printed word. They are equally familiar with informal channels, but, as will be shown, rarely use them in reference situations. Informal communication is what Finniston is talking about when he comments on the "unformalized value of conversations."

> *Such information conversations (a form of gossip mongering called the grapevine) are uncritical (the loose expression in speech would never be*

[13]W. D. Garvey and S. D. Gottfredson, "Changing the System: Innovations in the Interactive Social System of Scientific Communication," *Information Processing and Management*, vol. 12, no. 3, 1976, p. 166.

accepted on paper), liable to misinterpretation and misrepresentation, repetition and uncodified—all the worst characteristics of good information service—and yet how many good ideas and innovations have stemmed consciously or subconsciously from such a service. How often has it been said that the value of a conference is not the programme itself but people one meets.[14]

The information in phase 2 of the communications chain may be labeled in many ways, but essentially it is the familiar "inside information," or "inside dope." Knowledge of this information may give the receiver a certain status because of knowing something few others know, or it may help the receiver in an instrumental way by adding evidence for a decision—a decision on whether to go ahead on this or that experiment, business deal, or research project or a decision in terms of how to modify this or that. The content of the informal message varies, but the transmission process is somewhat the same in all disciplines:

1. Informal channels of transmission
   a. Face-to-face discussion with colleagues and those interested in the project
   b. Discussion via the telephone or private correspondence
   c. Drafts of manuscripts which may be circulated among friends and colleagues
   d. Discussion at meetings and seminars
2. Semiformal channels of transmission
   a. Works in progress. If this channel is open, the communicator will often report to it the current status of the project. In the case of the author this may be totally informal and picked up in a variety of sources, from *Publishers Weekly* to *The New York Review of Books;* i.e., a note may appear to the effect that Y author's next novel is just about finished. In the case of the mousetrap consortium, there may be a formal outlet such as a series in a journal which reports works underway by X and Y scientists.
   b. Semipublished studies. If one accepts "semipublished" in the sense that the work has not been offered for general circulation but is in a printed form, then this includes mimeographed copies of the speech the head mousetrap inventor gave at a conference or meeting, a completed report or summary of the study, the corrected, or even

---

[14]Sir Montague Finniston, "Information Communication and Management, *Aslib Proceedings,* August 1975, pp. 349–350.

corrected and edited, manuscript of the author, and in some cases, preprints (i.e., articles which are to appear in Y journal and are circulated beforehand by the author). In this group, some would also include theses and dissertations.

What is peculiar about both the informal and semiformal channels of transmission indicated here is that generally the information packages are not available to libraries. "Generally" is used advisedly because efforts are now being made to make many of these relatively inaccessible forms part of the reference process. For example, the alert reference librarian may tap into the semiformal levels of transmission when those are committed in some form to print—works in progress are often parts of journals and books; reports which are unclassified or not private are now better indexed and abstracted and many are available to librarians; dissertations are generally available via well-organized indexing.

However, this only skims the surface, tapping only the obvious aspects of the semiformal channels of communication. Much more is needed in terms of bibliographic control of traditional print or nonprint materials. The advent of data bases, the computer and sophisticated networks, may make this possible in the decade ahead.

Phase 3—Formal communication of the message

Time passes and the communication chain is completed. In terms of our model, this means the communicator's message has been codified, having been transmitted formally in a format which may range from a periodical article to a book. The time from gestation of an idea until publication of a report or journal article varies with individuals and disciplines. However, in most disciplines this is usually two to three or more years.

It is generally only when the chain is complete that the reference library comes on the scene by (1) acquiring and organizing the message in whatever form it may take; (2) acquiring the necessary indexes, abstracts, bibliographies, cataloging cards, etc., to gain ready access to the message; and (3) organizing the reference system in such a way that the message may be retrieved with the minimum of effort and the maximum of relevancy for the user.

The communication packages in phase 3 include the standard resources found in any reference situation. They are listed here in the general order of most current, next most current, etc.

1. Numerical data bases, particularly those updated hourly for business purposes, e.g., stock market reports
2. Reports (printed and other, including tapes of televised news shows and news events)
3. Periodicals, the timeliness of which increases when they are published as videodisks or tapes
4. Indexing and abstracting services. Data bases are usually, though not always, available faster than printed versions.
5. Annual reviews and state-of-the-art reports
6. Bibliographic reviews
7. Books
8. Encyclopedia summaries
9. Almost any other resource in print or in nonprint form, i.e., textbooks, conference proceedings, the card catalog, audiovisual materials, etc.

Library access to communication forms

The guides to this morass of information become increasingly scarce as one moves from published to semipublished sources. In fact, some information is extremely hard to come by because it is private (office memoranda, for example) or has never been indexed, abstracted, or otherwise made available. Totally unpublished material has little chance of circulation except via conversations, conferences, meetings, and the like, where one might learn about, and sometimes even view, the materials.

What is needed is effective access and retrieval indexes and abstracts—and other such forms which will make it easier to acquire, control, and access records. The records available should include not just those in libraries, but others—as long, of course, as they are available to the public, as limited as the public may be. A method of discrimination and evaluation must be built into these devices to eliminate the records which need not be maintained. To date we are closer to a system of acquisitions and control than we are to devising a means of evaluation. It is likely that for generations to come the essential task of the librarian will be the establishment and implementation of standards in information storage.

Selective dissemination of information (SDI)

Selected Dissemination of Information, or SDI, is a term commonly employed in the computer-assisted search. SDI, as a catch phrase, is no more than a way of saying that once a day, or once a week, or once a month the librarian searches the available new literature and prepares a bibliography of materials likely to be of interest to an individual. For example, if X client is involved with hospital administration, the librarian would search, via the computer terminal, data bases likely to give the latest information on the topic. The printout of the computer's findings is then sent to the client. In this way the material is "selected" from the latest periodical indexes, i.e., data bases, and the "information" is "disseminated" to the user.

Actually, this can be done almost automatically in that a search is made each time the data base is updated or new data bases are added. The key search words or phrases are built into the standing search. The user mentioned above, for example, is notified each month how many citations are available for "hospital administration" in university libraries. The user can then modify his request (if he feels there are too many or too few citations) and receive an updated printout of the citations and/or abstracts.

The normal system allows each user to draw up a profile of his or her needs, interests, and other pertinent factors. Given the profile, the librarian delivers relevant items to the user as they become available. The items may be citations (usually with abstracts), actual copies of the text, or microfiche.

How does the librarian know X document or Y article will be of interest or value to the user? The profile is consulted, and it indicates that X document falls within the user's field of interest, while Y article is probably only peripheral. Then the librarian will inform the user when the library has received X document.

Among the commercial services offering SDI are those which publish printed "current contents" magazines. (These services may also approach the same subject via the distribution of machine-readable tapes for use with automated systems.) For example, the Institute for Scientific Information, publisher of *Science Citation Index,* offers a number of *Current Contents* titles: *Life Sciences, Physical and Chemical Sciences, Social and Behavioral Sciences,* etc. These publications reproduce the title pages of journals—usually at time of publication or even several weeks ahead of publication. The user can then scan the current contents and indicate to the librarian what might be of particular interest—or the librarian can first check off what he or she thinks will be of value and then send the user either the citations or the hard copy of the article.

In one study it was found that libraries tend to differ in their approaches to this current-awareness service. The differences seem to be based as much upon the type of the library as upon the service offered. Academic libraries rely heavily on simply sending around accession lists that note all acquisitions for a given period or acquisitions selected on a subject basis. A few offer SDI through the use of computer data bases, but the number is fairly limited. Very few of these libraries have any way of telling whether or not the current-awareness service is useful. Public librarians seem even more lax in their service. It was found, though, that efforts are sometimes made to alert government officials about particular books, articles, and reports; and some libraries engaged in the production of formal bulletins. Special libraries, not surprisingly, have the most highly developed type of service, and the larger the company or the government agency, the truer this seems to be.

THE "INVISIBLE COLLEGE"

How do most people collect the information they need to make a decision or simply to answer some persistent query? Most often the answer is found by the researcher in the so-called "invisible college," and by the layperson at the "back fence." Although more analysis has been made of the phenomenon of the "invisible college" than of the "back fence," there seem to be similarities in both approaches.

Several, possibly scores of, studies indicate the procedures in information gathering that are common to us all.

(1) The first, and possibly the single best, source of information for both laypeople and subject experts is conversation with a friend who knows the subject matter. Lacking someone next door or in the next room, the bothered individual may pick up the telephone or even write a letter to the expert.

Most studies of the "invisible college" have been limited to the scientific community, but the few profiles available of other information seekers confirm the general pattern followed by scientists. When scientists, social scientists, and humanists are asked to list their information sources, all note that informal personal contact is valuable. When asked the method most often employed for locating a reference, all include personal recommendation, although in different orders of importance. Social contact through conferences and meetings is also cited as valuable for information gathering.

(2) A second source of information is in the informal approach, which may be used when and if the person seeking information has a personal library of books, periodicals, newspaper clippings, or like material. Here, the inquirer may turn first to the personal library, second to the friend. The rank of order is more a matter of

convenience and timing than of preference. The inquirer is most likely to use the closest library—in her building, if available—and lacking that, she may raid a next-door office or a small library of a friend in the vicinity.

(3) Should the personal library fail, the user then is forced to turn to the formal library—even ask a reference librarian for assistance. The order may be reversed; the user in a company or special situation may think first of the library before looking for material in a next-door office. A student or layperson with a special need, such as material for a formal paper, may also go to the library after a cursory search of his own collection of books.

The common denominator of these various approaches is convenience and ease. Most people turn first to what they can find with the least amount of trouble. Most of us are willing to sacrifice an in-depth article available in a library for a quick, possibly much more shallow answer from a friend. Even so, parallel studies almost always show that user expectations are highest for the formal library— although this may be the last place one goes—and lowest for the personal library.

THE INFORMATION INDUSTRY

In the nineteenth century and through much of the twentieth, storage and retrieval of information was left to libraries and librarians. After World War II, the information explosion that came with expanded technologies required a new approach, new sources of control. Today there are, in a general descriptive way, numerous depots of information: (1) the library in its many forms as public institution; (2) the private or special library which is associated with a company or organization and serves only its master; (3) government libraries and information centers—federal, state, and even local— which may serve the needs of the public as well as a limited government constituency; (4) private information brokers, managers, or industrialists who see information as a commodity to buy, market, and sell to anyone with the need and the money; and, of course, (5) the publishers and producers of all other media, from magazines to recordings. These last are sometimes classed as part of the information industry; sometimes separated out.

What is the information industry? There is no satisfactory definition, although the following would all be included as members of the information industry: (1) publishers of books, indexes, periodicals, etc.; (2) publishers of special reports and conference proceedings and companies that organize and index such materials; (3) data-base producers, which may be subsidiaries of publishing companies; (4) online data-base vendors and distributors; (5) free-lance, retail information-on-demand services, sometimes called information brokers; (6) television and aspects of the television industry involved with supplying information to the consumer via the television set and other hardware; (7) computer manufacturers; (8) micropublishing; and (9) information consultants.[15]

In the United States the industry has its own organization, the Information Industry Association (IIA), which is active in establishing itself as a private, for-profit group. The IIA has sponsored the development of the Associated Information Managers whose members come from corporate and government libraries and information centers.

Attitudes of rivalry

All is not smooth in the relationship between private and public information services, and, if anything, the antagonism is likely to increase in the decade ahead. There are those in the information industry who feel that there may not be enough work for both types of service, particularly as librarians now threaten to break out of their traditional role as passive agents of service. The argument is familiar. Some claim that private information services should be given first chance to make a profit, that libraries should not be allowed to give services that can be provided by a company or individual.

Unquestionably the three-way split between the information industry, publishers, and libraries will continue until each realizes there is more than enough space (and funds) for all. The solution will come when each has a better understanding of the function and the scope of the other. Meanwhile, the information industry is likely to continue to call for measures unlikely to appeal to librarians. Publishers, who serve both groups, are likely to be divided (from points of view of dollar and sympathy) between the two.

The conflict between private and public information interests surfaces in discussion of networks and national resource centers. Private companies such as Lockheed naturally favor networks which connect their product—access to data bases—with libraries, but are somewhat less enthusiastic about networks operated by nonprofit agencies such as OCLC. Some publishers and information organiza-

[15]"The EEC and the Information Industry," *Outlook on Research Libraries,* September 1979, p. 3.

tions are opposed to the proposed National Periodicals Center, where thousands of periodicals and articles would be available to libraries throughout the nation. They see the center as a threat to library and individual subscriptions. Information groups, which now supply periodical articles for fees, see a competitor which could deliver at much lower rates. Why would anyone subscribe, they argue, when he or she could get an article from the center within hours or days?

The familiar lines are drawn in the 1980s between private industry, operating for profit and giving service to the few, and public agencies giving service to the many. The situation was seen clearly by Major Owens, a state senator from New York who spoke at the White House Conference on Libraries and Information Services:

> *Citizens deserve the best that is available. Terminals for computerized data bases, video cassettes, oral history tapes, teletyped lectures, newsletters from the radical right and the radical left; nothing should be off limits for the public library. . . . To guide this national policy body we must adopt the concept of information as a public utility. . . . The federal government is the greatest single sponsor of research and surveys and it is also the greatest single generator of decisions of public significance. . . . Since the people own the raw material, then it is reasonable to require that certain entrepreneurs who wish to refine and package such raw data be either charged at the outset or taxed on the basis of actual usage. Such a requirement would allow for the creation of a special fund to subsidize library users of commercial machine retrieval services. . . .*[16]

Beyond all this is the sometimes condescending attitude toward librarians of those in private information services. Here is a private consultant on the subject: "Libraries are not connected in any significant way to meeting the most significant priorities of either individuals or society as a whole. They are seen as something it is nice to have, perhaps somehow even essential, but completely separate from what is important in people's lives or for social progress."[17]

Of course, the critic fails to give a definition of "significant" or of "what is important in people's lives." Those who disagree are quick to point out that there is something more to a satisfying life-style than "significant" statistical data that help one make decisions on how to invest money, construct a new automobile, or go to the distant planets.

The quality of life is not necessarily improved by vast amounts of information. As one observer puts it: "There is no greater mistake

[16]"Cadres for the Library Future," *Library Journal,* January 15, 1980, p. 154.
[17]Giuliano, op. cit., p. 1839.

than to confuse culture with consumption. What matters in culture is the power to distinguish and to cross refer, not the input of information."[18] The computer now makes it easier to store and to find information, and it is possible to call up citations to many human experiences, from scientific discoveries to rock concerts to television dramas and poetry. But the undifferentiated mass of information means little unless someone—and in this case it may be the librarian—evaluates, selects, and validates the data. If culture is about differentiation, then the librarian, on almost every frontier, is the guardian of that culture.

The library response

The library reaction to the efforts of the information industry to assume reference service work (at a fee, of course) has varied. On the whole, though, the librarians' response has been to take a new, harder look at traditional patterns of service.

One response to private competition has been to recognize that free enterprise is not likely to meet the information needs of more than a few—the few who can pay. In addition, there is recognition of the fact that many people who use a library do so for the type of information not likely to interest someone in the private sector. Everyday reference questions and answers will continue to be the major part of reference service—a part that is of little or no interest to private information brokers.

Another library response has been to "join 'em." This response has usually come at the university, special, and sometimes public library level where some of the services provided by private firms are now being given by librarians. Librarians have devised methods of adopting some of the techniques used by the industry. Here the basic notion is that a person should be as willing to pay the library as anyone else for a service. (Fees will be considered later in this text.)

There have been several innovative responses to competition from private information services.

1. INFORM is a service of the Minneapolis public library. It provides much the same work as done by free-lance information brokers. Charges vary with the time involved and the

---

[18]John Russell, "Putting Back the C in Culture, Inch by Inch," *The New York Times,* December 30, 1979, p. DX11. A good summary of culture in the 1980s with considerable space given to the dilemma of defining the term.

complexity of the question. (Note, however, that there is a separate free service.)

2. Facts for a Fee at the Cleveland Public Library provides in-depth searching for $25 an hour.

3. Research Information Marketplace of Rutgers, New Jersey, is a state-funded service which answers some 45,000 questions annually, primarily from New Jersey industries and business. About half the cost is paid by the state, the remainder by the firms.

4. Research Information Service for Education, offered by the Ontario (Canada) Institute for Studies in Education, has, over the years, not simply helped educators to find information, but has actively prepared information packages for both administrators and teachers. In so doing, the Institute has followed the practice of information brokers, giving the customer the information, not just instruction in how to find the data. Similar services are offered by the San Mateo (California) Educational Resources Center as well as by the Chicago Crerar Library—and, of course, by the private information brokers.[19]

MODIFICATIONS OF REFERENCE POSITIONS

Some librarians, and many library schools, see in the information industry a major new employer, an answer to the severe cutbacks in public support of libraries. This is unquestionably true and will become even truer in the 1980s. Most of the training librarians receive makes them highly qualified, certainly more qualified than nonlibrarians, for information industry positions, both in and out of the government. Library schools are now tailoring basic studies to consider the information industry needs and are even offering specialized courses in this area.[20]

New careers related to reference work are becoming increasing-

[19]Linda W. Corman, "A Library Alternative at the Ontario Institute for Studies in Education," *Canadian Library Journal*, April 1977, pp. 79–85. This is not only a discussion of the Institute, but a good overview of total, or maximum, library service, its costs and its problems.

[20]Robert S. Taylor, "Educational Breakaway," *American Libraries*, June 1979, pp. 364–368. The dean of Syracuse University's School of Information Studies is a staunch advocate of expanding the scope of library education to encompass information careers outside the library. He has many followers.

ly available. Reference skills may be easily turned to related fields of information practice.[21] But before considering new positions suitable for reference librarian's skills, it is advisable to take a cursory glance at various careers in reference service, both traditional and innovative. Documentalist, information scientist, and librarian as subject specialist are traditional roles; the search analyst, information manager, and information broker are relatively new positions.

Information science

"Information science" is an umbrella term for almost all the services offered by librarians, or nonlibrarians, outside of the regular reference service framework. How does information science differ from basic reference work?

(1) Materials. Most of the emphasis is on highly specialized materials, such as those used in organic chemistry or criminal law. The form of the material is usually a report, monograph, journal article, manuscript, inner-office or company study, etc., since there is a particular interest in timeliness and currency not associated with books.

(2) Services. The basic difference between the information scientist and the reference librarian is that the former will find specific bits of information for the user and will "package" that information for individual needs, usually with the aid of a machine-readable data base, while the average reference librarian will generally find sources for the user, but will rarely perform a literature search. More specifically, the services of an information scientist are likely to include: (a) giving direct answers to questions, rather than leading the user to a likely source where the answer may or may not be found; (b) preparing indexes, abstracts, and other bibliographical aids; (c) preparing bibliographies for individual users; (d) preparing and disseminating analytical studies; (e) preparing state-of-the-art reports; (f) evaluating data and information for individual users; (g) offering various publications aside from those mentioned; and (h) offering selective dissemination of information, i.e., keeping individuals advised of new material pertinent to their studies.

Information science puts more stress on specialized— particularly esoteric, technical, scientific, and theoretical—approaches to information. Broadly speaking, information science is involved in

[21]Betty-Carol Sellen, *What Else You Can Do With a Library Degree* (Syracuse, N.Y.: Gaylord Brothers, 1980). In this joint publication with Neal-Schuman Publishers, the author describes related jobs in other fields.

three major fields: (1) design of information systems and services, (2) basic techniques and tools, and (3) applications. The first and second of these are likely to involve engineering problems generally outside the knowledge of the average librarian. Still, a reference librarian can help in the design, say, of a computer terminal, if only to suggest what is wrong with present terminals. The third field, applications, is much broader and involves communications. Here the information scientist is interested in clarifying fundamental concepts and working with basic communication theory which will aid eventually in information retrieval.

One might say that the reference librarian deals on a day-to-day basis with users in a library situation. The information scientist deals with the larger implications of the interaction of librarian and user, and as such, is usually divorced from the nitty-gritty service aspects of library work.

If information science is somewhat more than fielding questions from a comfortable library chair, it may also be made to seem much too complex, too concerned with technology. D. J. Foskett, a literate and well-informed librarian, makes the point that systems, computers, and management is not all.

> *Some of those who are active in promoting the use of computers seem to be in danger of erecting a science of "information" based on the false premise that what is not reducible to mathematics has no claim to be scientific. . . . In developing the necessary scientific basis for library and information services, it is vital that we should not let the means turn into the ends, nor the production and circulation of information obscure the real purpose: benefit to the community of users.*[22]

Subject specialist

At one time the argument about whether a reference librarian should be a subject specialist or a generalist was a heated one. Today the argument is rarely heard because librarians are more concerned with other problems.

Ideally, the librarian should know all subject areas, all disciplines well; but this is not possible in an age of increasing specialization. One group responds to the situation by pleading for specialized training for the librarian. Here the rationale is that it takes an expert

[22]D. J. Foskett, "Information Service and Social Needs," *International Forum and Information and Documentations*, No. 4, 1977, pp. 30–31. This is a review of a book which covers the very subject—K. J. McGarry, *Communication, Knowledge and the Librarian* (London: Clive Bingsley, 1975).

to assist an expert, and the generalist will be lost. Points may be made for the specialist here, although in a much broader way than is normally employed in the discussion. Someone serving scientists and technologists should have a background in, or, at a minimum an empathy with, science and technology. The same is appropriate for the humanities and the social sciences.

The real specialization every reference librarian must have is not in a narrow subject area, but in the area of handling information— acquiring, storing, finding, and relating it to individual need. This is a specialization which was not appreciated by many laypeople until recently. Taught, usually by the well-meaning librarian, that anyone can use a library, many people believe that the actual finding of information is not a skill, but a power given from on high to anyone who stumbles into a library. This misconception is rapidly disappearing, at least among people who depend upon information for daily existence. It has slowly dawned upon even the most expert of experts that it is one thing to know a subject, quite another to find the necessary bits of data in the masses of information generated on that subject. A skillful search requires a trained reference librarian, and when a computer terminal is added to the picture, it becomes increasingly evident that a skilled mediator, i.e., the librarian, is even more necessary.

As more and more information becomes topic- rather than discipline-oriented, the old argument that the librarian is better as a generalist than as a subject specialist is increasingly true. A well-trained generalist, for example, has the ability to cross over many disciplines to find citations and documents for questions ranging from energy policy to methods of fighting fires in hospitals. Most reference work requires an answer to a given problem which may, and often does, employ sources from numerous fields. An expert in the social sciences must know something about the sciences and the humanities if he or she is going to make a study of unemployment patterns, legal questions regarding conservation issues, etc.

The term "interdisciplinary" became as common in the 1980s as "specialist" was in the 1960s and early 1970s. The fragmentation of information is one of the hazards of an overabundance of information, and the librarian is in the unique position of being the "master of the interdisciplinary," the one who brings meaning to the fragments.

There are times, of course, when the queries are of such a narrow range that the librarian first and foremost should be an expert in a subject rather than in a wide range of sources, but even in a medical, legal, or scientific library, it is possible that this very specialization may be detrimental since it blocks consideration of allied areas.

The reference librarian should be able to wander freely in the forest of specialization but be equally agile in looking about for other areas. In fact, this ability to look outside a narrow scope is what makes reference work a specialty. And the error, or so it seems to this writer, of those who argue for specialization is that they ironically ignore the specialization of the broad view, a specialization which makes reference librarians a unique link in the information chain.

Search analyst

A favored term to describe the librarian who searches for citations in data bases via the computer terminal is "search analyst." The analyst does what any reference librarian does; that is, he or she carries on a reference interview with the information seeker, attempting to discover the precise nature of the question, and determining how much information and what type of information is needed. (In some cases the questioner need not be present, but this will be discussed in detail later.) The next step is equally familiar to the reference librarian. A source, or sources, must be determined to match the query. In this case, it is one or more data bases, usually indexes or abstracting services.

But when the analyst sits at the terminal she parts company with the average reference librarian. The search analyst is likely to modify the search pattern during a discussion of the topic with the person being interviewed. The reference librarian, on the other hand, rarely changes the search pattern since she is not likely to receive any more questions once the user has been sent to an index to find his own answers. The analyst also usually prepares a printed bibliography for the user; the citations can be printed out at the terminal or sent to the user later. The reference librarian, on the other hand, rarely lists sources for the questioner.

Information manager

When information was recognized as a commodity and became the basis of an industry, a new career field developed.

"Information manager" is a broad title given to almost anyone in the private or public sector who manages information. Broadly speaking, an information manager decides what types of information are needed for X or Y organization and then selects personnel, technology, and organizational patterns to deliver the information effectively and efficiently. The manager is a coordinator who works not only with traditional reference sources, but with data bases, records, archival programs, reports, word processing, printing and publishing, paperwork management, mail and copying programs—in fact, with anything connected with the communication of information.

Information managers do not work exclusively for corporations, publishers, or data-base vendors. They are now considered an integral part of many special libraries, particularly at the federal level. In such a capacity, a primary problem for the manager is simply to solve the paperwork puzzle. Because of an excessive concern with paper and a lack of understanding of librarianship, the government has, at times, hired information managers who are less qualified for these positions than librarians.[23]

In the text *Industrial Information Systems* (Stroudsburg, Pa.: Dowden, Hutchinson & Ross, 1978) Jackson and Jackson give an explicit explanation of the organization and administration of a typical special information system. A close look shows it to be similar to most libraries, or at least to almost any special library. Where the system differs from the library is in such things as word processing and correspondence control. Except for the consideration of these functions, the text might be equally useful for a study of special business libraries or technical libraries. An analysis of *Fortune's* top 500 corporations reveals that the majority have libraries and that "librarians" are clearly designated as such.

By any other name the information manager is a librarian. True, the librarian must learn some new skills, most particularly how to handle the correspondence and reports which seem to flood a corporation, but the other skills required are much the same, even if one gives proper value to the knowledge of computerized data bases, networks, and the new information technology. For there is no librarian who can afford not to know as much about these systems as an information manager.

Information broker

Another broad category of information experts is that of the information broker. Essentially the information broker sells information service.

[23]For a discussion of the attempt to cut through masses of paper and forms, see "Librarians Seen as Information Managers," *FLC Newsletter,* May 1978, pp. 1–6. Note, too, that in 1980 a law was signed requiring all federal agencies and departments to designate officials to manage information needs. The information industry hails this as a victory, although in many cases it will be (should be) librarians, not managers who are hired. It is with some concern that *The Information Manager* (November/December 1979, p. 5) editor notes the need "to develop an official definition of the term information manager." It is hoped that when the position is defined it may command salaries as high as $50,000 a year. Where, oh where, is the library profession?

S'il Vous Plait (SVP) was apparently the first private information broker. Established in 1948 in Paris, the firm delivered answers to questions put to them by subscribers. The idea developed and SVP now has independently operated affiliates throughout the world. One of the largest is FIND/SVP, which in 1977 earned over $1.5 million. Some 30 professionals are employed by FIND to answer 3000 to 4000 reference questions each month for fees ranging from $10 to $55 an hour. Asked why people should pay fees when the same information FIND provides is available at New York Public Library, one source quotes Garvin as saying that "[his] clients can't afford to wait for library service; they need their answers yesterday."[24]

There are three basic types of private information services.

1. The information broker or search service tends to deal with specific questions and problems and to come up with citations and documents which will aid the user in the solution of the problem. The documents are screened and only those thought to be of benefit are presented.

2. The consultant, who may have one or more information brokers in his employ, goes a step further and not only validates the information, but evaluates it in such a way that recommendations for action are made based upon the documents.

3. A third type performs both services and often will advise corporations or small businesses on how to establish their own library and/or information system.

The number of for-profit information brokers grows each year, and by 1980 there were at least 100 operating full time, as well as several times that number of individuals operating part-time in the business.[25] Charges depend upon the size of the information brokerage and the complexity of the question, but fees generally run from $25 to $100-plus per hour, or so much per problem, or, under contractual arrangement offered by larger concerns, so much per month of service.

Who uses these services? Business is the primary user; the business may be a firm without a library or a company with a large

[24]Karl Nyren, "Information Entrepreneurs Stake Claims . . ." *Library Journal,* June 1, 1979, p. 1200.

[25]*Information Sources: The Membership Directory of the Information Industry Association* (Bethesda, Md.: The Association, 1978 to date, annual). This lists about 100 companies which supply information to the business world, i.e., publishers of reference works, data bases, etc. It does not include names of individual information brokers.

library but still in need of fast, expert searching. Government agencies are also good customers.

There are several specialized journals concerned with information brokers and information management. One of these is *The Information Manager,* a bimonthly title which concentrates on the practical day-to-day matters likely to face those in the information industry, including search analysts and librarians. According to the editor, "the goal is to give top management an awareness of the importance of what's happening in the information field. We talk about information usage, information networks, information brokerage, information suppliers, data bases. . . ."[26]

The librarian's role

The practical aspect of finding just what bit of data is valuable and how many documents may be discarded is the raison d'être of the librarian, the search analyst, the information manager—whatever the title given the person who sifts through the garbage for the gems. One sharp-tongued critic summarizes the situation this way:

> *If you just want to retrieve documents, information barbarians will win. But if you consider the real function of information systems—which is to grab information and not documents, to analyze it, correlate it, and help make decisions—the machine is a long, long way off.*[27]

Under the pressures of private business and new technology the librarian cannot save the day by retreating to old practices, old methods of reference work. Conversely, the librarian need not give up the traditional for the electronic in the library. The librarian now has many choices, many more avenues to find information. Instead of being someone who simply stores and collects data, the librarian must be someone who is an evaluator. The entire trend as we enter the 1980s is toward the librarian as intellectual and against the librarian as drone.

SUGGESTED READING

Berry, John, "ALA Colloquium Debates Information Agenda," *Library Journal,* August 1980, pp. 1560–1568. A description of a special conference to discuss "an

---

[26]Rodd Exelbert (ed.), *The Information Manager,* December 1978, p. 6.

[27]Wolpert is quoted in an article by Tefko Saracevic, "Collection, Generation, and Analysis of Information, . . ." *Bulletin of the American Society for Information Science,* February 1979, p. 21.

information agenda for the 1980s." Leaders in the field considered such things as how to improve the quality of information, the future of the library, and who should pay for information. See, too: "Information," a special issue of *Library Journal* (July, 1981) devoted to similar problems of the 1980s.

Cuadra, Carlos, "The Role of the Private Sector in the Development and Improvement of Library and Information Services," *The Library Quarterly*, January 1980, pp. 94–111. A member of the information industry makes a case for the private sector as a source of information for individuals and for industry. Of particular value for its description of the various types of information concerns operating in the private sector.

Felicetti, Barbara, "Information for Fee and Information for Free: The Information Broker and the Public Librarian," *Public Library Quarterly*, Spring 1977, p. 20. A private information broker clearly explains what her firm does in the way of supplying information and gives a candid appraisal of such an operation. She thinks there is no real competition between libraries and brokers as there is too much work for both. See, too, the current bibliography for other readings in this field.

————, "Information for Fee and Information for Free: The Information Broker and the Public Librarian," *Public Library Quarterly*, Spring 1979, pp. 9–19. The president of a "for-fee" company explains why there is a need for independent brokers outside of the library.

Herther, Nancy, "Free Lancing—A Personal Experiment," *RQ*, Winter 1978, pp. 177–179. A student explains the joys and the drawbacks of working as an information broker.

Williams, Patrick, and Joan Pearce, *The Vital Network: A Theory of Communication and Society*. Westport, Conn.: Greenwood Press, 1978. A survey of communication theory with an emphasis on the proper approach to communication and the individual in society. Beyond that there is a second chapter on varieties of literature. It raises many questions, but too often the authors give all the wrong answers. Still, it is useful for the queries.

*INTERVIEW
AND SEARCH*

CHAPTER THREE

The Reference Interview
and Levels of Service

THE REFERENCE INTERVIEW is a dialogue between someone in need of information and someone—the librarian—able to give assistance in finding it. Such an interview presents numerous fascinating possibilities and is a challenge for communication students who seek to analyze and explain not only the actual words spoken (or not spoken) but such other factors which help or hinder the interview as: body signals; dress; attitudes towards fellow human beings; and the influence of surroundings, from color to furniture and lighting.

An analysis of the interview is valuable because success in negotiating an answer for a user depends upon how well the librarian is in command of the interview situation. Failure to carry out a satisfactory reference interview may leave the librarian unaware that all is not well, and yet leave the user frustrated. An improper interview creates an insurmountable obstacle to service.

The discussion in this chapter presumes a reference interview. Actually, about 50 to 60 percent of all library interviews are not reference interviews. Directional queries such as, "Where is the catalog?" or "Where can I find a telephone?" rarely need an interview, nor do ready-reference questions such as, "What is the population of New Jersey?" One may argue an interview might be desirable in all cases, but that is a matter not treated here.

The barrier many people have to face when approaching a reference librarian is the suspicion that their queries are not worthwhile. "I know this is a dumb question, but . . ." That opener, in one form or another, is familiar to almost all librarians, few of whom take it as an excuse to agree. Any question is worth consideration, at least to the person asking it, or the question would never have been put.

Oscar Wilde noted, "There are no indiscreet questions. There are only indiscreet answers." The comment seems appropriate for reference librarians to remember, particularly as some people are reluctant to approach the reference desk when they think the librarian will "through words and actions . . . reinforce the user's feeling that he is a bother or he is stupid."[1]

The type of question asked will influence the extent of the reference interview that follows. The librarian need not get into a prolonged conversation, for example, with someone who asks the population of the United States or the name of the president of the local hairpin factory, although, as many experienced reference librarians know, the initial query may be only a prelude to a more involved question. Good librarians will sense a further need and, if in doubt, will try to switch the monologue to a dialogue. For example, the person asking about hairpins may really be interested in local employment or in the development of hair styles and will require more aid.

What type of reference questions are likely to be asked? In the average library, the majority are likely to be directional. Forty to 50 percent will be specific search-type questions, usually looking for general information on a topic. Another 30 to 40 percent will be ready-reference, i.e., quick facts about dates, persons, statistics, and the like. The rest, a small percentage, are miscellaneous queries which fit no real pattern and those which entail research. The actual percentages will vary with size and type of library, but even in a special situation where experts are being aided, the majority of users will present specific search- or research-type questions.[2]

All of this adds up to the fact that about 50 percent (give or take 10 percent, give or take different times of the year, etc.) of the questions are likely to require some type of interview, some form of a dialogue.

In a study of reference service in public libraries Zweizig offers further useful clarification of typical questions. He classifies queries by the various needs they tend to reveal: (1) a decision has to be made and the user seeks alternatives. Example: Which car to buy? (2) A person must resolve a worry which broadens the decision query.

[1]Mary Jane Swope and Jeffrey Katzer, "Why Don't They Ask Questions," *RQ*, Winter 1972, p. 164.

[2]Herbert Goldhor, "An Experiment in Literature Service to a Group of Local Decision Makers," *RQ*, Summer 1978, p. 307. Service was provided for a group of city executives, with the result: "In 59 percent what was wanted was information itself or a substantive answer."

Example: Do I really need a car, and isn't it too expensive as well as bad for my health? (3) A person is trying to overcome a barrier. Example: Where can I get money for the car? (4) The individual wants information on how to live with a difficult situation. Example: How can I find a way to cut down on the use of my car? (5) Finally, the individual may want to learn how to analyze the situation. Example: Just why do I need a car, and aren't there some likely alternatives?

This system of categorization is only one of scores that have been devised, all of which show the simple reference question is rarely simple. Zweizig continues:

> . . . a quite simple situation can give rise to a multiplicity of information needs depending on how the client views the situation at any given point. It is no wonder that a librarian may feel confused and uncertain about how to respond with service. To further confuse the picture, clients may change their views of the situation from one instant to the next, for they continue to consider the situation even as they make information requests. A client may begin by asking for information that relates to a decision-making process, for that is the kind of information request libraries are expected to respond to best. But as a librarian listens attentively, the librarian may notice that the client focuses on other aspects of the situation, and the information need may change. If a librarian ignores or remains unaware of this shift, the information delivered may not allow the client to make the new sense he or she requires.[3]

CLARIFICATION OF THE QUESTION

The common criticism in almost any discussion of the reference interview is that the person asking the question tends to do so in general terms without being specific enough to allow the librarian to respond with specific answers. This is such a normal condition of the reference interview situation that too many librarians fail to consider its implications. The interview, at least from the point of view of the user, should be of assistance not only in finding an answer, but in formulating the question itself.

When the average person approaches a reference librarian (and here it may help to think of your own experience), so many potential difficulties of communication and personality seem built into the situation that many users may try to defuse all problems by asking their questions in general terms. They hope this will elicit short, useful answers. For reasons to be considered, they do not want to get

[3]Douglas Zweizig, "The Informing Function of Adult Services in Public Libraries," *RQ*, Spring 1979, p. 242.

into a dialogue with the librarian. As a result, the initial query is couched in generalities.

> *One of the greatest difficulties in determining the patron's actual information need comes when that need is hidden under an "indirect" or "faulty information" question . . . .One observational study in an academic library reports that 25 percent of all questions were indirect in some respect and 73 percent of these indirect questions were successfully resolved. . . . On the basis of these studies we might expect that 20 percent to 25 percent of questions asked in an academic library might not represent patrons' actual information needs.*[4]

Numerous suggestions have been made to indicate why the average individual tends to phrase a question in a general way. The one most often cited is that the typical person believes this is the only type of question the librarian is willing to answer.

Beyond that, Mount[5] has observed that the lack of effective communication at the opening stage of an interview may result from (1) the user's lack of familiarity with the library and its collection; (2) the user's ignorance of the service likely to be offered by the librarian; (3) the user's instant, and perhaps, mutual dislike of the librarian; (4) the user's lack of faith in the librarian's abilities to find answers; (5) the user's sensitivity to the personal nature of the question; (6) the user's discomfort because of his ignorance of the reference works and the facilities; and/or (7) the user's embarrassment that the question is too simple (or too complex) for the librarian.

Another reason given for the oblique approach is that the person simply does not want to bother the librarian. One wonders just how often this happens, particularly when the librarian seems less than approachable.

But the overriding explanation for the failure of effective communication is the simple truth: Most people are not sufficiently familiar with reference service or with methods of finding answers to their questions.

The specific query

People may ask specific questions even when they are not sure of the nature of the question. Instead of asking, "Where are the airplane

---

[4]Egil Halldorsson and Marjorie E. Murfin, "The Performance of Professionals and Nonprofessionals in the Reference Interview," *College & Research Libraries*, September 1977, p. 385.

[5]H. Mount, "Communication Barrier and the Reference Question," *Special Libraries*, vol. 57, 1966, pp. 575–578.

magazines?" the user may ask, "Where is *Flight?*" Instead of asking what the library has on whales, the user may ask, "Where is *Moby Dick?*" The person with questions about sex will usually resolve the problem not by asking the location of books on marriage, but by asking for such an innocuous title as *Marriage and the Happy Family.*

The user may be quite specific in asking for an index or encyclopedia or other reference work by name. This may indicate that the person has a real knowledge of information sources, but it more likely indicates that the user does not know of the existence of other indexes and has limited his hopes to finding an answer in one specific index. For example, it is not uncommon for the student to ask "Where is the *Readers' Guide?*" when it would be more suitable to ask "Where is the *Business Periodicals Index?*" The few studies available indicate that as much as 65 to 75 percent of the queries on sources are for inappropriate sources.

Actually, there are times when a specific question is a tried-and-true research method for the user. The person has found that by asking for a book, periodical, or film she will be led to the other books, periodicals, or films in the subject area where she will then be free to browse and dig about for more specific information. Such an approach is perfectly acceptable and has been used as long as there have been libraries. But it should not be accepted by the librarian without clarification of the actual question. When the user is simply wandering about in the vague hope of finding data, the librarian must direct her in how to proceed.

The first situation—in which the subject expert asks a specific question and is pointed in the direction of a field of interest—is legitimate and may be the only way the individual is able to begin study or research. This is a common enough procedure, often employed by people who may be more expert in finding their way around the library than the librarians.

Summarizing the specific-type-of-question problem, Benson concludes:

> *Source . . . questions can mask or stand in place of both extraordinarily simple and extraordinarily complex information needs. The apparent specificity of these questions is misleading. Too often the deceptively simple questions about source locations are simply answered, not questioned.*[6]

[6]James Benson, "The Hidden Reference Question," *The Southeastern Librarian,* Summer 1979, p. 92.

"Yes, but . . ."

There are times, in fact some claim more times than librarians are willing to admit, when a person asks a question—just a question, no more, no less. In a Canadian study, for example, it was found that "75 to 85 percent of the client questions in an academic milieu are valid in the sense that the question asked is the question intended."[7]

In a public library study much the same result was evident:

> It has been assumed that library patrons do not ask for what they "really" want and therefore must be interviewed. But the query changed substantially in only 13 percent of the transactions observed in this study. . . . Perhaps those who write about the reference interview are misrepresenting the situation by concentrating on the idea that library patrons do not ask for what they really want. It seems that in many cases patrons do ask for what they want.[8]

The able research by Ms. Lynch is valuable on several counts, but its greatest value is that it challenges ancient assumptions about the reference interview. It is often assumed that people cannot ask clearly for what they want, but some studies indicate this is hardly the case—that the question asked is the question meant, and often it does not require an extended interview.

INTERVIEW TECHNIQUES

Thus far there have been some suggestions as to what the reference librarian should be doing in the reference interview, but there are more specific approaches to be considered. Here we may consider only a few of the time-tested techniques.

Using the "Open" Question The librarian's response to questions is sometimes a matter of using an "open" or a "closed" query approach. The open question is broad and allows for a dialogue. For example: "Do you want just airplane magazines or do you want related types of magazines, such as in the hobby field?" Such a question allows enough latitude for a discussion. In fact, its very purpose is to open up the possibilities for more questions and answers in order to pinpoint the precise data needed by the user.

[7]"Audience Participation" in *Proceedings of the Symposium on Measurement of Reference* (Chicago: American Library Association, 1974), p. 18.

[8]Mary Jo Lynch, "Reference Interviews in Public Libraries," *The Library Quarterly,* April 1978, p. 137.

A closed question limits the dialogue considerably. Such a question as "Do you want *Flying* or *Flight* magazine?" is closed because there can only be a single, direct answer. In her study of public library reference interviews, Lynch discovered:

> When the analysis was completed 8 percent of the questions were classified as open (for example, Have you found anything at all?) and 90 percent were clearly closed questions (for example, Do you need pictures of frogs or material about them?), while 2 percent fell into the intermediate category (for example, Patron: Do you have any books on music conductors? Librarian: Are you looking for any ones in particular?).[9]

If 90 percent of questions are closed, does this mean 90 percent of interviews are bad? Hardly, although the figures may be interpreted in different ways.

Expanding the "Closed" Query When the user asks for a specific source, the librarian may respond, "The *Readers' Guide* is on the table, but what was it you wanted to look up? We may have better indexes for your purpose." In fact, several studies show that this type of reply is quite common among experienced reference librarians.

Using a "Why" Question Where appropriate, the librarian will ask the user "why" in order not only to clarify the query, but to establish the types of sources wherein the query may be answered. It has been suggested that this method may be useful, but may not always be necessary or advisable, since it may be seen by the user as an infringement on privacy or an indication of rudeness on the part of the librarian.[10]

Listening Listening is a major factor in the successful reference interview. Impatience—whether because of lack of time, lack of interest, or a dislike of the user asking the question—often results in the librarian forcing the interview by jumping ahead of the individual in the conversation. For instance, the user may ask about material on mushrooms and the librarian, rather than listening for more clues,

[9]Ibid., p. 131.

[10]Robert S. Taylor, "Question Negotiation and Information Seeking in Libraries," *College & Research Libraries*, May 1968, p. 185. In those cases where the librarian feels no need to ask the inquirer what type of information is desired for what purpose, the usual reasons given are that the librarian thinks "the inquirer (a) knows what he wants, (b) knows more than the librarian, and (c) is aware of the search strategies necessary to satisfy his need. None of these assumptions appear to be wholly valid."

may immediately respond, "Try the card catalog," or "The books about mushrooms are in the third stack from the right." The user, perhaps by now upset with the reception, wanders off unsatisfied. Why? Because the real query, which would have been apparent had the librarian taken time to listen, was "I'm looking for material on starting my own business. Someone suggested growing mushrooms. Actually, I'm interested in just reading about small business concerns."

The ability to listen is a major virtue. Sperry, the American conglomerate, ran a series of advertisements in 1979–1981 which began: "It's about time we learned how to listen." That ad illustrates another point—people not only fail to listen, most don't know how to listen. The advertisement goes on: "Listening is one communication skill we're never really taught. We're taught how to read, to write, to speak—but not to listen. And listening can be taught."[11]

Listening is important, but an immediate response, if only a nod or a "Yes, I think I can help," is required. Librarians find that an indication of interest is necessary to begin the communications pattern. To stand, no matter how attentive, and say nothing for a minute or two is to drive the average person into a state of mild shock. The individual so treated will probably think he is not being heard at all. Some positive indication of attentiveness is always necessary.

Isolating the Type of Question The librarian must be able to classify the type of question. The exact nature of the query may be brought out by a few courteous questions. For example, if a user asks for airplane magazines, the librarian might point to the rack, or might respond with: "The airplane periodicals are over there, but we could give you more specific information about airplanes in some sources we have. Do you want anything in particular, or do you just want to look at the airplane magazines?"

Making the Person Feel at Ease Obviously someone who is relaxed is going to be more comfortable in dialogue and in revealing his specific needs. There are numerous techniques for making a person feel relaxed during the reference interview. Benson observes that:

> *Often the user is responsive to clarification efforts while the librarian escorts him to the materials requested. To attempt clarification while at the reference desk can suggest a lack of responsiveness to the question*

[11]*The New Yorker,* September 17, 1979, p. 10. Their sales pitch is that *their* employees do listen to customers.

posed by the user. In contrast, clarifying questions during the trek to the sources may often be received cordially by the user. This approach reassures the user. The librarian provides an immediate acceptance of the question posed. Therefore the librarian's clarification questions are less apt to be perceived as prying.[12]

A librarian who is "out and about" in the reference section may invite greater feelings of comfort than one not so accessible. In fact, some libraries have rules suggesting the reference librarian stay no more than five or ten minutes behind a desk, as the desk is considered a barrier between the librarian and the user. But there is no consensus on this point as sometimes the barrier works to an advantage, i.e., the user feels safer having something between her and the librarian.

Correcting the Question   Often the patron may confuse the issue and give the wrong clues as to the information needed. For example, in seeking an author, the user may have the name spelled incorrectly, or in seeking the source of a quotation, the user may misquote the passage. The librarian must then hope that the quotation is accurate at least in terms of subject matter so that a subject search may be launched.

The librarian's response in many such cases is almost intuitive in that he or she will recognize an error in information, a wrong spelling, a misconceived notion about a subject. The librarian may then suggest other possibilities, while trying to discover, through courteous cross-questioning, another approach to the query. Often a single clue obtained this way will give enough information to correct the mistake in the query.

When working with the students the librarian sometimes finds it helpful to ask to see the teacher's question in writing or to see an outline of the material. The librarian may have enough personal knowledge of the subject to make mental corrections of user errors and to go on from there with the search for materials. Knowledge is the great asset shared by most professional librarians, and it is no surprise that

> *the professional librarians . . . were clearly superior to the nonprofessionals in achieving successful solutions on "faulty information" questions in the reference interview. . . . Professionals personally arrived at the correct solution in the reference interview on 52 percent of questions, while nonprofessionals did so on 20 percent. These results are, to some extent, in line with those of Bunge, who found that the speed and*

[12]Benson, op. cit., p. 91.

efficiency of professionals was slightly but significantly greater than that of nonprofessionals.[13]

Expediting   When there are numerous people waiting to ask questions, should the librarian take time for an interview? Yes and no. The answer depends on who is asking the question. In this world of less-than-equal treatment, the librarian is likely to spend some time with the president of the university, even if there are many people waiting. Conversely, the average student may be lucky to have the librarian point him in the direction of the card catalog.

But in the best of all possible situations, the librarian would then take the individual to the section of the library where he would most likely find pertinent sources. Later, when the pressure was eased, the librarian would return to see if the user found what was needed. Where there is a need for a greater investment of time, the individual would be asked to come back, or would be called on the phone. Optionally, the librarian would ask the user to write down the question and would then work on the query as time permitted, giving the person the required data or documents on a subsequent visit.

Unfortunately, lack of budget, staff, and patience combine in too many libraries to create a condition in which the harassed librarian habitually takes the quick way out of a pressure situation—he or she points toward a likely source and moves on to the next questioner. The interview simply never takes place.

Should the librarian offer assistance to a person who does not ask for help, yet seems to need it? The question is meaningless in a busy, understaffed library, although even there some librarians rightfully pride themselves on finding time to help the silent ones who do need assistance. Lacking help, many libraries have attempted to solve the problem by establishing easy-to-see, easy-to-use access points where a librarian is on duty. This makes it much simpler for the reluctant user to ask questions.

The silent interview

Nonverbal communication, body language, or, as Edward Hall called it 20 or so years ago, "the silent language."[14] is of some importance in the reference interview, although too much may be made of how the

[13]Halldorsson, op. cit., p. 388.

[14]Edward Hall, *The Silent Language* (New York: Doubleday and Company, 1959). One of the first of scores of books on this subject, it remains one of the best. For a later study see Desmond Morris' *Gestures* (New York: Stein and Day, 1981). The author studies communication gestures employed by people in 25 different countries.

librarian smiles, stands, or places his hands on the desk. Too much, in fact, of the growing literature on this topic borders on the satirical, more fit for a Woody Allen or Mel Brooks comedy than for serious consideration by librarians. This is not to denigrate the topic, only to ask for a more practical and intellectual approach. The relative emphasis given nonverbal communication is important. While of questionable value for the librarian's self-improvement, an awareness of body language is of inestimable value for the librarian in evaluating the needs of the questioner.

It is obvious to anyone but a hermit that physical presentation is important, that it is easier to approach someone for help when that individual seems pleasant rather than preoccupied. Still, it is easier to advise librarians to look cheerful, be receptive, stand tall, and smile than it is to actually perform such rites of nonverbal communication —particularly when one has a headache or is plagued by bad lighting, unruly patrons, and a less-than-sympathetic working companion. The "chin up, all should at least look well" routine is admirable, but not always possible or even advisable. The real key to successful nonverbal communication is an intuitive sense for human relations discussed earlier.

The true value of nonverbal communication lies not so much in helping the reference librarian to shape up for the encounter as in assisting that librarian to understand the person who wants help. If, as some experts believe, 50 to 75 percent of a message is nonverbal, it is useful to be able to read that content of the message. Again, experience, common sense, and intuition are the best guides, although reading in the literature may yield some helpful information. For example, most Americans who "close in" on the librarian (i.e. stand no farther than three feet away and speak in a low voice) have something confidential or personal to ask. On the other hand, a nonpersonal query can be expected from the person who stands beyond four to five feet and speaks in a normal voice.

The person's appearance

Does the appearance of a person influence the way the reference librarian conducts the interview? The personal appearance of a user may, or may not, govern the quality of the interview. Most people react negatively to others who have apparently totally different life-styles and attitudes. At the reference desk when a stranger asks a question, the librarian's casual summary of the patron's physical appearance will sometimes make the librarian more, or less, receptive to carrying on an interview.

That is the way common sense and some experience tell us the librarian will react. But sometimes—though one would prefer *all* of the time—librarians rise above their psychological set and do not discriminate according to the appearance of a person making a request. In one study, conducted in a southern city, two women—one dressed as a college student, the other dressed as a "hippie"—asked the same question in eight public libraries. The results were contrary to expectations. The libraries offered both users equally good or bad service.

> *Five librarians took the deviant ["deviant" is the unfortunate descriptor applied to the hippie] directly to the shelves to find books whereas four offered the same service to the student. Five librarians answered questions thoroughly with useful information for the deviant whereas two provided useful information to the student. Five librarians were rated very friendly toward the deviant whereas four were considered very friendly toward the student. When the experimenter was dressed as the deviant, one librarian laughed and made derogatory comments about her appearance after she left. There were no such reactions from any librarian when experimenter was dressed as a student.[15]*

LEVELS OF REFERENCE SERVICE

An important consideration in analyzing the reference interview involves the level of service that the user is likely to receive. If, for example, the user knows that, whatever question is put, the librarian will respond with another question—"Have you looked in the card catalog?"—the form of the query is likely to be fairly simple: "I've checked the card catalog, but can't find anything on small dining-room tables. Where do I look now?" But when the user knows the librarian is going to pay considerable attention to the request, the question is apt to be more complex: "I'm thinking about buying an antique dining-room table. What is the current price, and how can I check to see if the table is authentic 19th-century American?" And the librarian is more likely to respond to such a query with a search for books and articles which will give direct answers than with a suggestion that the user try the card catalog.

[15]Howard Kroll and Deborah Moren, "Effect of Appearance on Requests for Help in Libraries," *Psychological Reports,* 1977, vol. 40, pp. 129–130. The study was replicated by a student at the School of Library and Information Science, State University of New York at Albany. The result was much the same; i.e., librarians as a rule do not discriminate between users according to the way they are dressed.

These questions and responses illustrate different levels of reference service. These levels may be categorized as follows:

Conservative or Minimum Service At its extreme, this type of service consists of no more than pointing out where a reference work may be found and, on occasion, helping the patron to help himself or herself. There is no concerted effort to educate, inform, or perform anything approaching reference service. The librarian who consistently takes this position, i.e., who offers minimal service, may argue that it is part of the educational process. It is not.

An example of minimum service might be:

User: Do you have *Audio?*
Reference Librarian: Audio?
User: Audio, you know the hi-fi magazine.
Reference Librarian: Let me check. Yes, we have it. It's right over there (pointing) on the shelves labeled "A."

Now, if the telephone rings or if the reference librarian is especially busy or lazy, the reference interview is over at this point. The user is sent off to *Audio* magazine with an unknown objective and an unknown information need.[16]

Moderate or Middling Service Here the librarian may make an active effort to instruct certain select patrons in the use of the library while answering their questions. On a slack day, considerable information may be provided. On a busy day, the minimal approach may be necessary. On any day, the librarian has mixed feelings about the extent of the service that should be offered.

Let us return to our previous example.

A better reference librarian, or a less busy one, might be able to extend the reference interview, perhaps by offering to take the user to the stack area where *Audio* is shelved.

Reference Librarian: Do you want the latest issue?
User: Oh, I don't know. I just want to browse through them to see if they have any evaluation of equipment.
Reference Librarian: Do you know what kind of equipment you're looking for tests on?
User: Sure.
Reference Librarian: These magazines usually have an index of some kind, and you can see what equipment they have evaluated.[17]

[16]Jack King, "Put a Prussian Spy in Your Library," *RQ,* Fall 1978, p. 32.
[17]Ibid.

Liberal or Maximum Service Here the librarian consistently comes up with the answer or with the sources of the answers. He or she is both willing and anxious to help the patron personally, but only when such help is requested.

Our example concludes:

Reference Librarian: Sometimes one magazine won't evaluate what you're interested in. If *Audio* doesn't have it, *High Fidelity* or *Stereo Review* might have done an evaluation.

User: Do you have those?

Reference Librarian: Sure. We even have *Consumer Index* which indexes all of those magazines. If you know what equipment you want to see evaluations on, you could look it up there.

User: I've got a list right here of the equipment I want to read about.

Reference Librarian: You must be in the market for a hi-fi set.

User: Just the receiver. I want to buy a receiver. I've been around to the dealers and looked at what they had. Now I want to see the evaluations.[18]

The ultimate response in our example would be for the librarian to come up with photocopies of the consumer reports and other studies needed by the user to evaluate equipment.

Rettig summarizes these service attitudes by making the point that they represent not only interpersonal levels of communication, but, more important, varieties of definitions of information:

> *Each level of service carries a narrow definition of what information is. Conservative service defines it as direction to information sources or instruction in their use. Moderate service defines it as sometimes information sources, sometimes instruction in their use, and sometimes messages from these sources. Liberal service defines information as messages received from information sources.*[19]

Few libraries limit their services to any of these levels of reference service. One user may receive minimal help, another maximum. One librarian may believe in one type of service, another in a different type.

How does a user know when a librarian is going to give minimum or maximum service? The user might be able to determine

---

[18]Ibid.

[19]James Rettig, "A Theoretical Model and Definition of the Reference Process," *RQ*, Fall 1978, p. 25.

her prospects by looking around to see how many people are making use of the service. Or she might go to a favorite librarian who inevitably gives maximum service. But, never knowing quite what to expect, the patron usually expects little or nothing. As a result, he tends to ask questions in an exploratory fashion, determining as things move along (if they do) what type of service is likely to be given.[20]

How much easier it would be if the library had a sign or a recorded voice explaining the philosophy of reference service, e.g., "We give maximum service," or "We give minimum service," or "Today we give maximum service, but never on Saturdays." But there is uncertainty, even unwillingness, in clearly establishing what the patron may expect when approaching the reference desk.

Determining the type of service given to individual users has been generally left to the librarian, and one strongly suspects that reference service is more often offered to meet the convenience of the librarian than of the user. The result is that few patrons have any concept of what it could mean if the library did offer maximum reference service.

A philosophy of moderate service only partially explains the reluctance of some librarians to go beyond finding a ready-reference source or an answer. Perhaps no further service is offered because the librarian is uncertain about specific reference sources to help the user and does not want to show ignorance. Worse, the librarian may know the source(s), but does not want to bother getting up from behind the desk to help. It may also be that the librarian is reluctant to become involved in a discussion or a reference interview with the person. This attitude is "probably due to constraints of the pressure of business in general. Professionals had developed the habit or policy of pursuing questions only up to a certain point—that point at which they could turn to a reference source for solution—and stopping short when the only resource was a difficult interview where prospects of success seemed low."[21]

---

[20]Ibid. Rettig rightfully suggests that "the type of service a librarian gives . . . should be determined by the type of information the inquirer wants, not by the librarian's allegiance to a level of service." This is more theoretical than real in that the attitude of service shades everything, even, one suspects, the way a librarian enters into an interview. However, Rettig later admits that reference service is really no more than interpersonal communication, and it is suggested that the best type of interpersonal communication occurs when the librarian is prepared to give the maximum amount of service, no matter what the need of the user.

[21]Halldorsson, op. cit., p. 391.

There are many different ramifications flowing from different attitudes of service. The interview, obviously, is modified by the librarian's feeling about helping people. The librarian who limits questions, or who merely waves a hand in the direction of a card catalog, is doing the user a major disservice. That librarian is cutting that patron off from much of the information in the library. Stumbling about looking for this or that document or bit of data, the average person is likely to settle for whatever comes to hand, no matter how limited or outdated the information found.[22]

An even worse consequence of little or no service is a subsequent wrong answer. In one study it was found that librarians frequently realized they should conduct a reference interview with an individual, but "were singularly reluctant to interview, asking only a few perfunctory questions."[23] As a result, the user left the library with a total misconception of reference service—and often the wrong answer.

Educating the library user

One aspect of the reference interview, an aspect closely related to the philosophy of level of service, is the education of the library user. According to the reference service "Guidelines," the reference librarian has two primary duties:

> (a) Reference or information services . . . [which] may range from answering an apparently simple query to supplying information based on bibliographical search. (b) Formal or informal instruction in the use of the library . . . rather than providing the information itself to users.[24]

The emphasis on instruction at the cost of providing "the information itself to the user" militates against maximum service and comes down on the side of moderate service. Some reference librarians, of course, do not interpret the ruling that way and suggest that instruction is a part of maximum service.

Excluding formal library education in bibliography classes "for credit," education in library use is limited. There are, to be sure,

[22]Harold N. Boyer, "Academic Reference Service: Conservative or Liberal Application?" *Southeastern Librarian,* Fall 1979, pp. 155–157. This is a cogent argument for liberal service and the author points out some sad results of minimum service.

[23]Halldorsson, op. cit., p. 391.

[24]"A Commitment to Information Services," *Library Journal,* April 15, 1976, p. 974. Similar support for instruction will be found in "Standards for College Libraries," *College & Research News,* October 1975, p. 292; *Standards for Media Programs* (Chicago: American Library Association, 1969), p. 4.

standard and worthwhile efforts to label the card catalog, to prepare mimeographed or printed guides to the library, and even to include audiovisual instruction in where to find what. Many academic and school libraries offer introductory tours of their facilities and give limited instruction in use of files and materials. However, in most reference situations—and this is the implication of the "Guidelines"— instruction is an ongoing process.

A typical instructional situation occurs when the librarian shows a person how to use the *Readers' Guide* or explains the classification system of the library. Nonformalized, usually highly personal instruction is second nature to many reference librarians, even those who may or may not have particular interest in a total library instruction program. Often the instruction has no formal content, but several libraries do employ printed handouts which explain various reference works; wall charts and posters are also favored tools of instruction. And as the instruction becomes more integrated with an overall program, the library is likely to employ slide-tape presentations.[25]

The amount of literature on the subject, the degree of interest shown at meetings and conferences, and results of numerous surveys all indicate a strong interest in user education by reference librarians.[26] There are numerous reasons for this, but one suspects that primarily it is because educating the user is more interesting than simply answering ready-reference questions. While not as stimulating as working with search or research queries, it has some elements of both and even becomes a part of the search or research situation.

Then there is the library-college movement, sparked by the Montieth College Library experiment, which links library instruction with the total academic experience. Although there is little disagreement with this program, to date the funds for other such programs have been limited. However, the library-college movement is consid-

---

[25] Peter Olevnik, "Non-Formalized Point-of-Use Library Instruction: A Survey," *Catholic Library World,* December 1978, pp. 219–220. A study of practices in 1333 academic libraries revealed almost all had some type of informal or formalized point-of-use instruction. Asked if it worked, 62 percent replied that it did, while only 7 percent were certain it did not work. The people who were instructed had no vote on that question.

[26] The number of articles produced in any one year is startling. See the annotated bibliography, H. B. Rader, "Library Orientation and Instruction," *Reference Services Review,* January/March 1980, pp. 31–46. See also the regular column "Library Instruction" in *The Journal of Academic Librarianship.*

erably more than simple instruction in library use, and, because of that, it is not considered in further detail here.[27]

There are numerous arguments for user education in the library. The most often heard include:

1. The library is the heart of education. The librarian is part of the system of education. Therefore, the librarian should be a teacher. As teachers, "their motive and style is to facilitate learning; help people make connections between ideas and books, serials, and nonprint media; and help them develop a sense of selectivity and critical judgment about sources. . . ."[28]

2. Lacking funds and staff, it is necessary to use time wisely, if everyone is to be served. Time does not permit maximum or even moderate service. Therefore, it is better to have an educated user who will not have to rely on librarians who may not be available.

3. "Information users trained as information scientists could, by eliminating the intermediaries, speed up the flow of information. . . . The possibility of such an arrangement depends upon the training of each potential information user."[29] The assumption of a "speed-up" is dependent upon a less-than-skilled librarian being about.

This last argument is often used in another context.

If scientists and engineers (here the reader may substitute any aware individual) are to cope effectively in the increasingly rich information environment, they must learn the skills of scientific communication—how to monitor, select, acquire, synthesize, use, and disseminate scientific and technical information relevant to their needs.[30]

Those who argue for maximum service believe that the librarian should furnish information, not instruction on how to find that

---

[27]It is important to distinguish the typical "how we use the library" effort from the fundamental educational approach of the college library movement, particularly at Montieth, Earlham, Swarthmore, Sangamon, etc. For ongoing news about this, see *Learning Today,* an educational magazine devoted to the subject, and *Education Libraries Bulletin.*

[28]Robert Spencer, "The Teaching Library," *Library Journal,* May 15, 1978, p. 1023. This is a solid argument for library instruction.

[29]J. M. Ross, "Information Science—The Views of Some New Recruits," *The Information Scientist,* September 1978, p. 97.

[30]Carole Ganz, "Education and Training for the User and the Information Specialist," *Library Science with a Slant to Documentation,* no. 2, June 1978, p. 67.

information, and that the user should be taught how to use the library only when he or she expressly asks. They argue their point this way:

1. Librarians are, by profession, experts in information and it is foolish to assume that a five-minute, or, for that matter, 15-week course will adequately train the individual in the use of reference sources.

2. Most people want information, not how to find that information.

3. If librarians were released for professional information duties, there would be enough personnel and money for maximum service.

4. The trained librarian has knowledge "which would allow him to provide users with information they do not even know they want—knowledge to organize the network of formal and informal channels of communication necessary to [their discipline], and knowledge of how to use information to forecast and interpret future [factors]."[31] This underlines the next point.

5. To assume that library education can equip an individual to everything he or she needs is to short-change the user. Having learned one or two indexes, for example, the user may think he or she has mastered the library and is hence effectively cut off from other knowledge.

6. Library education for the most part has not worked, has not made the library any more inviting, has not increased library use, and has, in fact, introduced still another frustration factor for the average user.[32]

There have been few studies of the librarian as teacher. Pauline

[31]Ibid., p. 71. After experimenting with training scientists to use library resources, the author concludes: "It is unlikely that basic researchers as a group and as individuals are going to take on many of the responsibilities for communication they should assume to be reflective users of information and, more important, self-reflective scientists."

[32]There are a number of articles which question the value of educating the user, but the two basic ones remain: Anita R. Schiller, "Reference Service: Instruction or Information," *The Library Quarterly*, January 1965; and J. E. Scrivener, "Instruction in Library Use: The Persisting Problem," *Australian Academic & Research Libraries*, June 1972. Schiller presents the arguments concerning education, pro and con, and concludes that reason and experience are on the side of those who do not insist on user education. Scrivener supports this view by citing 450 studies on the subject and concludes that there is a vast interest, but "it is a problem to which no generally acceptable solutions have been found." In the 1980s this conclusion remains true.

Wilson, in offering a fine summary of the situation, takes issue with the often unquestioned notion that librarians are teachers.[33]

There are difficulties encountered in arguing the pros and cons of library education. First, there are numerous interpretations of the term. Library education may mean one-to-one instruction, or formalized single courses, or even three- to four-year programs. The different methods employed tend to follow several well-known patterns. Second, there has been no objective evaluation of library education, at least on a national basis. Local evaluation, where it exists, usually has so many built-in biases that the results of the evaluation are often foregone conclusions.

Asked "Is library instruction making effective progress in significantly contributing to the college student's education?" librarians are likely to reply: (a) "The profession will welcome the efforts to measure the effectiveness of library instruction," or (b) "Library use instruction is starting to make very effective progress. . . . Evaluation of the effectiveness of these programs will be difficult. . . . I know of no large-scale attempts to evaluate library instruction," or (c) "Do user education programs significantly contribute to the college student's education? We don't know." or (d) "There is no doubt that wide interest exists in user education. . . . As to whether such instruction contributes significantly to the student's education no doubt depends on the individual.[34]

Until such time as there is any indication of objective measurement of education programs, the arguments will continue to rage.[35] Meanwhile, the library user and nonuser should be given a choice. It is important to stress "given a choice." The user should have the option of (1) learning how to use the library or any of its parts, or (2) not learning how to use the library while still expecting a full answer to his or her question(s) from the reference librarian. Furthermore, because particular needs vary at particular times, this option should be open, so that the user has the choice of either asking for

[33]Pauline Wilson, "Librarians as Teachers: The Study of an Organizational Fiction," *The Library Quarterly,* April 1979, pp. 146–162. This should be required reading for all involved with library instruction.

[34]"Library Instruction," *Journal of Academic Librarianship,* July 1978, pp. 160–161. Opinions are from three academic librarians and an officer of the Council on Library Resources.

[35]Larry Hardesty et al., "Evaluating Library-Use Instruction," *College & Research Libraries,* July 1979, pp. 309–317. The authors provide a model of evaluation but admit it needs modifications. See, too, David N. King and John C. Ory, "Effects of Library Instruction on Student Research: A Case Study." *College & Research Libraries,* January, 1981, pp. 31–41. Here the authors offer another model of evaluation.

instruction or avoiding it each time he or she approaches the reference desk.

Enter the computer

The computer has drastically changed the argument about levels of reference service and user education. Because of the relative complexity of searching data bases at a computer terminal, the search is almost always performed by a librarian or search analyst; this yields not only an answer, but a printout, i.e., list of citations or a bibliography. The inevitable result is service on a maximum level, whether the librarian wishes it or not. Technology has pushed many librarians into maximum service; given a computer, nothing less is possible.

The computer has revolutionized the very philosophy of reference service as well as the actual search process. The nondelegated search, in which the person who needs information conducts his own search, exemplifies the notion that the librarian should educate the user in methods of finding answers. The idea is to make the user self-sufficient, and the underlying assumption is that the trained librarian may make the average person as well versed in finding her way about the library as the librarian.

Much of this has changed because the computer simply refuses to obey the commands of the average user who is less than well acquainted with computer searches. As Atherton puts it:

> Searching the literature and compiling bibliographies with the aid of a computer requires skills, study, and training that one cannot expect library patrons to master. Accordingly, the reference librarian's role changes from that of "gate keeper" of the collections to that of being an active agent or advocate of a particular library patron with a specific information need or interest. The odds are against the do-it-yourselfer. Simple online searches, such as catalog checks for known items, may be done directly by the end user. However, the complex online searches . . . are still too demanding to be conducted successfully by any but the trained specialist.[36]

The relative complexity of using a computer to search for materials has resulted in a startling statistic: about 90 percent of the searches done today are done through an intermediary, usually a trained librarian.

The librarian has a definite advantage here because of knowl-

---

[36]Pauline Atherton, *Librarians and Online Services* (White Plains, N. Y.: Knowledge Industry Publications, 1977, p. 6, p. 117.

edge of the total system. The librarian is likely to find what is needed not only more quickly (no minor thing when costs are determined by time), but more efficiently. As a specialist he will know which sources to access. In rare instances, the layperson may operate just as efficiently because of an intimate understanding of the subject and of what specific information is needed. However, this occurs only when the subject expert has the same expertise in retrieval as the librarian. As this is rare, the best results come from a close collaboration between the two.[37]

The development of the new technology does not mean a decrease in library positions nor an instant library in every home. The information problem will more likely increase rather than decrease in dimension. Everyone will be able to choose what interests him or her from the mass of available information, but the difficulty will be in moving from general interests to particular, in being able to separate the necessary data from the mass of information available. This is likely to require an expert intermediary between masses of information and the consumer. Where and how the intermediary will operate remains to be defined, but he or she will be necessary if general information is to be translated into specific.

Lack of user access

Applaud as one may the new role of the reference librarian, it has serious drawbacks. In a manual search the user has the choice of calling upon the librarian or doing the search personally. (Actually, the librarian may be of little or no assistance, but that is another problem; the point is that theoretically, at least, the user has a choice.) There is no choice, however, when a data base is used. This lack of choice could present serious limitations, particularly as more and more information is "locked away" in data bases. It is conceivable that technology could carry us to the point where "big brother," ably assisted by a librarian, could control access to information.

The conventional way of helping users to master computer searches is via the traditional workshops and tutorials wherein the librarian shows the layperson the basics of searching. Because the systems are too diverse, too expensive and too difficult to access, such standard teaching vehicles are no longer satisfactory. The alternative, and one which by now is apparent to almost everyone, is to construct a

---

[37]Many tests have been run in comparing the patron's and the librarian's use of various systems, and the results are always much the same as explained here. See A. J. Harley, "An Introduction to Mechanized Information Retrieval," *Aslib Proceedings,* December 1978, pp. 420–425.

system which may be accessed by librarians and laypersons in a simple, direct fashion, much as one would use a printed index or encyclopedia. The steps necessary to make the computer data bases easy to use are called "transparent" by researchers in the field.[38]

Technological improvements necessary to make computer searches easy for even the most awkward layperson are the center of ongoing research by both public and private organizations. MIT is working on a simple command language, and the large television and radio conglomerates are seeking ways to give the computer simple voice commands. Eventually, the systems will be easy to use, but in the decade or so ahead it is unlikely that anyone but the most dedicated layperson can or will choose to eliminate the necessary intermediary —the librarian.[39]

Conclusion

The obvious question now is: Why does the person who uses a data base receive maximum assistance, while the individual who relies on traditional library service receives minimum help? Isn't this a bit unfair? It is, and some libraries counter by charging for the maximum service, i.e., for searching a data base.

The ultimate plea for maximum service is a plea for survival. If reference service is to continue as a viable part of the library, it must compete with numerous new technologies and, eventually, meet the higher expectations of service from individuals. When a person finds he can get the same information from a television set that he can receive from a reference librarian, and with considerably less difficulty, respect for that librarian is going to decrease. Respect—and better funding and higher salaries—will come only when the librarian performs that level of service which cannot be found elsewhere. At

---

[38]"Research is needed to make the [computer] steps transparent to the users of systems and networks and thus make them more user-oriented." Martha Williams, "Online Retrieval Today and Tomorrow," *Online Review,* December 1978, p. 361. The word is becoming common in a discussion of simplification of the use of computer searchers. There are numerous programs to train laypersons, but even the best depend upon the user being "someone who likes computers and likes to play with them"—in other words, a more likely scientist or technologist rather than the average expert or layperson. For one such training program see Charles T. Meadows, "The Computer as a Search Intermediary," *Online,* July 1979, pp. 54–59.

[39]Librarians are trying to educate users to find their own data at the computer keyboard. See the report on the ALA section MARS (Machine-Assisted Reference Section) effort to teach users, *Library Journal,* August 1980, p. 1589.

that time the average individual will see reference service as a necessity.

SUGGESTED READING

Boyer, Harold, "Academic Reference Service: Conservative or Liberal Application?" *The Southeastern Librarian,* Fall 1979, pp. 155–157. A clear summary of the various levels of reference service with good documentation.

Gardner, Trudy, "Effect of On-line Data Bases on Reference Policy," *RQ,* Fall 1979, pp. 70–74. The author identifies different levels and philosophies of service and shows how the introduction of data base searches will force modification of the traditional views of reference service.

Goffman, Erving. *Forms of Talk.* Philadelphia: University of Pennsylvania Press, 1981. A collection of essays by the American sociologist who probably makes more sense concerning the way people communicate (including interviews) than anyone else writing on the subject. The varieties of ordinary discourse discussed here should be required reading for those concerned with the reference interview.

Goldie, Judith, and Jacki Pritchard. "Interview Methodology . . ." *Aslib Proceedings,* February 1981, pp. 62–66. Various interviewing techniques are discussed, with particular focus on the telephone interview. While not precisely concerned with the reference situation, the brief paper is useful for the frank discussion of different approaches.

Goldhor, Herbert, "The Patrons' Side of Public Library Reference Questions," *Public Library Quarterly,* Spring 1979, pp. 35–49. Results of recording the reference interview and its techniques in the Urbana (Ill.) Free Library. The survey measured a wide variety of subjects, from who uses reference services to how well questions are answered.

Jahoda, Gerald, and Judith Braunagel, *The Librarian and Reference Queries: A Systematic Approach.* New York: Academic Press, 1980. A step-by-step approach to the reference process with exercises in answering reference queries. The real strength of this text is in the clear analysis of the reference query and the systematic description of basic reference works.

Jennerich, Elaine Z., "Before the Answer: Evaluating the Reference Process," *RQ,* Summer 1980, pp. 360–366. The author suggests several methods of evaluating the reference interview and, in so doing, points to good and bad interview procedures. She concludes with a useful list of references.

Lester, Ray, "Why Educate the Library User?" *Aslib Proceedings,* August 1979, pp. 366–380. A careful argument against the current theory that the typical user should be educated in the use of the library. Valuable for numerous quotes and the author's obvious familiarity with the field and its problems.

Lubans, John (ed.), *Progress in Educating the Library User.* New York: R. R. Bowker, 1978. A series of articles collected by one of the more able advocates of library use education. A similar work was edited by Lubans in 1974. See, too, Deborah Lockwood, *Library Instruction: A Bibliography.* Westport, Conn.: Greenwood, 1979. This is a relatively up-to-date bibliography which is nicely arranged and easy to use.

Marshall, A. P. (ed.), "Current Library Use Instruction," *Library Trends,* Summer 1980. A series of articles in which John Tucker opens up the discussion with a most useful history of user education in academic libraries. Both practical and theoretical steps follow. Of particular interest is H. B. Rader's "Reference Services as a Teaching Function."

McMurdo, George, "Psychology and Librarianship—an Appraisal of the Potential of Experimental Psychology in the Study of Librarian-Client Behaviour," *Aslib Proceedings,* July/August 1980, pp. 319–327. It had to happen. Here the author calls upon librarians to employ basic psychological methods to improve the reference interview and general communication patterns with users. The methodology is explained.

Norman, O. G., "The Reference Interview: An Annotated Bibliography," *Reference Services Review,* January/March 1979, pp. 71–77. The best selective bibliography available. The compiler not only annotates well, but has a feeling for what is or is not important in the area. A point of beginning for almost anyone interested in researching the reference interview.

The Reference Interview. Ottawa: Canadian Library Association, 1979. The proceedings of a 1977 symposium with papers by Samuel Rothstein, Bernard Vavrek, and shorter pieces on various topics.

Renford, Beverly, and Linnea Hendrickson, *Bibliographic Instruction: A Handbook.* New York: Neal-Schuman Publishers, 1980. A step-by-step guide for librarians, not users, who want suggestions on how to improve library instruction. Includes numerous charts, guides, etc.

Roloff, Michael, "Communication at the User-System Interface: A Review of Research," *Library Research,* vol. 1, 1979, pp. 1–18. The author examines several theories and studies of the reference interview and related matters. He provides a useful overview of the literature through early 1978.

Stewart, M. Massey, "Information Work and the Four Humours," *The Information Scientist,* September 1978, pp. 105–111. A unique approach to reference service and the interview based upon an interpretation of the classical four humors and how they are employed in dealing with inquiries.

CHAPTER FOUR

The Search

T HE SEARCH is an integral part of the reference inter-
view. Despite efforts to analyze, chart, and teach by
the numbers, it can be as subjective and intuitive a
process as the interview itself and just as complex. For
the search, as for the interview, the result is the
ultimate control. No matter what plan of attack is
used to discover the answer(s), success in finding the needed information is considerably more important than the process, no matter how
ingenious, which produces it. And the process varies. One librarian
may favor a type of "guerrilla warfare"; another may be more
comfortable with a considered, logical plan; a third may use both
approaches.

The secondary control in the search is the amount of time spent
in the process. "*Any* search which locates the desired information is an
effective search; the *efficient* search, however, is the effective one that
locates desired information with a minimum amount of time and
effort."[1]

The search tends to be more structured and more amenable to
close analysis than the interview. However, it is probably necessary to
point out here what is obvious to almost any reader who has ever used
a library: Not every search is a success; quite often the search is not

[1]James Benson and Ruth K. Maloney, "Principles of Searching," *RQ*, Summer 1975, p.
316.

even begun. Why can a search be even less satisfying to the user than the interview? One answer might be in the attitude of the reference librarian, or in the librarian's knowledge, or ignorance, of the subject matter.

Where there is no interview there is usually no formal search, although the librarian may look for a book, an index, or a periodical in a perfunctory sort of way in reply to a specific question about that book, index, or periodical, e.g., "Where is *Hamlet*?" "Where is the *Readers' Guide*?" or "Where is *Audio*?"

The search process generally begins with an interview, no matter how short. Once the librarian has received the message and has understood the question, if only tentatively, her next logical step is to match that question with the source(s) most likely to yield the answer. If someone asks for information on Tom Jones and knows this Jones is alive, well, and serving in Congress, the librarian sifts through a series of mental signals: Congressman, important personage, *Who's Who in America*. If the question concerns the literary figure Tom Jones, the signals are different: literature, Henry Fielding, encyclopedia for Fielding, or *Masterplots* for summary of *Tom Jones*, eighteenth-century literary criticism. But if the reference is to the popular singer, then the signal is the appropriate index, which may be anything from *Access* (which has more music magazines than *Readers' Guide*) to *Magazine Index* to *Popular Periodicals Index* to more specific music sources and/or *Biography and Genealogy Master Index*. And so the process goes. Matching the question with the logical source is as complex as the needs of the user; that is, depending upon the sophistication of the user's needs, one simple source may be used, or a more complex source, or even several sources, may be needed.

The search strategy a librarian employs depends primarily upon the nature of the inquiry. In its broadest terms the inquiry—and the search—may be divided into two types. If the inquirer seeks specific data, as in the case of a ready-reference query, the goal is predefined, and the search strategy can be laid out in a methodical, step-by-step fashion. A standardized pattern of routine movements can be prescribed, the purpose being to include, or exclude, certain alternatives. A more in-depth inquiry, as in the case of a specific search or research query, requires an investigative type of search strategy. Faith in routine must be replaced by faith in insight.

MODEL OF THE SEARCH PROCESS

The search is an effort to translate the user's query into terms acceptable by given reference sources. The analogy of the key and the lock pertains here. The proper interpretation of the query is the key which unlocks the source(s). The problem is in matching the key and the lock, not always an easy task—there are thousands of potential locks and, as seen, the key, the user's question, is always subject to change.

Logan provides a handy summary of the process:

> *Subject to limitations imposed by the amount of detail required and time factors, reference method can be seen as a four-stage process: (a) breaking the enquiry down into subject-headings; (2) deciding an order of search for sources of information on these subjects; (3) knowing how to carry out such a search effectively, by use of the library's catalogue, bibliographies or general reference books; and (4) following up the results of the search by finding material on the library shelves, suggesting a list of references, interpreting information found, or supplying photocopies. Ability in reference method requires an analytical mind, [and] good general knowledge supplemented by subject knowledge.*[2]

The reference librarian begins with a fundamental effort to bring the query and the library system together.

There have been numerous studies of the reference librarian in action, studies which attempt to analyze the complex search procedure. The results have often been charted; for one of the more ambitious mapping schemes, see the detailed charts of the reference librarian's search methods in Carlson's study.[3]

The process may be outlined in this way:

1. The query is first analyzed and clarified via the reference interview. From this, one determines the type of question asked, the parameters to be established (i.e., purpose, scope, time span, amount of material, level of material, etc.), and the source(s) or system(s) where the necessary information is likely to be found.

2. In the case of the majority of ready-reference queries, a source usually comes readily to mind, the source is consulted, and the answer is given.

3. In the case of search and research queries (and more difficult ready-reference questions), it is necessary to consider numerous sources or possibilities.

[2]Robert G. Logan, "The Process of Legal Literature Searching," *The Law Librarian,* August 1979, p. 27.

[3]G. Carlson, *Search Strategy by Reference Librarians, Part 3.* Sherman Oaks, Calif.: Hughes Dynamics, 1964). This is reprinted in F. W. Lancaster, *The Measurement and Evaluation of Library Services* (Washington, D.C.: Information Resources Press, 1977), pp. 113–129.

4. At this point, a likely source is usually one of two major possibilities:
   a. Bibliographies, indexes, card catalog—that is, not sources of answers in themselves but access points to answers.
   b. Form and/or subject sources, from standard reference books to magazines, newspapers, vertical file material, and a given subject area on the shelves.
      In most situations, because the searcher is not entirely sure of the avenues for an answer, (a) will be a first choice as a source.

5. Where bibliographies, the card catalog, etc., are to be searched for keys to sources, the searcher must determine likely subject headings. A helpful aid at this point is to list keywords most likely to be appropriate for such a search.

6. A choice of action must then be made. The searcher may:
   a. Broaden the search in terms of the subject headings.
   b. Narrow the search.
   c. Select more specific, or less specific, subject headings.
   d. Find more appropriate terms.

7. Through steps 4 to 6, there should be some type of dialogue between the user and the librarian. Or the dialogue may follow later when likely material is gathered. At any rate, adjustments in terms of which data can be used, which are peripheral, and which are useless, must be made throughout the total search process.

8. At this point in the search decisions are made.
   a. If there is more than a minimal amount of material, the librarian must decide in what order to search the material located via the bibliography, catalog, index, etc.
   b. Given some of the material, a judgment has to be made as to the relevance of the material to the specific question put by the user.
   c. If nothing can be found, the librarian must decide whether to try new or modified approaches, to give up, or to suggest to the user other avenues of approach (i.e., other libraries, interlibrary loan, a reframing of the request, etc.).
   d. In any case, the librarian must determine how much time can be given to answering the question.

Were the search process always this neat, the problem would only be one of finding specific sources or entry points to those sources. In practice, however, the librarian may decide that a given reference book has the answer but not find it; turn to another similar title but not find it; go to a bibliography but not find it; go to an index, find it, but then discover the article is too broad for the user; return to the index but not find additional materials; go to another index—and on and on until the patience of either the librarian or the user has reached a point of exhaustion. In most situations this does not happen, but it can. Because of the variables of both human judgment and resources, it is impossible to give a definitive outline of a search process. Even in a search in an extremely narrow area of interest, specialization becomes individualized and the definitive too often expands to the infinite.

THE SEARCH AND PROBLEM SOLVING

Everything from the clarification of the question to the probable location of materials may be almost a subconscious effort on the librarian's part. In the average reference situation each of these steps may be going on almost simultaneously. At any rate, rare is the librarian who consciously diagrams each step and moves neatly from square to square. Once the circuit of matching question with possible sources is closed, however, the librarian must have a strategy for finding the information itself. The strategy may involve no more than taking out a volume of an encyclopedia or looking up information in an index or in the card catalog. On the other hand, it may involve a more extensive search that leads to not a few dead ends and not infrequent returns to "Go."

The search process is strongly governed by the objectives and the philosophy of the reference service. If the service is minimum, i.e., primarily one of helping the user find citations and possible sources, the librarian's search is really directional. The user will be advised to search X index or Y reference book or to look under P subject heading in the catalog. The user may even be counseled to try another department in the library or another library. If the service is middling or moderate, the librarian may actually go to the index, card catalog, or reference source and help the user find what is desired. If the service is maximum, the librarian will follow through by gathering citations and possibly useful sources until satisfied the user has enough material to answer the question.

An analysis of the search reveals that it may take one or two different, sometimes simultaneous, paths. The first concerns the thought processes of the librarian. The second concerns the actual steps the librarian takes once the thought processes have been triggered. For example, some searching is almost automatic in that the librarian knows from practice where to look. But sometimes considerable thought may be given to the question and to the source of its answer. Once the mental process has evolved, the actual search is then a matter of locating materials in given forms. Obviously, even the simplest thought process requires a follow-through to a source and an answer; while it is possible in theory to separate thought from action, in practice it never quite works this way.

In short, analyzing the thought patterns of the librarian in the search process has a certain fascination and significance. Still, the feasibility of carrying this beyond generalizations seems fairly questionable, particularly so since trained psychologists and educators are far from certain how to explain the thought process. A major step in any investigation of problem-solving procedures is to observe the human behavior associated with it. Unfortunately, for the most part human problem solving is not directly observable.

The librarian goes through certain internal mental operations during the search process. And these operations vary from librarian to librarian. Decisions are made, decisions which may be rational or emotional, expressed or unexpressed. There is no way of generalizing this process; the human factor is the overwhelming and underlying variable in the problem-solving process.

One of the ways of understanding these internal mental operations is to have librarians describe what they are doing as they attempt to solve a problem, that is, to have them map their steps in the search process. Other approaches to fathoming the process vary from direct observation to questionnaires. By any of these methods the process can be verbalized (and possibly later reduced to a mathematical or logical formula), but the process of understanding the verbalization is not always easy.

Still, two basic approaches to analyzing the search process will be considered. The first is problem solving in terms of rules, the second in terms of testing.

Rules for searching

There is considerable amount of "automatic retrieval" of information by librarians. In some cases the answer is found with little or no difficulty. The system of automatic retrieval of information operates whenever the reference librarian knows (1) the solution or answer to a specific question or problem or (2) an unvarying, simple rule or set procedure for finding the solution or answer to a specific question or problem.

In the case of (1) this may be no more complex than knowing the name of the mayor of the city or the population of the state. Obviously, there is no need to consult any reference aid except memory. In the case of (2), which is more prevalent in daily reference service, the librarian employs a simple operation or procedure guaranteed to elicit a result.

Lindsay and Norman give an example of the difference between knowing specific solutions and learning basic procedures. They suggest the student consider two questions: "What is 8 times 4?" and "What is 262 times 127?"

> *For the first problem you have the facts stored in your memory and, when asked the question, you recall the answer directly. For the second problem, it is likely that you do not know the answer, but you know how to compute it. Thus, you could take a paper and pencil and, by following the rules of multiplication, procedure the response. These are two different strategies for dealing with information. The first is to store the facts directly in the memory. The second is to store a routine, a set of rules that generates the information when needed.*[4]

These two basic processes, memory and learning procedures, both serve the reference librarian (as they serve all of us), but because of the variety of queries, the most productive approach is to master the procedures. At the level discussed here, the procedures are no more complicated than mastering the multiplication table. Some examples will suffice:

1. The same search procedure can be learned and used time and time again to find the answers to questions about prize winners. The technique for learning the Pulitzer Prize winner for 1965 is the same as that for learning the Nobel Prize winner for 1977.
2. Once one learns to find the distance between New York and San Francisco, it is easy to apply the same procedure to find the distance between San Francisco and Tokyo.
3. The procedure for finding the first line of a verse using "love" is the same as that for finding the first line of a verse using "hate."
4. The procedure for finding X book in the library is the same as that for finding Y book.

The same techniques or set of rules (sometimes referred to in

[4]Peter Lindsay and Donald Norman, *Human Information Processing* (New York: Academic Press, Inc., 1972), p. 521.

the literature as "algorithms"), once learned, will automatically generate answers to the same set of questions or queries. The answers can be looked up or retrieved by what are essentially the same automatic techniques used when one masters any set of rules, from those for multiplication to those for boiling an egg.

Given what is essentially an automatic method of deriving answers for certain types of questions makes much—possibly too much—reference work no more difficult than any automatic process. The librarian simply masters a group of rules and equivalent sources for finding answers. Usually the more experienced one is in terms of types of questions and resources, the greater the number of basic rules or concepts one can acquire. For example, building upon an understanding of addition, one eventually learns how to subtract, multiply, and divide.

In general, completely automatic techniques for handling questions are limited to answering directional and some ready-reference queries—and possibly some search queries where it is no more than a matter of finding a group of documents. Research queries are rarely that easy to answer automatically.

Certain fundamental assumptions keep this essentially human-automated reference system operative.

1. The question is clearly understood, so there is no static between it and the rule for finding the answer. If, for example, one wants to know the distance between New York and San Francisco, this has to be the question—not the unexpressed query of what will this mean in terms of bus fare.

2. The rule for retrieval is as definitive as the rule for multiplication; that is, given X and Y quantity, the answer can always be found in Z source. For example, any biographical query which includes X (a deceased person) and Y (a famous American) leads automatically to Z source (either the *Dictionary of American Biography* or other sources, from general encyclopedias to almanacs, which "recognize" X and Y factors). However, introduce a variable and the result may not be predictable. When the deceased famous American is noteworthy in terms foreign to Z source (a criminal, sports figure, etc.), it may well be that Z source will not "recognize" the variable and refuse to provide the answer.

3. The librarian or the user has to know (a) the specific rule for retrieval and (b) the code or language to identify the source. In the example cited above, for instance, the librarian must

know about the *Dictionary of American Biography,* as well as alternative sources such as the general encyclopedia. Lacking this information is similar to knowing the numbers without knowing how to multiply. On the other hand, the librarian must also know the code used to locate the *DAB*. Although this information may be based on a recollection of its exact place on the shelf, it is more likely derived from a knowledge of the classification scheme employed in the library or from an ability to use the card catalog.

The obvious difficulty with learning rules that never vary in their anticipated results is that this implies that the librarian should memorize (quite literally) hundreds of sources and what answers they will provide. This might be similar to memorizing the multiplication tables—only a thousandfold. One might question the advisability of limiting the brain's imaginative powers by strapping it with rules. This type of training seems more suitable for a computer than for a reasoning human being. Perhaps the self-conscious opposition of many librarians to the computer is the sometimes naïve notion that reference work can be analyzed in purely algorithmic ways—that the perfect machine can replace the librarian if all that has to be done is to record and organize the data of usage and experience.

THE TRIAL AND TEST SEARCH

In a very real sense the search strategy is tantamount to making a hypothesis and then testing its validity through the search. For example, the answer to the question should be found in Y source (hypothesis). Y source is found, but the answer is not there. If it is not in Y, it is not likely to be in B, but it will probably be in C (hypothesis). A check of C proves the answer is there, and the hypothesis is correct. In initiating the search, the librarian can list all the possibilities, attach a success-probability function to each, and solve the problem by selecting what seems to be the best source(s).

The formulation and the testing of any hypothesis presupposes a careful analysis, but in practice how often is this really done? If the librarian is left out of the search process, the average user is more likely to browse (or as one student put it, "cruise") the collection until something likely turns up. It may not be the best source, but it is a source, and it at least serves the purpose, no matter how poorly, of answering the question. Even the librarian may conduct a "cruise," although usually with a little more direction. For example, a biographical query may simply lead the user to the biography section in the reference or the general collection in the hopes of finding what is needed without further effort. A question about a quotation may take the librarian, with no other thought about other possible sources, to the quote books.

This is not to say that browsing is not beneficial; in fact, with proper direction it may be a very legitimate search process. It needs only a minimum of thought or planning, and it can be modified as it goes along to produce the desired results.

The ability to solve the problem, that is, carry on the search process, depends not only upon the librarian's existing knowledge of the collection and the question, but on changes in that existing knowledge. The librarian begins the process by mentally testing and validating or invalidating given hypotheses and then accepting one hypothesis and testing it against the possible source. In a ready-reference question this may be quite enough, but if the source fails to provide an answer, the librarian learns to discount the hypothesis and, perhaps, the form for this type of query. Instead of an almanac, a yearbook may be more useful. This decision requires reorganizing the problem in terms of new hypotheses and building upon the state of knowledge existing when the question was first posed.

Throughout the search procedure the librarian is making decisions as to whether or not this process, this source, or this bit of information will be relevant to solving the problem of X question. Salton calls for multiple rather than single searches. One should not go "full steam ahead" on a request that has been translated into the terms of the information system without testing those translated terms first. After a partial search, it will be discovered whether the subjects chosen are adequate, or if there is a need for adjustment and refinement. Salton concludes, "One of the most fruitful ways of upgrading retrieval performance consists in using multiple searches based on user feedback information furnished during the search process."[5]

TRANSLATION OF THE QUESTION

Once the question is isolated, understood, and clarified, the next logical step is to "translate" the query into characteristics of the available information system. The "translation" process is essentially made up of two components. In the actual process of translation the

[5]G. Salton, "Automatic Text Analysis," *Science,* April 17, 1970, p. 343.

librarian may mesh the two components into one continuous process, jump from one to the other, or eliminate one in favor of the other. Nevertheless, for purposes of analysis, the translation process is made up of two parts.

1. The first of these . . . is analysis, clarification, or categorization of the question along various dimensions.
2. The other component . . . is choosing terms from the control and access language of the information system to represent the information need of the patron.[6]

The "translation of the question" is a rather academic way of saying several things about the typical question-analysis process—a process which is well understood in its broader dimensions by both the sophisticated reference librarian and the nonuser of libraries.

Form

Essentially, a basic step in translation is to isolate the form(s) for possible answers. The average television viewer or newspaper reader will translate his question—"Where can I find tomorrow's weather forecast?"—in terms of form and find his answer by turning to the paper or switching on the weather forecaster. In another situation, the question, "Where can I find the difference between the meaning of 'weather' and 'climate'?" would result in the translation of the query into the form of, say, a dictionary entry or an encyclopedia entry.

Of course, the translation of either question might be in terms of a human resource. "What's the weather tomorrow?" we ask the weather forecaster. "What's the difference between weather and climate?" the librarian asks the geographer.

Either question, too, might be translated in more depth. For example, the query changes if put by an airline pilot or by a geographer who wants a definitive explanation of weather and climate. In either case, the translation will be in more sophisticated forms, such as daily weather maps or scientific journal articles.

The most obvious type of translation is usually in terms of a librarian's self-questioning: "Is the answer most likely to be found in a book, a pamphlet, a periodical, or a government document?" This decision is usually based on the depth and timeliness of information

---

[6]Charles A. Bunge, "Reference Service in the Information Network," in *Interlibrary Communications and Information Networks,* ed. by Joseph Becker (Chicago: American Library Association, 1971), pp. 109–110.

sought, as well as on the sophistication of the user. Another decision is based on knowledge of the collection or of how easy it is to obtain materials from another library. For example, a library may have a good pamphlet collection, but the librarian who has not often used the collection may fail to consider it when a particular question is asked. Also, the librarian who realizes that technical materials on a given subject are well covered in a nearby library has the advantage of several options: he may go to the phone for an answer, or refer the user to the other library, or borrow the needed materials.

In the majority of ready-reference queries, as well as most search and research questions, the isolation of the form is probably the easiest bit of translating. And perhaps it is too easy. A librarian, for example, who has grown accustomed to equating certain queries with biographical sources, and, if he or she is typical, specific standard sources, is often overlooking equally excellent or better forms.

Subject

The next most decisive and generally the easiest translation of specific question to library system is made in isolating the subject field. Queries about where to find information on "X member of congress," or "Y American baseball player" or "Z totem pole carver" will take little translation. The librarian will automatically go to the biographical section. The "where" or "what" query, by definition, inevitably leads to a subject classification. Queries such as "What is the cost of living in New York City?" "What is the formula for water?" and "Where is the capital of Alaska?" inevitably lead to related subjects, whether statistical data or chemistry handbooks or geographical sources. Obviously, too, the relationship between form and subject is so close that often one is the other, as in questions dealing with biography and geography.

All these queries, though, are at a simple, telegraphic level where a connection between query and subject is self-evident. Problems arise when the subject is not clear or, more likely, when the librarian's knowledge of the subject field is too general or too inadequate to translate the query into a meaningful source.

What happens, for example, when the question is clear enough, but the librarian is uncertain what salient part of a large subject area should be tapped? If, for example, the user wants material on the classical theory of unchecked population growth, the librarian, in an interview situation, might try to gain a more specific insight into the needs of the user. But if the needs cannot be expressed in any more definitive terms, what next? The obvious answer, if the librarian happens to know of Thomas Malthus, is to begin either with his works or with essays about Malthus. Lacking that subject knowledge, the librarian will move from the known, population and population growth, to the unknown. The subject might be checked in a general encyclopedia for the historical background or in a subject encyclopedia. Inevitably the name of Malthus will appear. The librarian should then find subject material on Malthus and the Malthusian theory. If this does not prove satisfactory, a search of the encyclopedia (or for that matter, the card catalog or any general bibliography concerned with population) will provide other key subject terms to consider.

These steps follow the old tried-and-true principle of moving from the known to the unknown. Obviously, this presupposes an understanding of the general parameters and the vocabulary of the question. Lacking this, the librarian should return to the negotiation of the meaning of the question with the inquirer.

Success here depends upon a thorough knowledge of the library's classification systems, from cross-references in catalogs and indexes to storing and shelving systems. For example, the librarian may realize that a query has to do with the history of printing in Montana but be unable to make the association between the subject and the likely subject heading in the catalog or the place the material might be on the shelf, perhaps under Montana history, technology, or graphic arts.

The reference librarian must be able to move comfortably from the general subject to the specific subject. This presupposes a thorough knowledge of close subject classification. The librarian must have the imagination to move about in related subject areas. For example, if nothing can be found about the history of printing in Montana under the subject of printing, the librarian should then move instinctively to the broader area of Montana history or general works on printing history of the United States. If the material is not available in the given library, the librarian must also know what bibliographies and union lists to consult in order to obtain it from another library or to be able to advise the user what bibliographic sources to consider in larger libraries.

A thorough knowledge of the general collection is presupposed here, primarily because the query may be answered not in the usual sources but from a standard biography, history, or manual in the circulating collection.

Time

The element of time as related to spatial situations is fairly well determined in the question "Where can I find the per capita income of America?" The answer is going to be from a current, not a historical, source. However, the question "What was the per capita income of America in 1860?" leads the librarian to an obviously different era.

Sometimes, though, the time element is not clear. For example, when the user says, "I want something on the history of New York," he or she might be given a general history of New York City, but more likely something on a certain period is desired. A request for "something on President Carter" must be narrowed down in terms of today or yesterday, his term as president or his term as governor.

Once the time element is determined, it is relatively easy to move to corresponding sources—that is, if the library has those sources. One of the major problems in almost all but the largest libraries is currency. Retrospective sources are probably to be found in considerable number in libraries, but the question which demands information generated yesterday, the day before yesterday, a week ago, or even a month ago will pose definite problems.

Language

In the United States, in all but the largest libraries the collection is essentially in the English language. In large libraries, though, the librarian obviously must know whether the inquirer can handle French before including an article from a French periodical among his sources.

The level of reading comprehension is another aspect of language which must be considered. The specialist will be satisfied with one style, the amateur with quite another, and the young student with a third. The difficulty arises with the adult user who may be better educated or less educated than the librarian suspects.

Availability

It seems obvious the librarian cannot locate materials which are not in the library. But—and this is important—the right source may be precisely determined yet unobtainable. Everyone is familiar with the common situation of locating an article in the *Readers' Guide to Periodical Literature* and then going to the shelf and discovering that the library does not take the magazine or, more likely, that the magazine is there but the particular issue is missing, or that the issue is there but someone has cut out the article.

The librarian then turns to another source, which may be in the library or, if time permits, available via interlibrary loan. The factor of availability is often more important than recognized. Ease of use and ready accessibility, as countless studies have found, are the two major factors in determining which information is used.

While, in one way or another, all these translation devices are applicable to all types of reference queries, they apply primarily to ready-reference queries. By concept and practice, the average question is related first to a subject and/or to a form, which is normally a reference work. Beyond that, the librarian determines the specific reference work in terms of the other elements, i.e., time, language, and availability. The search can be complex, and even difficult, not because of a lack of proper translation procedures but because of a lack of specific sources.

When the question moves from the ready-reference variety to the search and research type, the emphasis tends to change. Here, instead of looking for a simple answer, or an extremely limited amount of material, the librarian is seeking the highest possible number of relevant and pertinent documents for the user's information requirements. This situation shows the importance of the use of bibliographical aids and adds the further challenge of matching the question with the access language of such aids.

ACCESS LANGUAGE OF THE INFORMATION SYSTEM

Once it is determined that the question cannot be answered quickly in a ready-reference source, the librarian must then choose methods of getting at the needed sources. To do this the librarian must know the control and access language of the collection and/or the reference sources chosen. Such knowledge presupposes an understanding of the language or terminology for tagging information used by the library or the consulted sources. This implies an appreciation of the indexing and cataloging subject terms; it also implies a knowledge of the classification scheme of the collection, the location of reference books on the shelves, even the place where, say, the ERIC microfiche are filed. In this broader, more general context the language of the information system is more directional than conceptual.

The directional language is probably the most familiar one to the average library user, particularly the user who either does not want to bother the reference librarian or has little faith in the librarian's ability to locate needed answers and information. Usually such a patron simply finds a section of materials—books, magazines, documents, etc.—which may answer his or her needs and commences to browse. In order to do this, though, the user must understand the language of classification or at least have learned through experience where the needed materials are located. That these materials happen to bear significant classification numbers may mean little.

The normal library-reference pattern of access via the language of the information system begins with specifics such as author and title, which, if accurate, afford exact entry via the catalog, index, abstract, or bibliography. Here, in fact, there is really no translation. Lacking a specific entry, the librarian must translate the query into a subject form which the catalog, index, abstract, or bibliography will accept.

The librarian should not hesitate to confess ignorance of the meaning of certain terms. If it is obvious that the user cannot help (particularly true in the case of students who may be as puzzled as the librarian by a teacher's specific wording), the terms should be checked in a general dictionary, encyclopedia, or standard work on the subject. A dictionary will suffice for definitions, but an encyclopedia may be necessary for an overall view, especially when the question involves a matter of judgment. For example, to understand a request for material on hydrometers a dictionary definition of "hydrometer" may be sufficient. However, if the question is "What is the dividing line between legislative matters of policy and executive matters of administration?" a dictionary definition of the terms will be of little help, whereas a quick check of an encyclopedia article on government may clarify the question.

Common failures at this level may come from misunderstanding as well as from failure to grasp the meaning of the terms. The user's mis-pronunciation may indicate one word, when she had another term in mind; for example, the user pronounces "neurglia" but means "neuralgia." Or the spelling of a term, name, event, etc., may be wrong and delay the search. This is particularly true when a user seeks information on persons or places. The difficulties of the situation may become apparent in the cooperative reference service when a request is channeled to a central library for material on china or on seals.

Searching bibliographies and indexes

About 50 percent of all searches of catalogs (and probably indexes) are by subject. Such subject searches are usually to select books or articles or, in the case of the catalog, to find the shelf location of books in order to browse in the area of interest. Normally this search is limited to one place; that is, the librarian or user goes no further than a single subject heading. Experiences may differ, but statistics show that about one-half the searches done by laypeople are effective, while the searches conducted by librarians may be 70 to 80 percent effective.[7]

While the figures for success and failure vary from survey to survey, there is a consensus that subject headings in catalogs and indexes are often less than satisfactory. The good reference librarian makes an earnest effort to become familiar with the subject headings employed in the library and with those in any cooperative system or network. This familiarity comes through practice and through knowledge of such things as the Library of Congress subject heading list or the Sears subject headings. It is supposed, too, that the librarian will learn the subject approach used by the major indexing and abstracting services and be acquainted with general indexing practices.

Here it is worth observing that if the librarian has difficulty with the translation of users' needs into subject headings acceptable to the system, how successful is the average user, who knows nothing about the system? Not very, and it is here that Taylor makes a wise observation which many beginners should consider:

> There really has been little empathy for the unsophisticated [i.e., nonnative] user. Within the conventional information system, the signs offered the inquirer pose too many alternatives without specification as to where each may lead or what each will do for the inquirer. . . . For the type of questions posed there is a great deal of "noise" in library catalogs, particularly in the subject section.[8]

Given this situation of self-help, Taylor suggests that the librarian who confidently expects the user to master the library should look to his or her own problems—more particularly the problems about question clarification and searching. In the question-negotiation reference process the librarian, knowing the particular system, has difficulties enough. When that same process is left wholly or almost completely to the user, the result can be a disaster in which no answer, the wrong answer, or too little information is found. This leads Taylor to rightfully conclude:

> The results seem to support the belief that the inquirer's interaction with a library or information system has certain similarities to the negotiations

---

[7]Marcia Bates, "Factors Affecting Subject Catalog Search Success," *Journal of the American Society for Information Science*, May 1977, pp. 161–169. Figures are from numerous studies and reports which the author summarizes.

[8]Robert S. Taylor, "Question Negotiation and Information Seeking in Libraries," *College & Research Libraries*, May 1968, pp. 189–190.

process. If this belief has validity, it means that libraries are frustrating to use and that library systems need considerably more experimental work to enhance this interface between user and library.[9]

Keywords

At any rate, to return to the librarian who is helping the mystified user, one excellent approach to subject headings that might be appropriate for the search is to check the keywords. When the keyword is not found in the index, catalog, etc., synonyms should be sought in the various subject-heading and authority lists, which are part of every library system.

Grimes and Doyle, for example, suggest that before any search begins the librarian should list the keywords which seem to be related to the subject.[10] For example, in the question "What teaching strategies utilizing educational media are available to meet the needs of the disadvantaged youth?" the keywords are "educational media," "instructional materials," "media research," "multimedia instruction," "teaching strategies," "urban education," and "urban teaching." As the search proceeds, these general terms may be translated into specific terms the system will accept.

The keyword analysis is helpful in the larger context of first writing down the question. This is hardly necessary for most ready-reference queries, but where it appears there will be any difficulty in translating, or where the search promises to be a relatively long or difficult one, the librarian (or the inquirer) should phrase the question, in writing, as clearly as possible. This obviously forces either party to think about exactly what is being sought. In this, one is not particularly influenced by the logical and linguistic constraints of the system. Doyle gives similar advice: "Define the problem. Write it down and rewrite until you are satisfied. Compile a list of relevant keywords or descriptions that describe your topic. Nearly all indexing systems use such terms and it's helpful to have them in mind."[11]

The librarian may be a bit optimistic in thinking the average index uses the same natural language terms as the user, but the suggestion is still helpful.

[9]Ibid., p. 191.

[10]George Grimes and James Doyle, *Information Resources: A Searcher's Manual* (Detroit, Mich.: Ohio Regional Education Lab, July 1969), ERIC Ed 034–559, p. 7.

[11]James M. Doyle, "Searching Educational Literature," *RQ*, Spring 1972, p. 227. Doyle is speaking here to a doctoral candidate, but it seems equally good advice for librarians in given situations.

Many data bases now have thesauri which isolate key words and related words and are useful in a manual search. For example, the *Thesaurus of ERIC Descriptors* is a primary source for anyone doing search which may involve the frequent use of synonyms. The *Library of Congress Subject Headings* and other such guides to subject headings discussed in Volume I of this text should be consulted before beginning any detailed search.[12]

RULES OF THE GAME

Over the years different reference librarians, through experience more than through scientific analysis or theoretical considerations, have compiled useful approaches to searching. Some of these are of the limited "how-we-do-it" type, but many others are of considerably more universal interest. Some applicable techniques are listed here:[13]

1. When you know the answer is in a source, it is. There are times, and we have all had them, when after checking all the possible places for an answer, one source stands out as the most likely key to the problem. But a check of the source helped not at all. Take heart: The answer is there, it will just take some proper page-shaking before it falls out. Admittedly, this course will occasionally fail, but if it does, the fault lies not in the stars, but in your choice of source.

2. Depend on no one's prior research for accuracy or completeness. This means fellow staff members. While the staff members of your department are renowned good guys and have never led you astray, the moment one of them hands you a question and specifies that A, B, and Z have already been checked, believe them not. It may happen that they speak the truth; it will, however, not usually occur that way. Of course if they have followed all the rules set forth here, trust can be extended—half way.

2a. Sometimes I trust, and sometimes I don't. If our own Business Library has transferred a call to us, we know that their well-trained staff

[12]No one is entirely satisfied with subject headings and there are countless methods of improving the subject approach, from citation indexing to PRECIS (Preserved Context Index System). The latter has gained some favor and is the subject of numerous studies. For a collection of papers, see Hans Wellisch, *The Precis Index System* (New York: The H. W. Wilson Company, 1977).

[13]Rules 1, 2, 3, and 4 are from Nathan A. Josel, Jr., "Ten Reference Commandments," *RQ*, Winter 1971, pp. 146–147. Rule 2a is from Lillina Tudiver, "Letters," *RQ*, Fall 1972, p. 103. Rule 5 is from Egil Halldorsson and Marjorie Murfin, "The Performance of Professionals and Nonprofessionals in the Reference Interview," *College & Research Libraries*, September 1977, p. 392.

has checked all of their sources, and we can eliminate those tools we both have in common. If a member of my own staff says that the answer is not in the Almanacs, Statistical Abstract, etc., and he gives me the subject headings he has checked under, usually I believe him, because I train every new staff member with Tender Loving Care, and he gets a minimum of four one hour lessons on the World Almanac, the same on Statistical Abstracts, at least an hour apiece on the other Almanacs, plus varying amounts of time on every open shelf reference book in our division. Nothing makes me angrier than a patron who has called half a dozen Special Libraries in New York City, and asks a question as if we were the first library he has called. All of us checking the exact same sources for nothing. If he tells me whom he has called, I can usually tell the tools we have in common, and what we may have in our collection that may be unique. When in doubt I'd call his prior sources to save our very valuable time.

3. Remember special indexes. Such a thought should be obvious from reading the preceding rule. There is hardly any point in compiling a query file or any other aid if they are not used. Although the compiler may have sought librarian immortality with his collection of alphabetized, subject-labeled index cards, his efforts are totally zilch if they are not consulted. And in your long and difficult search for why water feels wet you will be duplicating effort all the way. Another thought: You should be able to name all such files in your department; if you only have one file and feel that is all you need, you are missing some facets of the operation.

4. Keep a list of where you have looked. On a long question it is folly to try to remember all the sources checked and the results of each search. It is doubly silly to expect to transfer all of this negativeness to the next researchers and expect them to remember it too. So, mark, somewhere, the source checked and the result. It will surely happen that Rule 2 will be applied nonetheless by fellow staff members, but if your markings prove accurate, no one is hurt. On the other hand, having no such list will absolutely guarantee some duplication of effort.

5. Take your time. One professional librarian twice selected the correct reference source but overlooked answers directly under her eyes, due to being in too great a hurry. In another case, she obtained the key information from the patron but did not take sufficient time to examine it. Lack of time to interview and to consult sources appeared to be another major cause of professional failure.

6. Try various entry points. The subject approach is the most common, but consider the name of an author or an organization. Normally the author search is limited to those with some knowledge of the field, but it does no harm to ask the user (where appropriate) if an author or organization name is known.

Time

How much time should be given to a search? In practical terms, the time allotted is usually no more than a few minutes—which is to say that a good 90 percent of the ready-reference questions can be answered without much consideration for time.

In terms of ready-reference queries and search and research questions which are likely to take more than 10 minutes, the decision as to time will be affected by (1) the work load of the librarian and/or (2) the needs of the user who may have limited time to wait for a reply. Stych suggests "further factors":

Further factors may present themselves in particular libraries or particular situations. For example in an industrial or other special library the rank of the enquirer may influence time available for a given enquiry; considerations of security or legal liability may preclude the utilization of certain materials or information. Decisions involving factors such as these will, again, not be likely to affect the student but he had better be aware of the problems.[14]

An equally important aspect of the time element is what some call the "irritation quotient": i.e., just how long should the user be asked to wait for an answer? Potential irritation can be curbed at the beginning if the reference librarian indicates approximately how long the user should expect to wait for an answer.

In a related area, everyone is familiar with the sometimes long wait for an interlibrary loan item, the necessary wait in line until the librarian is available, the wait which culminates at the reserve desk only to find the wanted item is gone, etc., etc. Not all of this, of course, is the fault of the librarian, but he or she should be aware of how important a factor is time in influencing the use or nonuse of the library.

When to quit

Another major aspect of the time factor is deciding at what point one should give up the search. This situation is nicely explained (and with some suggested solutions) by a working librarian:

[14]F. S. Stych, "Decision Factors in Search Strategy," *RQ,* Winter 1972, p. 145.

> *"No" is never an answer.*
>
> *Despite your training, despite your unflagging devotion to duty, despite checking with all the greater minds, new approaches and faithful devotion to the Decalogue, the time will come when you fail to find an answer. To be sure, as good and as devoted as you are to the cause of reference, the question will remain prominent in your mind for years if necessary, until the answer is found. But what about the patron? Not many are named Job. So you must do the next best thing: Refer him to another source; suggest another likely starting place; find a special library, but never say nothing could be found. If reference has to go from information to referral, then for the patron at least, that is better than nothing at all.[15]*

In the majority of situations, the "no" should be hedged with Josel's referral. When the librarian concludes that the limits of the library's resources have been reached, the user should be referred to a larger library or to one with specialized materials. In smaller libraries the most frequent referral is to the state library; larger libraries may be part of a system or network that includes resources of public, college, or university libraries in the immediate area.

Search failures

Other than that caused by lack of system resources, failure may be attributed to two basic flaws in the search process itself. The first, and most inexcusable, is a simple lack of interest on the part of the librarian in either the user or the user's question. If an answer cannot be found immediately, the librarian calls the search to a halt before it even starts. The second, and more common, is a lack of communication between the user and the librarian. At times the user cannot communicate in terms which the librarian can translate into possible keys to an answer, and neither the librarian nor the user is sure what the latter is searching for. Put another way, the librarian may either misunderstand the query or may accept the query at face value, without analyzing whether the user has given all the vital information needed or has even given correct information.

Other causes of failure come from the librarian's failing to give sufficient time to the search or from the librarian's missing an obvious, but unexpected answer. For example, following an inquiry regarding the chemical treatment for gallstones, a librarian found the statement

[15]Josel, op. cit., p. 147.

that "no solvent for stones exists." However, because the user implied that such a remedy did exist, the librarian continued the search.

The conscientious librarian, realizing a search has failed, should be prepared to analyze the various steps taken and determine where the search went wrong. The following series of questions, suggested by Benson, can be "applied to guide in the analysis":

1. Do I know what I am looking for?

2. Am I sure I have not found it?

3. At what points did I make decisions?

4. Taking each decision identified in order, were there alternative approaches I might have taken?

5. Having made the decision, did I proceed properly in following through on the decision made?

Systematic failure analysis reaps not only immediate results regarding the search in question, but also is vital in developing one's future searching knowledge and capabilities.[16]

To state it another way, the benefit of this kind of analysis is suggested by Alice's remark from behind the looking glass: "There's one great advantage in it," she says, "that one's memory works both ways. . . . It's a poor sort of memory that only works backwards."

Then, too, the negative can be positive on either side of the looking glass. For example:

A full 30 percent of the [machine-aided bibliographical searches] at MIT yield nothing at all, and the researchers are delighted. It reassures them that the line of inquiry they have in mind [for present or future research] has not been preempted.[17]

Another difficulty, particularly for researchers who employ a number of periodicals in their search, comes from the inaccurate references in many journals. This is a real problem for a user of any of the citation indexes. In a study of scientific journals it was found that:

Problems in locating a cited item occur when there is an error in the journal title, volume, initial page, or year. The seven errors in journal titles were in the omission of a key word; for example, the omission of

---

[16]Benson, op. cit., p. 320.

[17]Roger W. Christian, *The Electronic Library* . . . (White Plains, N. Y.: Knowledge Industry Publications, 1975), p. 57.

Journal *from* Journal of Pediatrics *or* New Biology *from* Nature (New Biology). *Errors in volume, initial page, and year are probably the most commonly heard complaints. . . . The use of authors' names and initials is necessary if one is going to execute an author or citation search. Surprisingly, 77 percent of the errors occurred in this area. The two most distressing discoveries were the high number of errors in authors' surnames and the omission of initials. Unfortunately, the omission of both first and middle initials often occurred in the citation of names of the editors of books; this would necessitate more time wasted looking a book up in the card catalog.*

The use of previously published papers for a "quickie bibliography" is a risky business, because 15 percent of the references studied had at least one error. By the same token the high percentage of inaccuracy justified the library in asking for verification of inter-library loan requests in standard indexes, abstracts, and catalogs.[18]

THE ANSWER

Infatuated—some would say intoxicated—with the ability to retrieve millions of facts, a librarian may forget the essential point to all of this—how the information is used. The average search is not likely to turn up more than essential data, but harness the computer to the search and the results can be overwhelming. This leads many critics to ask some essential questions about results.

It is suggested that it is not enough just to locate a piece of data, a source, or a document. There should be some kind of subsequent evaluation, interpretation, or clarification on the part of the librarian. This should be as much a professional duty as the interview and the search itself—although always with two considerations: (1) A user who does not want assistance should not have it forced upon him. (2) There are numerous times, as in most ready-reference queries, when the answer speaks for itself. One hardly need take time to explain that "Yes, the population of Zewa is truly 323,000."

Unfortunately, in the average situation the librarian only indicates reference sources (from indexes to encyclopedia articles) and leaves it to the individual to determine the relevancy of the material. In the desired situation the librarian helps to determine that base relevancy. There are several factors in helping to focus on an answer in terms of an individual's need.

[18]Robert K. Poyer, "Inaccurate References in Significant Journals of Science," *Bulletin of the Medical Library Association*, October 1979, p. 398.

Level of Inquiry   The librarian is often able to determine the level of sophistication of the material required by weighing the age, experience, and immediate needs of the user. This judgment is made before the actual search is begun; the librarian is not likely to start looking for material on nuclear power for a scientist in the children's section. When the material has been found, the librarian, again in consultation with the individual, should be able to suggest what sources are too detailed or technical and what sources are not detailed or technical enough.

Amount of Information Required   This is the quantitative side of the level of inquiry. The amount of information needed will depend, of course, on the proposed use of the materials. A student preparing a paper for a junior high school class in history will need considerably less material than a student on the graduate level at a university.

Dumping   The information or materials required cannot just be dumped in the user's lap, but must be introduced step by step as the patron goes through a certain cycle of behavior. A wide variety of potential sources should be offered wherever possible, but only in some logical, easy-to-understand order.

Where there is little or no control the user may suffer from the excellence of the search, that is, too much material is retrieved and dumped upon him or her.

> *A National Bureau of Standards study asserts that 50 percent of the data supplied by scientific literature are unusable for one reason or another. Therefore, a selection has to be made, which is in turn time-consuming. As a result, the end user prefers selectivity to exhaustiveness and is content with a few journals or publications by institutions considered to be predominant in the field.*[19]

The role of the librarian is to evaluate and discard information.

> *Hardly a person alive, even a scholar in a very narrow subject specialty, is able to cope with the barrage of information our society has been generating in almost all fields of human endeavor. With such an over-abundance of available information, the discarding of information may become even more important than the retention of information. The intelligent management of this information flow is one of the most pressing problems of contemporary society.*[20]

[19]Magdeleine Moureau, "Problems and Pitfalls . . ." *Online Review,* no. 3, 1978, p. 243.
[20]Klaus Musmann, "Will There Be a Role for Librarians and Libraries in the Post-Industrial Society?" *Libri,* no. 3, 1978, p. 231. (The answer, naturally, is yes.)

Clarity When citations rather than data or material are presented, how much does the user understand? In this situation it is important that the librarian follow through with explanations, as needed, of the different kinds of references (from books to articles and reports), of abbreviations of journal names, and of any unusual term or library jargon. In fact, the librarian should exhibit a general willingness to help with an explanation of any questionable matter.

Location Where is the periodical or book located? It is not enough for the librarian to suggest the card catalog. He or she should help the user find the references, an act which in itself provides the librarian an opportunity to point out that material not in the library may be had via inter-library loan.

User-Anticipated Answers An answer may be anticipated, and accepted, by the user for a number of reasons. If the form or the scope of an answer is anticipated by the user, the essential question-negotiation reference process of the interview is negated. The odds are that the user will go away not with the *desired* answer but with an answer shaped by anticipation of little or no real help from the librarian. In this case the patron's preconceived notions of an accepted answer have at least cut short the painful reference-interview situation.

The type of answer anticipated by a user is usually revealed in the phrasing of his question. Such phrasing is dependent upon a given situation or individual, but some good examples are found in these common situations.

1. Time. The user thinks to herself: "The librarian has only a little time to help me." The user then says to the librarian: "I have to have an answer in the next 5 minutes."

   Another version of this situation occurs when the user either believes the librarian is saying to himself or even actually hears the librarian say: "I have only 5 minutes to assist you, so make the request simple."

   The result of this anticipated time difficulty is that the user either is confused or, more likely, frames a question to elicit a quick, simple answer.

2. Form. The user thinks to himself: "The librarian is helpful when it comes to suggesting periodical indexes or magazines, but he is likely to refer me to the card catalog if I ask for more extensive materials. The user then says to the librarian: "I need something out of a magazine."

One may reverse the thought process; i.e., the user does want a book, but only a short, easy-to-read title. Rather than ask the librarian for an easy book, he is more likely to say: "I'd like a magazine article, not a book."

The result of this conflict is that the user may end up with nothing, or several books, or the wrong periodical articles.

3. Currency. The user thinks to herself: "In the past I've been able to get current material without waiting, so, while I'd like some background material, it will be faster to ask for recent books or magazines." The result is a good current book which might not help the user, although in the process of finding the book on the shelves the librarian may show her where similar books of an older copyright date are located.

The reader of this text can frame his or her own examples of how a user anticipates an answer, or the form of an answer, through a preconceived notion of how the initial question is going to be accepted and interpreted by the librarian. The solution to the difficulties of anticipation is dialogue, which can build a mutual trust and understanding between the librarian and the user.

Another solution is found in subsequent follow-up by the librarian. If a source has been indicated, the librarian should try to discover whether or not the source was adequate. Where the actual data or document(s) are retrieved by the librarian an effort must be made to determine if these materials are precisely what is needed or wanted.

The point is that providing information is not the final step. In the best of all situations the librarian is as involved with the answer as in finding the answer; and this concept is badly in need of development. The step after the information is located may be the most important phase of the entire search process, particularly when the librarian is working with a user who has only a vague notion in the first place of what is needed. This category, of course, includes almost any student or layperson who is involved with more than a ready-reference question.

A teacher summarizes the situation nicely:

Librarians are truly in the informing *business, a business that involves helping their clients make new sense for themselves in their situations. This definition of the role may imply a difference in professional behavior, but, in addition, it will allow libraries more strongly and effectively to define their contribution to the community than they are able to do by merely providing counts of materials circulated or questions answered. . . . The providing of information in whatever form is only a step in that process, not an end in itself. We have intuitively understood this, but we have been frustrated in our attempts to cope with the complexity that such a definition of our function implies.*[21]

The true professional librarian is that one whose reply to "What's the answer?" is not simply a response, no matter how efficient, to "What's the question?"

SUGGESTED READING

Bates, Marcia J., "Information Search Tactics," *Journal of the American Society for Information Science,* July 1979, pp. 205–214. An expert shares her experience and research into methods of improving the search—both on-line and manually.

Fenichel, Carol, "An Examination of the Relationship Between Searching Behavior and Searcher Background," *Online Review,* December 1980, pp. 341–348. Using basic online searching methods, it was found (to someone's surprise) that "the moderately experienced searchers with ERIC performed the briefest, most cost effective searches." Along the way the author gives some interesting insights into search behavior, many times as applicable for a manual as for an online search.

Hafter, Ruth, "The Performance of Card Catalogs: A Review of Research," *Library Research,* no. 2, 1979, pp. 199–222. An exhaustive search of the literature with two distinct sections—methodology and results of studies. This should be a first source for anyone concerned with evaluation of searching via the catalog and related indexes.

————, "Type of Search by Type of Library," *Information Processing and Management,* no. 5, 1979, pp. 261–263. A report on various studies of the success or failure in the search of the card catalog in both academic and public libraries.

Marshall, Doris B., "To Improve Searching, Check Search Results," *Online,* July 1980, pp. 32–37. A plea for search analysts to check results of searches made at the computer terminal. In the process, the author gives tips on search strategy which will be equally useful to those using printed sources.

[21]Douglas Zweizig, "The Informing Function of Adult Services in Public Libraries," *RQ,* Spring 1979, p. 243.

ONLINE
REFERENCE
SERVICE

CHAPTER FIVE

The Computer
and
Reference Service

WHEN ONE SPEAKS of the role of the computer in reference service today, the topic necessarily touches upon a multiple number of approaches to answering questions. The types of queries and the answers remain much the same as they were a decade ago, but automation has made it possible today to recover data more quickly and with considerably less effort than in years past and to arrive at more precise answers.

In this section we will consider four basic aspects of the computer's role in reference service: (1) The delivery system—hardware, software, and vendors. (2) Bibliographic data bases, which are composed primarily of indexing and abstracting services. (3) Networks, which tie the libraries and bibliographic data bases together and help the librarian tap into another type of data base—the national or trade bibliography. (4) Matters related to computer use, from interlibrary loan to video.

Rapid development of increasingly sophisticated computers has brought us into a new era to the information age. Many see the approaching period—from the next 20 to 40 years—as a time of major technological developments, developments as historically important as the discovery of steam power and mass manufacturing. And the new technology is likely to bring a comparable shift in work emphasis. Before steam power, 80 percent of the United States work force tilled the soil; today, less than 3 percent feed the country—and the world. Computer power is expected to bring a like displacement in production lines and offices.

The shift of information storage from books to electronics is likely to have a major effect on libraries, at least in terms of where people gain information. Such inventions as Teletext can bring information directly into the home, thus possibly making the library no longer necessary for elementary factual questions and simple search queries. Conversely, the argument is that as the country and world become more aware of the availability of information, there will be an increased need for librarians, particularly reference librarians, who are able to make use of the vast amounts of information captured on tape or microchip.

HARDWARE TO SOFTWARE

The basic components of the average online information system consist of the machinery, i.e., hardware, and the commands, i.e., software.

The hardware consists primarily of an electronic computer and an input-output device. The computer, the function of which is to process data, may be an inexpensive unit, often called a minicomputer, or it may be a gigantic highly complicated maxicomputer or mainframe unit.[1] The computer has a central processing unit which controls signals passing through its memory store. The input and output device makes it possible to receive and give information to the central processing unit. In today's library—or even in today's home—the input and output device normally is a terminal unit consisting of a standard typewriter keyboard, with some additions and variations, and a cathode ray tube (CRT) or display unit. One types in messages and commands which are shown on the television-like tube, as are replies. This unit, connected to a memory system—which may be as simple as a cassette and player or as sophisticated as a floppy disk unit—gives the library the capacity for creating and using information. If a printout of the data shown on the tube is desired, a teleprinter may be attached to the unit. This teleprinter can take the place of the CRT, in which case the messages are typed out as sent and received, rather than displayed, on a screen.

---

[1]Nancy N. Perry, "Mini or Maxi . . ." *Audiovisual Instruction,* February 1979, pp. 16–18. This is a good summary article, in easy-to-understand, nontechnical language, on the differences between the two types of computers. For more data at a basic level, see Antonio M. Lopez, "Microcomputers: Tools of the Present and Future," *School Media Quarterly,* Spring 1981, pp. 164–167; and, in the same issue, R. C. Nicklin and John Tashner, "Micros in the Library Media Center?" pp. 168ff.

Printers and terminals are now a part of the retail computer trade and are sold at steadily decreasing prices through outlets which may handle a broad line of electronic equipment. For example, Radio Shack has a computer model for under $600 which is sold side by side with high-fidelity radio equipment. Numerous periodicals compare and explain the various pieces of hardware. In the October 1980 issue of *Radio Electronics* there is a 40-page buyers' guide to personal computer units, which are, for the most part, really little more than a keyboard, a CRT, and a memory system built into a tape-recording device. Pick up almost any popular science or electronics magazine today, and there will be articles and information on these units, usually of a comparative nature. For example, "Word Processing" in *Popular Electronics,* August 1981, explains differences in various available equipment.

The home, office, and library may use the same basic type of terminal for sending and receiving data, but the library's unit will generally differ radically in one respect; its terminal is invariably connected to a mainframe computer having a gigantic memory capacity. For example, the typical memory capacity of the home or office may be no more than 70,000 characters, but the memory open to the librarian at a terminal will be in billions of characters.

The terminal, which, like an electric typewriter, is simply plugged into any outlet, can be connected to the distant computer, and the data bases stored in that computer, in a number of ways. Most commonly, the user dials a number on the telephone. The telephone receiver is then placed in a coupler on the terminal and, after a series of commands, the terminal operator is connected to the data base within the computer.

Software

The software is the set of instructions which make it possible for the computer to perform work. The integral part of the software is the program, which is the operational plan controlling the input, storage, processing, and output of the computer. At the commercial level, software is best typified by the hundreds of games which one may use with a home computer outfit. Here is no more than a simple cassette loaded into the unit.

Today most libraries do not have individual programs, but purchase, lease, or otherwise tap existing software. In fact, there is a general feeling that it is more feasible for a library to make use of existing software than to develop its own programs. The library is likely to purchase a "turnkey system." This means one only has to "turn a key" to start the system. The turnkey system has been designed and programmed for general use, but can be modified to meet individual needs.[2]

Data bases

The data base or data file is a form of software. In this case it is the reference work captured in form other than printed. This usually means the information is stored on microchip, magnetic tape, floppy disk, or magnetic disk. Technologists are seeking smaller and smaller units of storage. They now have a minichip, often a sliver of silicon, and so-called denser chips, which will accept even more data.

The storage, or memory capacity of the computer, and the speed with which the machine can find the needed data are the primary concerns of today's computer people. In 1976 a 64,000-bit random-access memory chip (RAM), which can be read by a computer in roughly 125-billionths of a second, was perfected. By comparison, the first-generation chip, developed in 1971, had a capacity of 1000 bits. By the mid-1980s it is expected the capacity will jump from 64,000 to 250,000 bits of information.

The form of a data base may differ from the standard reference-book form, but the publisher is usually the same. Many of the more expensive scientific and technical data bases are issued by the government, or with funding from the government. Another large group of publishers is found among nonprofit organizations with specialized memberships, such as the American Institute of Physics. Finally, there is the private publisher, such as The New York Times. In sum, the greatest number of data-base publishers are found in the government and nonprofit organization sector. The balance is likely to shift to the private sector in the 1980s.

Data-base vendors

The majority of bibliographic data bases are produced by the same publishers that offer the library printed works. The base often begins as a byproduct of the printed work or is first produced in order to

[2]There are now numerous articles, books, monographs, etc., on the minicomputer. Some of the more suitable for the reference student: Audry N. Grosch, *Minicomputers in Libraries* (White Plains, N. Y.: Knowledge Industry Publications, 1979). This is updated from time to time. Kenneth Frost, "The Library Owned Computer," *Ontario Library Review*, June 1980, pp. 92–97; B. W. Williams, "The Potential of the Microprocessor in Library and Information Work," *Aslib Proceedings*, April 1979, p. 205; Gerald Lundeen, "The Role of Microcomputers in Libraries," *Wilson Library Bulletin*, November 1980, pp. 178–185.

make the printed work possible. The publisher may furnish the data base directly to the library, but more likely a middleperson, or vendor, will be used for distribution.

The vendor, sometimes called a distributor, is a person between the library and the publisher. The vendor is the equivalent of the book or periodical jobber. However, the vendor does not sell the book or the periodical, but only sells access to various data banks. The vendor pays the publisher a royalty for the library's use of the tape. The royalty paid usually is based upon the amount of use by the library.

There are three basic types of vendors: (1) A commercial service offering access to numerous data bases, which are normally produced by other organizations and publishers, but may have been produced by the vendor. (2) A government service, such as the National Library of Medicine, which offers the well-known MEDLINE (an acronym for MEDLARS on Line, a term which is itself an acronym for Medical Literature Analysis and Retrieval System). In addition, the NLM has a variety of other related data bases, including TOXLINE, EPILEPSY, CANCERLINE, HISTORY OF MEDICINE, and some half-dozen more. (3) A commercial service with one or more data bases which it publishes and distributes. The New York Times and Dow-Jones are examples; in this case there is no vendor and the library deals directly with the publisher, albeit in some cases, the publisher may offer the vendor limited access to the materials.

Some would consider the so-called bibliographic utilities— OCLC, RLIN, WLN, and UTLAS—vendor/distributors. Actually, these utilities do make data bases available and may, in time, expand this service. For example, OCLC announced a plan late in 1980 to offer access to data bases provided by Bibliographic Retrieval System, Lockheed, and the New York Times at discount rates of up to 30 percent. OCLC members take the service on a quarterly basis and are billed by OCLC. A more detailed discussion of the utilities' role appears in the chapter on networks.

There are three primary commercial vendors in the United States: Bibliographic Retrieval Services (BRS) of Latham, New York; Lockheed Information Systems of Palo Alto, California; and Systems Development Corporation (SDC) of Santa Monica, California. BRS has developed a software package, BRS/SEARCH, to access data bases; Lockheed has developed its own software program, DIALOG, to accomplish the same thing; and ORBIT is the program developed by SDC.

A library's selection of a vendor depends upon numerous factors, the primary one being whether or not the vendor offers the data bases needed by the library. Many of the popular data bases, and particularly those from government agencies and scholarly organizations, are offered by all the vendors. Conversely, a greater number of bases are unique to one vendor.

About 165 bibliographic data bases (as of 1981) are available from vendors, both the commercial services and the government agencies. Of these 49 are on two systems, and 18 are on three. So, there are at least 67 data bases for which a system choice can be made.

The cost for use of a vendor's system is another important consideration. There is a large cost differential between various data bases. For example, one government-developed data base may cost no more than $15 a connect-hour to use while a commercial base may be as much as $120 an hour. This same cost differential, of course, occurs in printed works where the price of X volume in hard cover edition may be $50 while a Y paperback sells for $2.50.

The other factors to be considered in selecting a vendor include: (1) The size and the number of records the vendor offers in each data base (these figures vary from vendor to vendor). (2) The format of the records and how much or how little information is given for each citation. (3) The nature of the program output, whether it is citations, abstracts, a combination of both, or some other form. (4) Currency of the file and frequency of update. (5) System features which increase the ease of use of the various data bases and the overall system. (6) Online printing speed. (7) Offline printing speed and the time it takes to get offline printouts. (8) The reliability of the system. Computers do break down; when this happens, of course, the data bases cannot be read and the information cannot be transmitted to the library. At least two vendors—BRS and Lockheed—now have large mainframe computers as backups to help prevent "down" time when something happens to the main computer. Some of these factors are subjective considerations; others can be judged as objectively as printed reference works are judged. There are many reasons why some librarians prefer one system and other librarians choose another. Studies have shown that librarians tend to prefer the one they first learned to use.

Other considerations to be weighed in choosing a vendor are the extra services offered. Does the vendor provide workshops, instruction manuals, and updates on what changes are taking place in the system?

Some efforts have been made to evaluate the three commercial on-line vendors. Hoover ran five similar searches on the three services and found: Orbit prices and costs were consistently higher than BRS or Dialog . . . [but] BRS's low prices are offset by the fact that for retrospective searches in large data bases, more than half of the file is offline and cannot be searched online. . . . BRS's nested search statement capabilities are very nice, allowing a rather complex search to be entered in a single statement. . . .[3]

ECONOMICS OF THE COMPUTER SEARCH

What is the average cost of searching a data-base online? The cost varies, but it is determined primarily by two factors: (1) the initial expense for equipment and its maintenance; and (2) the ongoing expense of the use of the data bases and the salaries of the librarians.

If one is going to measure only direct costs, then two factors must be considered: (1) hourly connect time rate and (2) cost of the telecommunications for access to the data base or bases. Here an average of the two may be from $50 to $65 an hour. Estimates of a "typical start-up expense for online searching" will differ, but Saffady used these figures in 1979: (1) teleprinter with acoustic coupler, $2400; (2) teleprinter installation, $75; (3) site preparation, i.e., electrical and telephone installation, furnishings, $1210; (4) search aids such as thesauri, directories, and dictionaries, $300 to over $1000; (5) initial searcher training, $1500. Saffady also noted an annual cost of about $1890 for maintenance, telephone rental, and searcher training. Some would consider these estimates too low or too high, but the figures do give some notion of types of expenses involved in initiating an online system.[4]

The operating expense depends primarily upon the online charge for the individual data base. Here, too, costs vary, but rough

---

[3]Ryan E. Hoover, "A Comparison of Three Commercial Online Vendors," *Online*, January 1979, pp. 12–21. Since this study was made BRS has been purchased by Information Handling Services of Englewood, Colorado, which, in turn, is owned by Thyssen-Bonemisza N.V., a Dutch firm. What acquisition of vendors, data-base producers, etc., is likely to mean in terms of service (good or bad) has yet to be established; but the conglomerate is more likely to play an increasingly important role in the years to come.

[4]William Saffady, "The Economics of Online Bibliographic Searching: Costs and Cost Justifications," *Library Technology Reports,* September/October 1979, pp. 567–654. It is important to stress that the figures employed in this section are relative, subject to change, probably upward. Some, for example, see data-base searches going to $200 to $300 an hour as well as more formula pricing which makes it difficult to determine hourly costs. So, the discussion can only be employed to indicate trends and what to look for in making comparisons. See, too, Ryan E. Hoover, "Computer Aided Reference Services in the Academic Library," *Online*, no. 4, 1979, pp. 28–41; and Laura G. Harper, "A Comparative Review of BRS, DIALOG and ORBIT," *Reference Services Review,* March 1981, pp. 39–51 (she has an excellent section on "Price Comparisons").

estimates established in early 1981 for the average online search for the average user quoted figures of: (a) a low of $7.50 to $10, (b) a medium range of $35, (c) and higher rates from $50 to several hundred dollars.

Where the library carries most of the expense, as is sometimes the case in academic libraries, the charge to a user may be minimal, not more than a few cents for the printout. In special libraries there may be no charge at all. This is the case in some public libraries where the charges are met by fundings from a specialized program. Still, as the online operation becomes more standard in the public library, fees become the norm. Conversely, when an individual calls on an information broker the charge may begin at over $150 and skyrocket thereafter.

Charging plans, schemes, systems, and mechanisms

Sara Knapp, an experienced search analyst, explains the rate schedules (as of mid-1981) from a practical point of view. Direct online costs of a search consist of three elements: the vendor's (BRS, SDC, etc.) charges for use of the system; the royalty paid to the producer of the data base (Biosciences Information Service for BIOSIS, etc.); and the communication charges paid to the communication network (Telenet, Tymnet, etc.) and/or the telephone company. Except for the telephone charges, the vendor collects all these fees from the user and, in turn, pays the royalty to the producer and the communication charges to the communication network. The balance then goes to the vendor for the use of the vendor's system on the vendor's computer. Exceptions exist in the case of some government-produced data bases, such as ERIC and AGRICOLA, which are royalty-free. Here the only charge for their use is the vendor's charges.

Because not all vendors describe their rates in the same terms, it may, at first, seem a bit confusing. However, it can be sorted out and is really quite simple. Two of the vendors, SDC and Lockheed, simply "lump together" their own charges and the data-base royalty charge and quote a flat rate per hour for the use of each data base. The plot thickens, though, when the library's total usage exceeds a certain number of hours and discounts are offered. For example, Lockheed offers PAIS at $60 an hour. With a discount of up to $15 an hour, that price could go as low as $45 an hour. Of that $45 or $60, a certain portion must always be returned by Lockheed to the publisher of PAIS as a royalty for use of the data base.

In contrast to Lockheed and SDC, BRS itemizes its charges. It publishes the royalty rates which it is required to remit to the data-base producers as well as the rates for use of the BRS system computers. To take the same example, BRS rates for use of its system (also dependent upon volume of usage) are $16 an hour for high-volume usage and up to $20, $25, or $30 for very infrequent users. BRS must pay PAIS a royalty of $20 an hour. Naturally, this cost is passed on to the user. The result is that PAIS may be accessed on a BRS system for $36, $40, $45, or $50 an hour, depending on the user's connect-hour rate. In general, it is the royalty which makes data bases so expensive.

All of the vendors provide separate accounting for the communication charges and itemize the Telenet or Tymnet charges for each search in the total monthly bill.

"Subscriptions" are simply an annual contract whereby a library agrees to purchase a minimum number of hours from a particular vendor within a specified 12-month period. Subscriptions, which are available on both BRS and Lockheed, have an advantage for libraries in that they provide lower rates for use of the system. For some libraries, a subscription helps in budgeting for the service, while for the vendor it assures a certain volume of business and income for the year.

Manual search costs

Once the librarian has some notion of the cost of an online search service, the next obvious question becomes: How does an online search cost compare with the cost of a search using printed materials? Which one is less expensive?

Actually, the first question will be: Which type of search is most efficient, best suited for the particular needs of a given situation? In most cases it is the online approach, but as this is not the best of all possible economic worlds, the librarian usually has to go a step further and justify the choice in terms of dollars.

There have been, and will continue to be, studies of comparative costs. Generally the conclusion is the same, at least for the majority of searches of bibliographic data bases: the online search cost is less than the cost for a manual search. (1) "Manual searches were more expensive than online searches in 65 percent of the cases."[5] (2) "The

[5] D. R. Elchesen, "Cost-effectiveness Comparison of Manual and Online Retrospective Bibliographic Searching," *Journal of the American Society for Information,* March 1978, p. 59.

average cost per relevant citation retrieved manually was 86 cents, compared to 65 cents for the online mode."[6] (3) Online "bibliographic literature retrieval is considerably more cost-effective," with the exception of the case in which a search requires "a high number of offline prints such as searches covering whole business or technology areas."[7] (4) Online searches "cost much the same as the staff costs for manual searching."[8]

Again, in calculating costs of a manual search much more is involved than the time it takes the librarian to find the material or point the user in the direction of an index. In order to maintain comparable figures, it is necessary to assume that the end-product will be the same—a bibliography prepared by the librarian for the user. In most cases, of course, it is not the same. The librarian at the terminal is forced to offer maximum reference service; the librarian at the desk may offer only minimum service for precisely the same query. It is obviously important to recognize the potential differences. If one compares mediocre average reference service with first-rate online service, the online will cost more only because so much more service is rendered.

PUBLISHERS

Given the fact that the computer-aided search is often less expensive, and usually always more efficient, and given the fact that there are numerous indexes and abstracts, as well as a growing number of ready-reference books online, why should the library continue to purchase the printed versions of these works? The question is particularly valid when a given index is used only occasionally or not at all. As online searches accrue charges only for the time the index is in use, the potential savings on subscription costs are impressive.

The possible elimination of standing orders for indexes, abstracts, and other reference works has not been a serious question in the past and in the next few years is not likely to bother those librarians who lack access to computerized data bases. However, where data bases are employed, it is a major consideration, and by the

[6]T. Flynn, "Cost Effectiveness Comparison . . ." *Journal of Information Science,* May 1979, p. 83.

[7]Richard W. Boss, "The Library as an Information Broker," *College & Research Libraries,* March 1979, p. 138. The study was made by the Lawrence Livermore Laboratory Research Information Group at the University of California.

[8]Susan M. Johnston, "Choosing Between Manual and Online Searching . . ." *Aslib Proceedings,* October/November 1978, pp. 383–393.

1990s will be a problem faced by more and more librarians. What happens to publishing when all that is needed is a data base on a magnetic tape instead of thousands of volumes of Y index?

The possible substitution of the magnetic tape for the printed work has, of course, occurred to publishers. One answer for the publisher, if not for the librarian, was indicated by *Science Citation Index* in early 1981. When a library subscribes to the printed service (about $3500 a year), the cost of online searches is $30 per connect-hour. The library that cancels a subscription will have to pay four times as much for subsequent use of the computer, i.e., $120 a connect-hour, plus extra charges for offline printouts.

Similar balancing acts have been, and will continue to be, tried by other publishers. Congressional Information Services, for example, requires that online users purchase the printed version before going online. Others try to solve the problem by making only a limited amount of material available online—the rest is to be found in the printed version. Here the usual procedure is to have the citations online and the abstracts in print. Conversely, a publisher may offer more, not less, in the online version. In 1980, for example, *Psychological Abstracts* began to add some 25 to 30 percent more abstracts (including heretofore overlooked monographs) to the online service.

Despite the fourfold cost increase for nonsubscribers, the economics of use may still dictate that the online charge is less costly than the subscription, especially in view of the extra expenses—space needed for the volumes, cost of processing, etc.—which the subscription entails. One university, for example, compared the amount of use, the online cost, and the total subscription price of *Science Citation Index*. They concluded that service online, even at a more expensive hourly charge, should prove to be less expensive than maintaining the print index subscription for years to come. At the same time, the much-less-costly *Social Science Citation Index* (about $1400 for a year) is maintained in printed form because it is heavily used and the print cost is relatively low.

It seems most likely that in the future costly print services will be eliminated, or, at the very least, certain duplicate sets will be cancelled in favor of online service. Standard, relatively low-priced reference works will continue to be purchased both in print and in data-base form, excepting those titles that are little or rarely used.

Other action taken by the publisher is likely to vary. The publisher may raise the royalty rates, i.e., charges to the vendor for the use of the data base, rather than double the rate based on subscriptions. Up to this point the bulk of profit for even the most successful online data-base publisher has been in selling printed works. As this part of the profit disappears, it is apparent that bibliographic data-base royalties, which now account for 20 to 40 percent of the direct costs of online searching, may roughly double in real terms over the next five years.

In daily reference work there is little question that the library will continue to support printed works. As long as there is a need for a librarian at a terminal, the library will have to either have more searchers or, and this is more likely, retain printed works which the user can search. In view of the numerous variables, librarians are not apt to cancel subscriptions to various services in favor of online searches very quickly. Kent raises a valuable point about a psychological mind-set and the printed work. Librarians, he says, find it difficult to buy a service which is not as "lasting" as is a printed index.

THE QUESTION OF FEES[9]

Today the major point of contention concerning computer use in libraries is neither the question of mechanical or intellectual mastery of the computer search nor the problem of whether it is better to use the computer or the traditional printed sources for reference work. It is the question of fees—to charge or not to charge for computer-aided reference service—and, by extension, whether to begin charges for such other library services as interlibrary loan. Wanger found in 1976 that 77 percent of all educational institutions charged for online searches, often at a modest fee.[10] In government libraries that figure dropped to 29 percent. In a 1978 study of health science service, it was found that 90 percent of the educational institutions were charging fees, although across the board, in various other types of libraries, from commercial to government, the figure was only 53 percent.[11] There was an extremely broad range—from $2 to $50—in the actual charge. The mean charge for MEDLINE was just under $7.50.

Basic ideology underlies the contention. The debate centers on whether some of the people or all of the people should have access to

[9]The American Library Association library in Chicago offers "Fees and Costs of Machine-Assisted Reference Service" on interlibrary loan. This is a packet of information "collected in 1978 from libraries on their policies and methods of charging for online bibliographic services." *RQ,* Summer 1979, p. 380.

[10]Judith Wanger et al., *Impact of On-Line Retrieval Services* (Santa Monica, Calif.: Systems Development Corporation, 1976), p. 155.

[11]Gloria Werner, "Use of On-Line Bibliographic Retrieval Services in Health Sciences Libraries . . ." *Bulletin of the Medical Library Association,* January 1979, p. 9.

information. If the advocate is on the side of "some," the inevitable stance is a plea for charging for information services, or at least those services which now involve computers. The opponent, believing that all people require—indeed, are entitled to—free information, will say fees should not be charged.[12]

Before briefly presenting these pro and con arguments, the author must state his position: fees should not be charged in public institutions. That opinion is based upon a conviction that information should be free for the public and upon the pragmatic notion that the moment people begin to pay for information in the library, they will turn away from the library. Information seekers will likely turn to the more convenient, possibly even less costly, retrieval and information systems in the home.

Arguments for fees

Should the library charge for these services?[13] Those who favor, although sometimes reluctantly, charges for computer searches argue:

(1) The library normally charges for photocopying, and computer searches are but another form of a service most users accept as a necessary expense in library use.

(2) The computer-assisted search is complete and individualized, and, therefore, the individual should pay for such exceptional services. (Another related argument is that all reference service should be as complete.)

(3) Users are really not denied access to information. They still have printed sources available for most of the data bases. The user is only denied the personalized search and the personalized format.

(4) Fees do not discourage the use of the computer service. In one study of a large health science library it was found that:

(a) [Users may not] be as highly sensitive to changes in user fees as is

[12]Fay Blake, "Let My People Know," *Wilson Library Bulletin*, January 1978, pp. 392–399. Outlines the social (and practical) argument against fees. Ms. Blake has written extensively against the fee system and is a good name to check when searching out arguments in this area.

[13]There are hundreds of articles on the necessity of charging, but for an objective analysis, see Marilyn Gell, "User Fees I, The Economic Argument," *Library Journal*, January 1, 1979, pp. 19–23, and "User Fees II, The Library Response," *Library Journal*, January 15, 1979, pp. 170–173. For a good, relatively current overview see James Rettig, "Rights, Resolutions, Fees, and Reality," *Library Journal*, February 1, 1981, pp. 301–304. Note the bibliography.

*widely thought. . . . (b) As user incomes (and thus expenditures) in-
crease, a more-than-proportionate increase in the demand for library
service is likely to occur. . . . (c) Society will demand more and more
specialized informational goods and services as real income increases.*[14]

Cogswell states that "similar findings are reported from numerous large academic and research libraries where the faculty, if not
always the students, 'are willing to bear a portion of the costs for
online searching.'"[15]

In one year of operation, 1977, it was found that the specialists
who used the data-base service available in Kansas City libraries rarely
complained about the average search cost of $18.15. The reason:

*Patrons view online searching as cost-effective and a tremendous
time-saver. The reference staffs of most public and academic libraries
have never had the time to compile extensive bibliographies for patrons
involved in research. Online searching provides this new capability to
those patrons willing to pay for the added convenience.*[16]

Arguments against fees

On the other side of this question, the arguments not to charge for
online searches include:

(1) The American Library Association, in a resolution approved
by the majority of librarians, has gone on record against charges.[17]

(2) American libraries have been built on the democratic notion
of accessible free information. Charges are in direct opposition to this
heritage. Anita Schiller and others believe that librarians are being
catapulted into the pivotal role between the consumer and informa-

---

[14]C. A. Casper, "The Impact of Economic Variables on the Demand for Library
Services," *Information Choices and Policies,* ed. by Roy Tally (White Plains, N. Y.:
Knowledge Industry Publications, 1979), p. 48.

[15]James A. Cogswell, "On Line Search Services . . ." *College and Research Libraries,* July
1978, p. 277. The author cites other studies which confirm his opinion.

[16]Gary D. Byrd et al., "Minet in K.C.," *Library Journal,* October 1, 1979, p. 2047.
Actually, more than specialists use this system, and both teachers and students did not
complain about the charge. The obvious "yes, but . . ." is that those who did not
complain did not use the service, and they might be the majority.

[17]The American Library Association has taken a position against fees. The membership
has confirmed the concept of "access to information, without charge to individuals
in . . . publicly supported libraries." *American Libraries,* July/August 1977, p. 378. The
position is reiterated time and time again; e.g., at the White House Conference on
Library and Information Services the delegates (in late 1979) strongly endorsed library
service without fees.

tion technology—as only one element in a developing national pattern of costing, pricing, etc. There is a major shift emerging, a shift to the financing of individual information services by those able to pay. Libraries are being utilized to accomplish this shift. And that has many implications for the role of information in a democratic society.[18]

(3) Libraries are not free in that they are tax-supported. People who have paid for library service are now asked for a surcharge for services which have been paid for previously.[19]

(4) Since much of the progress of computerized searching was made possible by federal research grants, the "people" have already paid for the pioneering efforts and should not be charged again for the resultant success.

(5) The most serious danger in charging is that once those who control the budget realize that the library can charge for services they will be sorely tempted to decrease rather than increase funding. The step would be perfectly logical; if you can charge for one service and make it self-sufficient, why not charge for another service, and still another, etc.?

(6) Despite arguments and studies to the contrary, fees *do* cause the average user to hesitate in calling for a computer-aided reference search. In one survey of the subject it was concluded that demand for such service decreased by 50 or even 75 percent when charges were imposed.[20] The point is that too little is now known about the real effect of fees on service, although one suspects that common sense gives the answer. People who have money will use the service; those who do not, will not use the service. And in the latter group, many believe, are the majority of Americans.

(7) The paperwork involved with charges is so great that it is often less expensive not to charge. "Not charging for searching eliminates billing, collecting of fees, and the extensive accounting required."[21]

[18]Karl Nyren, "The Online Revolution in Libraries," *Library Journal,* February 15, 1978, p. 440. Ms. Schiller is being paraphrased here, not quoted precisely.

[19]California's attorney general wrote an opinion in 1979 that it is not legal to charge users for service. "Taxpayers have already paid for library services . . . and should not be charged again for such services. The California Library Services Act clearly states that the public should be granted free access to the resources of the libraries." This may be equally true in other states. *Library Journal,* February 15, 1979, pp. 451–452.

[20]Mary Huston, "Fee or Free," *Library Journal,* September 15, 1979, pp. 1812–1813.

[21]Don R. Swanson, "Evolution, Libraries, and National Information Policy," *Library Quarterly,* January 1980, p. 88.

(8) Computer search generally costs less and, therefore, is seen as a replacement more of the expensive manual search, not an added feature. As a replacement it may save enough money to more than counter the need for fees.[22]

Compromise

Free service, or a minimal charge, would be possible if the librarian were able to be objective about certain cost savings of the online search. The librarian may argue that the money saved in time and effort when using the online service more than pays for the search.[23] Though such might be the case when the user is an employee of a private firm, this is not true when applied to a user such as the average layperson, student, or teacher. Another argument is that money is saved in cutting back on subscriptions and on reference book purchases, and in a corresponding saving in librarian labor. This, unfortunately, depends as much on the amount of service offered as on accounting, and, again, the saving normally does not materialize.

The real question remains quite simple. Is the library going to offer maximum reference service to all patrons, whether they are using online service or printed sources, or will the library, by necessity, offer maximum service only to those who can pay for the online search? The author suggests that once maximum reference service, in all its forms, becomes an accepted rule rather than the exception, the library will find it much easier to request central funding—not individual fees—for the online/manual searches at a level required by modern need and technology. And more important-ly, such maximum service will ensure that the library has a major role in the lives of *all* people seeking information.

RELATED AREAS OF INFORMATION

There are several newly developed areas which are closely related to reference work. The reference librarian should have some acquaint-ance with the terminology of these fields, particularly as that termi-nology is used by information managers and specialists.

[22]John Berry, "The Westport Model," *Library Journal,* May 1, 1980, p. 1021.
[23]Robert Fiskes, Jr., "User Charges: A Debate in Search of a Premise," *News Notes on California Libraries,* no. 2, 1978, p. 13. While several years old, the questions still remain unanswered, at least in objective terms.

Word processing

Word processing is an umbrella term which covers all processes that eliminate the early stages of typing on paper. A word-processing unit will generally include a typewriter keyboard with additional special function keys, a CRT (television screen), and a printout unit, which may be a separate component or may be part of the keyboard/CRT unit. Many systems include a memory unit—normally no more than a floppy disk capable of holding 50 to 250 pages of material.[24]

The word processor has no use for typing paper. The material is entered on a standard keyboard and appears on a CRT screen the size of a piece of standard typing paper. The material may be edited—words, lines, or paragraphs added or deleted and spelling corrected—as it is entered. Once the material on the screen is letter-perfect, the typist touches a button and a nearby printer produces one or more copies of the finished material on paper.

More expensive word-processing units feature a memory system which allows the typist to call up standard form letters as needed. Again, corrections may be made, names and dates added, etc. Or rather simple programs, which allow the typist to prepare payrolls, keep ledgers, handle inventories, and carry on general bookkeeping functions, may be available.

While essentially associated with offices, word processing may be used by reference librarians for preparing copies of standard bibliographies, current contents, selective dissemination of information, and like materials.

A writer for *The New Yorker* explains word processing, or WP as it is often called, in this way:

> . . . *is work done by people known as word processors, or as word-processor operators, on machines that are also known as word processors, or as word-processing machines. And these machines, though they are available in many models—for instance, some have video screens and some do not—are in essence electronically bolstered typewriters that can store typed material, can be instructed to alter the stored material in a variety of ways, and can automatically reproduce the stored material again and again, operating as efficiently as good bread-slicing machines. . . . Although many of the machines nowadays are extremely sophisticated*

[24]"Behind the Reports," *Consumer Reports,* March 1980, p. 138. A clearly written library-related article on word processors is J. B. Whitehead, "Development in Word Processing Systems . . ." *Aslib Proceedings,* March 1980, pp. 118–133. See, too: John Whitehead, "Progress in Documentation. Word Processing: An Introduction and Appraisal," *Journal of Documentation,* December 1980, pp. 313–341. Gay Courter, "Word Machines for Word People," *Publishers Weekly,* February 13, 1981, pp. 40–43.

—some are hooked into computer networks—a word processor is really just a machine that is capable of storing information and then retyping it, pursuant to your instructions. Basically, it's the simplest thing in the world.[25]

Paperless information systems

The "paperless office" is often the final result of a word-processing system.[26] Jointly employed, the two phrases, "paperless information" and "word processing," define a method of ensuring that the typical office products—letter, manuscript, and report—need not be endlessly typed. The work is duplicated by the word-processing machine as required and then stored on microfiche, floppy disk or other form rather than filed away in its paper state. This system creates the "paperless office."

In the context of the library, the paperless information system is one where most printed matter is confined to the computer data base. The technology and convenience of this system assure the library user of the future—and this may include everyone, from scientists and students to businesspeople and how-to-do-it fans—the capability of using "some form of online terminal to compose text, transmit text, receive text, conduct searches for data or for text relevant to a particular . . . problem and build personal information files."[27]

Where paper is nonexistent the message has to be recorded in some manner. An oft-used form is Computer Output Microfilm (COM), a film produced from material fed into the computer's data base.[28] This microfilm can be used and read independently or employed as a step in the printing out of the message.

More than 10,000 pages, equivalent to the total contents of a drawer size filing cabinet, can be stored in a space four inches by 1/2 inch. Thirty microfiche contain as much data as an entire mile of computer printout. And a single ounce of microfiche, equivalent to about a thousand pages

[25]"Words," *The New Yorker*, March 10, 1980. p. 38.

[26]F. W. Lancaster, *Toward Paperless Information Systems* (New York: Academic Press, 1978). This is an excellent overview of the possibilities of doing away with most printing and paper.

[27]F. W. Lancaster, "Whither Libraries? or Wither Libraries," *College and Research Libraries*, September 1978, p. 352.

[28]The basic book in this area for librarians is William Saffady, *Computer-Output Microfilm: Its Library Application* (Chicago: American Library Association, 1978).

of printout, can travel through the mails [for the prevailing postal rates].[29]

COM can be updated, via the computer, as often as needed and offers the individual a complete file. With COM there is no need to search the library—one simply calls up the microform. This is precisely what is done when one uses the updated *Magazine Index* or the *Biographical Dictionaries Master Index* (Bio-Base). Numerous libraries are now using the same basic process for their card catalogs, which are referred to as microcatalogues.[30]

The word-processing system and COM promise many potential uses.

Electronic publishing[31]

Electronic publishing, an expression which has several meanings, employs many of the word-processing machines. Some publishers and newspaper people consider it a method of short-circuiting traditional ways of preparing copy for printing. Others use it to explain the complete, or nearly complete, bypassing of printed forms. There is a familiar path in current publishing methods: author to publisher to print form to library (and to index or abstracting service for analysis so it can be retrieved in the library). This time-consuming process can now be cut several ways. (1) The publication, generally produced from a computer-readable tape, can be made available via the computer through printout or screen. (2) Where a more permanent form is required, the work may be printed from computer-output microform, or the microform itself used, or it may be transferred to a videodisk or other form of inexpensive duplication.

Publishers will distribute new issues of trade magazines or scientific journals, for example, in digital form over satellite networks, advanced

[29]Truett Airhart, "Computer Output Microfilm," *IMC Journal,* First Quarter 1978, p. 40.

[30]Carolyn K. Murray, "Teaching the COM Microcatalogue," *RQ,* Fall 1979, pp. 52–57. See also James Thompson, "The New Catalog and the Unfinished Evolution," *American Libraries,* June 1979, pp. 357–360; and Brian Aveney and Mary Ghikas, "Reactions Measured: 600 Users Meet the COM Catalog," *American Libraries,* February 1979, pp. 82–83.

[31]Joseph Raben, "The Electronic Revolution and the World Just Around the Corner," *Scholarly Publishing,* April 1979, pp. 195–209. This is a clear step-by-step explanation of how the computer is employed in publishing. See, too: "Electronics and Publishing," *Publishers Weekly,* March 20, 1981, pp. 24–30; March 27, 1981, pp. 21–27. The two-part series offers an excellent overview.

networks like AT&T's service, or possibly through the mails on a videodisc. Customers will be able to scan information on a CRT and select that portion which they want to see in hard copy. With the new generation of printers, they can specify the typeface and very soon will be able to choose color if they so desire. There are obviously questions concerning copyright and pricing but the big question is how long it will take before electronic publishing and distribution of full text information becomes widespread.[32]

Another aspect of electronic publishing is on-demand (OD) publishing, which "means simply the production and supply of copies of a work in response to orders, or demand, one by one (or perhaps few by few), rather than supply from a pre-produced stock of copies."[33] There has been a long-standing relationship between Xerox and libraries, through the *Books on Demand* listing, which allows the library to order one of over 100,000 out-of-print titles in hard-copy xerographic prints or on microform. Similar systems allow on-demand publishing of back copies of periodicals, newspapers, etc.

Today, however, on-demand publishing refers to a new approach to original material (i.e., material which has never been printed or has reached an out-of-print status). There are numerous facets of this new approach. A storehouse of information and data, never published in the traditional fashion, may now be published for individual readers via microfilm or xerographic prints or may be displayed on a video screen. After a detailed discussion, Singleton points out that as "reprographic technology improves it may well become tempting for research and learned institutions increasingly to adopt do-it-yourself OD publishing."[34]

HOME INFORMATION CENTERS[35]

Employing much of the technology of the computer-aided reference search and the various word-processing systems, the so-called home information center is a distinct possibility; it is, in fact, an ongoing operation in several parts of the world. One group of home reference systems employs a television set, which may or may not be of a special

---

[32]Robert Badger, "Smart Printers . . ." *Information World,* April 1979, p. s/2.

[33]Alan Singleton, "On-Demand Publishing," *Aslib Proceedings,* December 1979, p. 561.

[34]Ibid., p. 579.

[35]Susan Cherry, "Telereference: The New TV Information Systems," *American Libraries,* February 1980, pp. 94–110. This is a clear overview. See also Elizabeth Ferrarini, "Move Over Electronic Mail Here Comes Viewdata," *Interface Age,* December 1980, pp. 77–82.

type, and a push-button-affair control for turning to needed information. Another group of systems, considered at the end of this section, provides a minicomputer in the home.

The television-oriented systems include two basic systems. One *(teletext)* is non-interactive in that the viewer can only see the material and cannot respond by asking or answering questions. The more sophisticated system is *viewdata,* an interactive approach which allows the user to communicate with the system, something on the order of searching data bases.

(1) Teletext (called Ceefax in England and operated by the British Broadcasting System).[36] Here the message is received over the television set and appears as a picture or as print on the screen. The viewer, equipped with a control unit similar in appearance to the hand-held box used for cable television, can call up various messages as needed. Selection is limited to about 1000 or fewer printed pages, which are shown, in part or in whole, on the television screen.

If, for example, the user wants tourist information, a catalog gives him a number to key on the control panel to begin the process. When he pushes the appropriate button, a page of print appears on the television screen. This "tourist information" page gives a listing of subheadings, one being "events." Keying the appropriate number for "events" brings up a page of activities in the local area, or in the next city, or state, or country.[37]

Such a system is, in fact, little more than turning pages in a gigantic book. Actually, only about 100 pages are held in the system at one time, and it takes about 12 seconds to "turn" from page 1 to page 99. This slowness militates against large storage of data, hence the trend toward another system, discussed next.

(2) Viewdata (called Prestel in England and operated by the British Post Office since 1979). This is much the same type of system, although it is considerably more sophisticated and has promise of being more useful. Here information is in data bases, with no limit to the amount. (In 1981 advertisements for the system claimed over 150,000 pages available.) The greatest difference between Viewdata and Teletext is that the former is interactive, with Viewdata, the user, perhaps the librarian at the computer terminal, has limited ways of communicating with the computer. Teletext, however, is little more than a broadcaster sending out a set number of pages. Because there

---

[36]The private station, ITV, has a similar system called Oracle.

[37]There are, and will be, numerous variations on the Teletext system. For example, the French are perfecting Antiope which overcomes some of the problems with the "page-turning" block of Ceefax.

is no computer and no data base, Teletext involves no need for expensive specialized equipment other than the command unit. But Viewdata, by comparison, is costly. A special television set, at about $2,000, is required. In England the set may be rented for about $50 a month and connected via the telephone line to the computer. There is a fee for this information service—from a few cents up to ten cents a page. Currently, the English system has about 136 different sources of information, sources as varied as "Where the Action Is" (news on nightclubs), *The New York Times,* and consumer reports.[38]

Specific library uses of Viewdata are numerous. In various experiments in the United States, OCLC is to provide catalog information from local libraries to users. The system also opens up possibilities for paying bills, participating in discussions, etc. OCLC has sponsored a *Home Book Club* which makes it possible for people to participate in an hour-long discussion. Viewers vote "yes" or "no" on certain questions and are given the opportunity to select the next book for discussion.

The Canadian variation is Telidon, which now includes over 1000 pages of data and graphics. Sponsored by Bell Canada and the Department of Communications, the system was in the experimental stages in the early 1980s. It has a wide number of possible applications, which generally include: "electronic mail, electronic banking, news, weather, sports, stock market information, entertainment schedules and ticket booking, travel information, educational TV. . . ."[39]

When will the average person be able to push a button and activate a data base to give up the same kind of information now located at a computer terminal in a library? Quite likely, not for many, many years.[40]

Library comparison

The home systems are controlled by the users only to a limited extent. Basically the user makes a selection through an index system and reads a "page" of information on the television set. But the material on the page is predetermined in context and organization and cannot

---

[38]*The (London) Financial Times,* March 24, 1980, has a special section on Viewdata which gives a clear explanation of what is involved. Librarians may write the Prestel center International House, Canterbury Crescent, London SW9 7QT) for packages of information.

[39]Lydia Dotto, "The Information Revolution," *Canadian Business,* May 1979, pp. 58–67.

[40]For a detailed analysis of the difficulties with these home systems, see Hans Karlgren, "Viewdata—Something to Be Crazy About?" *International Classification,* November 1979, pp. 172–176.

be modified by the user. This differs radically from the library computer terminal where information is searched to meet a special need. Neither of the home systems described above allows the user to employ the same type of logical searches employed in the library.

Stripped of the hoopla, the systems are little more than a television screen acting as a printed page. The user has the option of calling up a particular subject, or even a particular page, but there are no citations, no abstracts, and certainly few or no options for making the sophisticated searches required in the library.

The fact is that the librarian who envisions the home becoming the Library of Congress may be correct in the sense that it will be possible to deliver up texts on the home screen. But the texts will be primarily undifferentiated, except in broad subject areas, and there is little reason to believe the average user at home will be able to cope without the reference librarian. At best, the home television screen will deliver up answers to many ready-reference queries, give current news events, and even furnish professional people with paging services. But there is little reality to the assumption that every home will soon have ERIC, MEDLINE or any of the bibliographic data bases which are the heart of the library information system. Granted that such bases are even made available, until such time as they are simplified, the problem will be the same as it is today with printed works in the library—most people either cannot or will not learn to use the system, and they will rely instead upon the librarian.

To this point most work has been with technology, *not* with potential audiences. No one is quite sure that any of the systems will be accepted by users; for that matter, the particular needs of users are not known. Given, too, the fierce competition between networks, publishers, and other information sources, few producers are willing to commit the billions needed for development of more sophisticated systems.

The Columbus, Ohio, system has cost over $20 million, but of the 100,000 potential subscribers, only 30,000 have expressed interest. Without more subscribers the home-information suppliers will not be able to spread fixed costs widely enough to bring prices, which today average about $5 an hour, within range of the average user.[41]

The question as to the feasibility of systems involves many factors: the cost, now alarmingly high for the average home; the ease of use, now satisfactory but hardly sophisticated; the visual effect— much of the material is difficult to read; and the speed of use, e.g., the words flow row after row down the screen or a complete page may

---

[41]Edward Meadows, "Why TV Sets Do More in Columbus, Ohio," *Fortune,* October 6, 1980, p. 73.

appear but one must wait for this to happen. In any event, will people be willing to take the time and the trouble even with interactive systems?

There is another major consideration. Information can be packaged and sent almost as well, sometimes better, via such existing systems as radio, television, telephone, the daily newspaper, and the weekly magazine. Some critics of the various existing home information centers believe that it will take a major change in human habits to draw people to a television screen as a substitute for the printed page.[42]

Given the negative point of view, there is no question there is an argument for the other side. Video media is considered one of the most promising fields today, and some believe that by the late 1980s the various services that fall under the video umbrella are likely to offer a greater challenge to magazines and other print media than either cable television or home video equipment. In fact, the complete list of companies in this country that are spending millions of dollars on research and development of videotext systems reads like the list of the Fortune 500.

Home computers

Viewdata and Teletext rely upon a television set and upon a knowledge of limited commands on the part of the user. These systems are not to be confused with the popular home minicomputer. The usual home system consists of a keyboard, a CRT, and floppy disks or less expensive cassette tapes. The disks or tapes usually offer programs for games, but more expensive models carry programs for numerous activities, from accounting to inventory procedures. Some estimate that "by 1985 seven out of ten households will have home computers."[43] Others are not that optimistic, but grant that there is a large

---

[42]If, however, it is found that delivery of information can be cheaper via the home system, the print media may be doomed, at least for some services; e.g., AT&T is experimenting with the replacement of the phone book with a teleprocessor system. Why? Because the cost of the printed book, plus other services, comes to over $2 billion a year. The tentative plan is to have users find needed numbers via television sets which have been modified for Viewdata. See David Burnham, "Tests Point Way to Use of Home Teleprocessors," *The New York Times*, April 28, 1980, p. D12.

[43]Deborah dePayster, "Having a Serious Talk with Your Computer," *American Bookseller*, January 1980, p. 53. Space does not allow development of the use of microcomputers in libraries. In 1981, the American Library Association organized the ELA—Electronic Library Association—to consider uses and problems of microcomputers and home delivery systems. For an excellent outline, see Ted Hines, "Library Applications of Microcomputers" (processed, 5 p.), available from the Library Science/Educational Technology Dept., University of North Carolina, Greensboro, NC 27412.

market to be developed by firms such as AT&T, IBM, and Texas Instruments.

Librarians may lose sight of the real significance of the minicomputer to the average citizen. In the future, as in the past, it is likely that only a relatively few home computers will serve as information sources. Most will be devoted to such practical applications as computerized heat and light control or the remote reading of utility meters. It is with development of systems for these daily preoccupations that the giants, from AT&T to IBM and Xerox, are most concerned.

The closest a current system comes to offering reference work is SOURCE, a product of the Telecomputing Corporation of America. There the homeowner buys a terminal, the necessary telephone coupler, and possibly a CRT, but the actual program is a data base on a mainframe computer. The user draws upon this just as does the librarian who sits at a terminal searching a bibliographic data base. Among the 2000-plus sources of information are "games such as Startrek and Adventure, payroll accounting and cash flow programs, income tax preparation, daily financial and stock quotes, availability of airline reservations, weather conditions in many cities, comparative shopping, movie and book reviews, horoscopes and biorhythms, etc. . . . The system is also capable of handling electronic mail."[44] By late 1981 the SOURCE also included news summaries and limited stock information. Commands are simplified and there is no Boolean logic employed. Cost, excluding hardware, is an initial $100 connection charge plus $2.75 to $15 an hour, depending upon the program and time of day used. Eventually this is seen as a method of tapping bibliographic data bases, possibly programmed for easy home access and supplied by the nation's major vendors.

Variations of the minicomputer/television telereference systems are likely to be of considerable popularity. However, although they do offer a tremendous potential, as of this writing they do not seem much of a challenge to library reference service.

SUGGESTED READING

Barwise, T. P., "The Cost of Literature Search in 1985," *Journal of Information Science*, October 1979, pp. 195–202. An objective analysis of the factors which go into the cost of an online search, with a fascinating projection into the years ahead.

[44]*Database*, December 1979, p. 8. In mid-1980 OCLC announced it would test-market SOURCE to libraries, with emphasis on the information data rather than the games. The fee for libraries will be about $300 to $400 a month for 122 hours of use. *IDP Report*, April 10, 1980, p. 1, 4. This may change as *Reader's Digest* purchased controlling interest in the firm in early 1981. The *Digest* hopes to broaden the base of SOURCE and make it the first really popular electronic system for the home.

Cawkell, A. E., "Will Information Flow to the Citizen Be Improved with Videotext Systems?" *Aslib Proceedings,* June 1980, pp. 264–269. A frank discussion of the promise and the reality of gaining information via the tube in the living room. See the rest of this issue of the *Proceedings* for a discussion by several other experts on this same topic, i.e., "Computers and Information for the Citizen."

Hawkins, Donald, "Online Information Retrieval Bibliography," *Online Review,* April 1981, pp. 139–182. Some 401 references from mid-1979 to the middle of 1980. The bibliography is divided into seven sections; there is an author, but not a subject index and there are no annotations. Earlier bibliographies appeared in the same journal in March 1977, 1978, 1979, and 1980. To date this is the most comprehensive and current bibliography in the field.

Jensen, Rebecca, et al., "Costs and Benefits to Industry of Online Literature Searches," *Special Libraries,* July 1980, pp. 291–299. Clients of NASA Industrial Application Center were interviewed to determine user-identified dollar costs of online searches. The point is made that there are times when a manual search is more economical and that there is a need to educate the user as to when and how to request help online.

Kidder, Tracy, *The Soul of a New Machine.* New York: Atlantic–Little, Brown, 1981. By way of being a best-seller, this is the story of how the Data General company developed a sophisticated minicomputer. For a detailed review, and an insight into the engineering and financing of minicomputers, see also: Jeremy Bernstein, "Modern Times, *The New York Review of Books,* Oct. 9, 1981, pp. 40–41.

Klempner, Irving M. (ed.), "Information Technology and Special Libraries," *Special Libraries,* April 1981. The complete issue, some 180 pages, is turned over to current concerns with technology and information. Most of the dozen or so articles are as applicable to other libraries as to special libraries, and the issue is a good introduction to computers.

Knapp, Sara, "Beyond Fee or Free," *RQ,* Winter 1980. Librarians from three different academic libraries offer suggestions on how to mediate the fee debate. Along the way they describe their different systems of online searching.

Kranich, Nancy, "Fees for Library Services: They Are Not Inevitable," *Library Journal,* May 1, 1980, p. 1049. A thoroughly objective discussion of the pros and cons of fees and the need for the library to continue offering free, integrated reference service with data bases.

Lancaster, F. W. "Some Considerations Relating to the Cost Effectiveness of Online Services in Libraries," *Aslib Proceedings,* January 1981, pp. 10–14. The author finds that a comparison of search costs "greatly favours online operation." Note, too, the use of the H. R. Collier study (in the references) which is dated, yet still useful.

Miller, Inabeth, "The Micros Are Coming," *Media & Methods,* April 1980, pp. 32–35. A clear explanation of how the home-type computer will be, and is being, used in education. Some of the material is applicable to libraries in general. For specific application of these smaller units in library online cataloging, see S. Michael Malinconico, "Mass Storage Technology and File Organization," *Journal of Library Automation,* June 1980, pp. 77–87.

Pope, Nolan F., "Database Users: Their Opinions and Needs," *Special Libraries,* May/June 1980, pp. 265–269. Searchers give their opinions on what publishers and vendors should do to improve systems, from making those systems much easier to use to supplying better indexing. Only three of the 52 users polled cancelled, or did not order, printed versions of sources after having the material online.

The Professional Librarian's Reader in Library Automation. White Plains, N. Y.: Knowledge Industry Publications, 1980. A collection of articles by Martha Williams, Susan Martin, Michael Malinconico et al. on networks, online catalogs, bibliographic data bases, etc. While uneven, the collection gives a solid overview for the beginner.

Raben, Joseph, "The Electronic Revolution and the World Just Around the Corner," *Scholarly Publishing,* April 1979, pp. 195–209. A clear explanation for the layperson as to the various factors and equipment involved in the "paperless society."

Salton, Gerald, "A Progress Report on Information Privacy and Data Security," *Journal of the American Society for Information Science,* March 1980, pp. 75–83. The problem of automation and the threat to privacy is discussed by an expert who is as clear in his writing style as he is in his thinking. A solid overview of an increasingly important topic.

Serban, William, and Elizabeth Vandersteen, "Computerized Bibliographic Retrieval," *Louisiana Library Association Bulletin,* Spring 1980, pp. 100–105. A discussion of costs and fee structures for online service in a typical midsized university library.

Tyner, Sue, "Checklist for Printing Terminals" *Journal of Library Automation,* June 1980, pp. 108–118. A checklist of points to look for in good printers' and allied equipment. Useful as an overview of the major types of hardware likely to be found in a library with an online search service. For data on specific brand-name equipment see Joseph Becker, "Printer Terminals for Libraries," *Library Technology Reports,* May–June 1980, pp. 231–292. See also ongoing issues of *Library Computer Equipment Review* in which hardware is carefully analyzed and advice given on what to purchase or avoid. Ably edited by William Saffady.

CHAPTER SIX

The Online Search

WHETHER SEATED AT A COMPUTER TERMINAL, searching a
card catalog, or wandering through the stacks of the
library, the reference librarian has the same basic
skills. No amount of automation will change what
some consider an almost intuitive ability to find
answers to questions.

The author does not subscribe to the too-commonly heard
dictum that "Anyone can do a computer reference search." It
requires the reference librarian's skills, and these are skills which are
not given to everyone. It is true that we know discouragingly little
about just what those skills are and how they are developed. Still, a
broad outline of the interview-and-search methods used at the
terminal may be drawn and contrasted with the techniques needed
for a successful search in printed materials.

Online searching is a complex, confusing, and sometimes frustrating process for the beginner. The difficulty is that the online
search (1) does not follow a well-prescribed sequence of events, (2)
does not lend itself to assessment while in progress, and (3) is highly
language-dependent.[1]

---

[1]Charles T. Meadows, "The Computer as a Search Intermediary," *Online*, July 1979,
pp. 54–55. For an overview of who searches what and problems involved see: Marjorie
M. K. Hlava, "Online Users Survey 1980," *Online Review*, September 1980, pp.
294–299. See too: Connie Lamb, "Searching in Academia; Nearly 50 Libraries Tell
What They Are Doing," *Online*, April 1981, pp. 78–81.

Even after several years of research into the search-and-find operation at the computer terminal, basic questions on the process remain to be answered. Some claim that the answers may never come or that the questions can only be resolved in compromises between people and technology. For example:

> *How do people search? What makes them decide to take certain actions? What effect does the particular choice of commands or even the manner in which a machine converses with a user have on the user's performance? What makes the intermediary function effectively? Even with humans in this role, when is it successful and when not? What can be done by either intermediary or user to enhance the interaction between the two?*[2]

The same general methods are employed in the search of a data base as in the search of any index or abstracting service.

1. There has to be a clear analysis of the search question(s) and the real, as opposed to the sometimes badly expressed verbal, question clarified.

2. The question must be compared to access points available in the data base(s), and determination made as to which point(s) will most likely yield the answer.

3. One must determine the most likely search elements—subject, author, title, or keywords from abstracts—and begin. The idea is to match terms used in the search with terms used by the indexer, or terms present in the title or abstract of the documents in the base. For example, the user may want material on "jumping beans," but the vocabulary in the data base may be limited to "spurge family" or to the Spanish term "brincadora."

4. The librarian must recognize all possible approaches to retrieving the needed information, and these may be infinite in number. Now at the actual level of the search, the librarian makes another judgment—whether to call up nearly everything on a subject, limit the search to a more precise area with low recall, or compromise. For example, in quest of material on Henry James the librarian might enter a broad search for everything written in the past 30 years about the author or a narrow search limited to critical American writings of the past five years on James's later novels.

---

[2]Ibid., p. 59.

MANUAL OR ONLINE?

Cost aside, how is the judgment made to use an online or a manual search? Assuming the choice exists, there are some general considerations to be used in determining which method serves better. The decision requires an analysis of the needs of the particular user.

(1) A manual search is generally the better method if a broad, undifferentiated search is called for; an online search is better if the need is for a specific topic or fact.

(2) The manual method is preferable when the user wants only one or two citations. An online search is better when the user wants an exhaustive examination of the literature.

(3) When more than one index has to be searched, the convenience of paging numerous data bases at the terminal makes this the obvious choice, rather than dashing about the library looking for various services.

(4) Such services as the citation and many other science indexes are more difficult to use in the printed than the online form; therefore, an online search is preferable.

(5) Finally, one must take into account the much-mentioned benefits of the online search—depth of indexing, ability to coordinate terms, free text searching, etc.

Then, too, there is the librarian. No matter what may be said about the ease of use of the online or the manual service, the deciding factor is how comfortable the librarian feels with either form. A user may also have developed a bias for the printed index and make this the choice even when reason says an online search would serve better.

Some of these differences should be examined in a bit more detail. A manual search is preferable when the user/librarian is dealing with a broad subject. For example, a patron looking for an overview of the common cold would be better started at a printed source where it would be immediately clear how much information was available and where a further check of several citations would narrow the search to, say, the cold among children, the cold in New York, etc. Using a computer for a broad subject is somewhat analogous to looking for your home by using a microscope. Conversely, if one is dealing with a particular strain of the cold, then it would be preferable to begin at the computer in order to find the exact citation among countless possibilities.

When the search is for an uncomplicated subject or the work of one author it is often faster and even easier to use the printed sources.

For example, if the layperson wants to discover the various pros and cons of using aspirin, a single article in a popular magazine is likely to suffice. Here the searcher would use one of several general indexes. Conversely, if a specialist is doing research on the relationship of aspirin and heart attacks there are numerous approaches possible— authors, subject terms, tag terms, etc.—which can best be sifted online.

There are times when, no matter what arguments favor the efficiency of the online search, a manual search is preferable. Too much may be made of these reasons, but they are at least worth recognizing.

(1) A glance down a printed page is an excellent method of focusing a search. (This same approach is possible via the computer, but it can be more complicated.) For example, in looking for material on "Newcastle disease" in the *Bibliography of Agriculture Index* the searcher could infer a matched term of use. This is done by noting that the title of articles under "Newcastle disease" often included the term "wild birds," i.e., the two terms are synonymous in many cases. "This advantage produced higher recall than the computer search. . . . Wild birds is impossible to express fully in free-language—all possible birds' names could not be included in the computer search, although the manual searcher could easily interpret them. In this search the manual searcher's use of interpretation outweighed the physical constraints of the printed index."[3]

(2) An experienced search analyst may browse with a computer terminal, but generally in an online search, there is a certain lack of what many consider a high road to gaining information— serendipity.

(3) Sometimes it is forgotten that no suitable display exists whose information capacity matches the processing power of the brain's eye. When a user needs to scan for information, the printed page is much faster and more efficient than waiting for a printout or a CRT display.

PRESEARCH INTERVIEW

When the decision is made to employ an online search, most libraries ask the individual to fill out a preliminary form on which the question

[3]Susan M. Johnston, "Choosing Between Manual and Online Searching . . ." *Aslib Proceedings,* October/November 1978, p. 391. The interaction of traditional reference work with online searches is discussed by Simone Klugman in "Online Information Retrieval Interface With Traditional Reference Services," *Online Review,* September 1980, pp. 263–272.

is stated. Sometimes this is done systematically, other times it is suggested that the user write a brief "narrative" in which the question is framed. For example, in one model form the following is requested: the name and address of the user; the title and purpose of the search; the terms and the synonyms likely to be used in connection with the topic; a list of important people in the field; and, sometimes, a note on maximum cost.

The use of the preliminary interview-search form is almost universal, simply because it saves valuable time. The form forces the user to consider the question and to be precise in its formulation. As one teacher points out, a similar form for any reference interview would no doubt improve all type of searches. The form also serves as a good departure point in formulating and negotiating new vocabulary as the librarian and patron work together.

Synonym search

The majority of bibliographic online searches are via subjects, although the search may be conducted through an author's name, keywords in the title, geographical points, etc. Still, proper descriptors are the secret to the success or failure of many searches.

Experienced librarians tend to make up lists of keywords and synonyms before they begin the search. It is no accident that most presearch forms ask the user for such words.

Here one must understand the difference between a controlled-vocabulary search and a free text search. A controlled vocabulary exists where subject headings, or descriptors, are assigned. In a manual search, if one wants to know what subjects have been used, a list of subject headings, such as the ones published by the Library of Congress or Sears, are consulted.

Matters are somewhat different for an online search. While Library of Congress subject headings may be consulted, the searcher is more likely to depend upon a thesaurus. Many of the data bases, although not all, have their own specialized thesaurus. Here the field of possible terms is more limited than in the Library of Congress list, certainly more specialized, and is less likely to depend upon numerous synonyms.

The advantage of a controlled vocabulary is that the user may immediately check the subject headings used by the indexer. For example, if someone wants material on the aged and insomnia, he or she turns to a list of subject headings or to a thesaurus and finds that X data base uses the term "elderly" for the aged; "geriatrics" is a related term, and "sleep disturbance" is used along with insomnia.

Many bibliographic data bases now have a thesaurus, and, in addition, several vendors have loaded the thesauri online. Searchers have the option of requesting a list of alphabetically related terms. In another instance of failure of the vendors to standardize, Lockheed calls their thesaurus option "expanding," SDC calls theirs "neighbor," and BRS refers to theirs as "root."

When the proper command is entered, the online system gives the searcher an alphabetical display of the dictionary file, or the inverted file, which includes, but is not limited to, the controlled vocabulary. Hence, the systems include not only the thesaurus but all other searchable words in the same alphabetical order. One may expand time after time to get related, broader, or narrower terms.

For example, one may look up online "consumer behavior" (a descriptor) in *Psychological Abstracts* and find 15 expanded, related terms. The number of items in the file is indicated for each, that is, there are four citations containing the term "consumatory" (not a descriptor) and 956 containing the term "consumer" (a descriptor).[4] Parenthetically, in the printed thesaurus there are only five descriptors, i.e., basic controlled-vocabulary terms (from "consumer-attitudes" to "consumer-research"), although each does have related, broader, and narrower terms. The point is that online one may find many more mnemonic hints as to search areas than in the printed thesaurus. (Note: Not all data bases have this online service; e.g., Lockheed has thesauri online for only a few data bases.)

Free text searching is searching of fields or paragraphs where the vocabulary is not standardized or "controlled." The librarian must try to outguess the data base. For example, lacking a place to find terms of "aged," the librarian may turn to a book .of synonyms, a thesaurus used by a related data base, the patron (who may suggest synonyms and related terms), or simply try a few terms to see what develops in the search. This natural-language approach forces the librarian to make up a list of many

---

[4]The thesauri, of course, only indicate controlled-vocabulary terms, but how is one to determine what uncontrolled, free-language, common speech terms to enter into the system? For example, the thesaurus may indicate one can use "jazz music," but there is no indication of "fatal jazz rock," a new term, in the thesaurus. How is the searcher to know that "fatal jazz rock" is likely to be found in an abstract or title? She cannot unless (a) the user knows the term and suggests it or (b) she knows the term and tries it at the terminal. A solution is suggested: an online thesaurus of vocabulary to be used in free-text searching. This might include terms not found in the thesaurus because not adequately indexed, not organized to use subject headings, or not current. In one proposal it was pointed out that "one of the advantages of these [free language] thesauri over existing vocabularies is that they would incorporate current vocabulary and would be constructed in part from actual searches. They would therefore be more useful to practicing searchers than existing controlled vocabularies."

more terms than would be necessary were the controlled descriptors known.

The free-text approach may be more scattered and less precise, but it does have such advantages as being able to locate terms—new expressions and descriptors—not yet in the indexer's vocabulary. Command of a broader group of terms in turn may lead to more articles and less reliance on the skill of an indexer.

Useful as a free-text search may prove, the best type of data base is one that offers both a free-text and a controlled-vocabulary approach. "A database constructed without any editing or intellectual effort at input (i.e., without controlled vocabulary) requires considerable expertise on searching—it becomes more an art than a science."[5] Most of the more frequently used data bases offer both a controlled-vocabulary and free-text searching capacity. This means that the librarian, failing in a search for assigned subject descriptors, may search for single or combined terms in all searchable paragraphs, from abstracts to titles to content-classification codes.

In no case should the librarian underestimate the knowledge of the user. The expert quite likely is not only familiar with basic terms, but has probably built up a group of terms which have been useful in previous searches.

Basic steps

Let us now return to the librarian and the user. A decision has been made to use the computer search, and a definition of the basic concept has been reached.[6] What are the next steps in the presearch interview?

1. An explanation, in as much detail as is needed, of the structure of the individual data bases likely to be of value. Both the capabilities and the limitations of the bases should be explained.
2. An exploration of possible synonyms.
   (a) Where a thesaurus is available, relevant terms are discussed with the client and those most likely to be of use are isolated. In the process, the question is likely to be more closely defined.
   (b) Lacking a thesaurus, the likely subject headings, names of authors, titles, geographical locations, dates, or any other

---

[5]A. R. Jackson et al., "On-Line Retrieval . . ." *The Information Scientist,* March 1978, p. 16.

[6]Arleen Somerville, "The Place of the Reference Interview in Computer Searching: The Academic Setting," *Online,* October 1977, pp. 14–23.

tags which may help in the search are discussed with the user.

Experience soon familiarizes the librarian with the essential language of the subjects covered by the data bases, and the librarian's knowledge of the terminology may be more advanced than the user's. A good dictionary at hand is an almost indispensable aid. Where the area is likely to be new to the searcher, or at least relatively new, it is useful to ask the user to bring in advance one or two articles on the subject which the searcher may read; where the time permits, the user herself may do outside reading on the subject, although this is a luxury few have time to consider.

3. An explanation of all possible limitations on the search, from language to type of source publication to time frame. Other limitations might be imposed by requests for works by (or not by) certain author(s) or by a maximum or minimum number of citations, authors, institutions, etc. (If citation indexing is employed, of course, the author entry becomes the most important factor.)

Most of the presearch interview will be conducted before the actual search begins. Several steps, of course, may be extended, modified, or possibly even skipped when the search is begun.

Remote or personal interview

Is it necessary for the searcher to have the questioner present when the search is being conducted? There are various opinions and two distinctive approaches to the question. In some situations the user is not present when the search is made. Instead, the individual fills out a form, often with the help of a librarian, but not the librarian likely to make the search. For example, the New York State Library has a system whereby librarians may submit search queries on a special form to the Library. The name and phone number of the person putting the question are given so that the search analyst may call, if necessary, to discuss the question with the individual.

This method is not as satisfactory as the personal interview, but it does allow the computer to be brought into every library. The service, even if indirectly, is made available to everyone. Ideally, there would be a terminal, as well as a trained searcher, in each library. But in libraries where there is hardly enough money for one professional librarian, the ideal is not likely to be reached very soon.

An expert's advice

It is probably most instructive to hear how an expert search analyst handles the interview. The following are comments on the presearch interview written by Sara D. Knapp, an experienced search analyst at the library of the State University of New York at Albany:

> *I use the term "computer-based setting" rather than speaking of the "presearch" interview, for my observations are drawn from the practice (by no means universally accepted) of requiring the patron to have an in-person interview with the search analyst and* to be present *with the analyst at the online terminal while the search is entered and results are sampled. This practice reduces the shortcomings of the delegated search.*
>
> *Appointments for searches are scheduled in advance by the section secretary, with advice when necessary from librarians at the reference desk. At the time of scheduling, patrons are given a search form to complete and bring with them when they come to their appointments. The form is in two parts so that one copy can be retained and the other returned to the patron with the search results. The form includes space for a brief narrative statement; categories for limitations such as "human language only"; and a request for one recent relevant citation, if known. The form does not make a request for key terms or descriptors, although some patrons like to include them.*
>
> *During the half-hour appointment, the search analyst is seated at the terminal. User and analyst discuss search strategy and the user's needs. Search statements are entered at the online terminal, with immediate feedback. Generally, only the titles and descriptors of a sample of citations are printed. If the total number of citations retrieved seems reasonable and the sample is judged satisfactory, then offline printing is requested.*
>
> *Usually requests which can be readily answered using a printed index are not searched by computer. But if the material is complex or difficult to locate using conventional sources, then the search is online; therefore the preponderance of computer searches tends to be research-related.*
>
> *If the problem is not well articulated at the outset, the analyst must try to help the patron to clarify the specific need. The problems and processes tend to require greater use of cognitive skills than is necessary during the more personal interview, in which emotional support plays a greater role. When problems lean toward the personal, subjective end of the continuum, the patron may have an urgent need to feel accepted and understood as a person. With relatively more objective types of problems,*

the patron may be more concerned that the subject or the content be understood. The techniques for inviting patrons to "open up" have less importance in this setting. (I do recall one patron who could hardly bring himself to utter the word "rape," although most clients for computer-based searches have few emotional problems in describing their requests.) Seldom does altruism or sympathy play a major role in the computer interview; i.e., the approachability of the librarian is less a factor than the ability to relate to complex research problems.

Nevertheless, personalities do play a part. Etiquette can be an inhibitor when analyst and user are uncertain of their roles. Inferential confusion is a problem when some queries are not clearly stated. An inhibitor possibly unique to the computer situation is the fear that ideas for research, a proposal, a grant, etc., may be pirated and used by someone else. And the belief that the search analyst may not understand the actual need of the user may lead to confusion in stating the question. I would not for a minute suggest that personalities and personal accept-ance are not important. Still, good manners will probably suffice and "cotton-batting" is usually not required.

The best communication probably occurs when both user and analyst are perceived as having relatively equal status. Search analysts who come across as "This is your Captain speaking" are as inhibiting as they are annoying. At the other extreme, we have "your obedient servant" at the terminal, wasting time and money by doing exactly what the user commands, even to sinking the ship.

Self-confidence is important because the analyst must be able to admit she does not understand a request. The search for meaning is the heart of the interview. The librarian must be able to ask, "What do you mean by . . .?"

Users often give long, detailed statements of their needs. The analyst must be able to cut the statement back to essentials. How? Thesauri can provide synonyms; e.g., "You want swamps. Shall we also look at marshes, bogs, moors . . .?" But only human intelligence and dialogue can help in the sort of intellectual Ping-Pong needed to narrow the search to particular terms. The thesauri offer one aid, but a greater aid is the dialogue with the user.

At the same time, it is important to realize that silence can be important. Intellectual concerns require serious thought. The babbling conversationalist, whose insecurities mount with every second of silence, will interfere with the process. If the babbler is the patron, it really doesn't hurt to explain politely that one could probably do a better job given a few moments of quiet to consider the request and perhaps to consult the thesaurus. If the analyst is insecure, the sources of the insecurity should, if possible, be identified and remedied. Searching requires full attention, and distractions, whether from within or without, can only lessen one's effectiveness.

THE SEARCH

The online search requires two distinct, yet related talents. The first is mechanical—the searcher must be able to type and must master the commands necessary to get the material out of the system.[7] The second is logical, but also intuitive, and is ultimately the more important. The searcher must be able to interact with the user and the computer in order to produce the required results.

Mechanical procedures

The first step, after sitting down at the terminal, is to connect. This is normally done by dialing a phone number, and when a high-pitched tone is heard, placing the receiver in the coupler on the terminal. A code is typed into the system which connects the user and, of course, allows the vendor to know to whom to bill the services about to be rendered.

Once the password is entered, the terminal gives a message indicating the connection is complete. The next step is to enter the name or number of the data base to be searched. Most systems then automatically give a "user prompt," which may be the first search statement number. This is a way of keeping track of commands entered and a method, too, of calling up a previously entered term by number rather than by spelling it out each time.

The next step is to proceed with the search strategy via terminal input. The last of the mechanical steps is the "sign off" at the end of the session. In response to a signal given by the searcher, the vendor reports, via the terminal, how much connect time the search required.

The format and the commands which activate a given data base depend upon the format of the data base itself and the format of the vendor's system. Lockheed, SDC, BRS, Mead Data Center, etc., all

---

[7]The too-common idea is that keyboard mechanics is enough. "Undue concentration upon keyboard mechanics without intellectual substance during training may create a . . . monster. This is a novice searcher with a tunnel vision view of searching who thinks he sees the light at the end of it when actually he only equates mastery of commands with mastery of searching." Donna Dolan, "The Quality Control of Search Analysts," *Online*, April 1979, p. 13.

display a data base in a slightly different manner. However, the end result (i.e., the citation or abstract or text) is usually the same.

Search strategy[8]

While the sophisticated searcher may use numerous methods of extracting information from the data base, at its most basic level the procedure usually begins with keywords or phrases which are concepts of interest to the user. These have been formulated in the presearch interview and, except in the case of a particularly simple search, are likely to be modified during the search itself—usually in consultation with the user. If, for example, the user wants information on the effects of aircraft noise on hearing, the key concepts to be typed at the terminal are "aircraft noise" and "hearing." If neither, in any of various combinations, produces results, then the searcher must turn to other terms, authors, or tags.

The procedure is much the same as following a printed abstract or index, i.e., the searcher must try to discover the keywords, subject headings, author's name, etc. One must suggest as many synonyms as possible for likely search terms.

Parenthetically, a problem for beginners is spelling or typing. Failure to enter the correct spelling causes the computer to spit back "keyword not in dictionary." The Lockheed system returns what was typed and a zero results, if it does not receive the proper word.

Boolean logic

The search is conducted by the use of Boolean connectors.[9] That is, the computer will report results according to certain conditions dictated by the searcher. The librarian will input combinations of logical connectors, called Boolean connectors, to limit the search.

[8]For a detailed analysis of terminology of search strategy see the excellent article by Marcia Bates, "Information Search Tactics," *Journal of the American Society for Information Science,* July 1979, pp. 205–214. It is worth repeating that the literature of search strategy is continuing to develop, and anyone who plans to do more than cursory searching should be a constant reader of *Online, Database,* and related journals which carry one or more articles on specific search patterns for specific data bases. Then, too, the user should have the publisher's manuals at hand, as well as those issued by the vendor.

[9]Boolean logic is named after George Boole (1815–1864), who used three operators (plus, times, and minus) for combinations of logical statements. Essentially it is a method of combining terms in searches, particularly as few searches are begun using only a single term.

1. The operator "OR" (A or B). The use of the disjunctive "or" is simply a way of asking for more and more material. In common speech, one is more likely to use "and," e.g., "I want material on science courses and science instruction and science units." But in a search this is translated into "science-courses *or* science-instruction *or* science-units." Actually the user wants any article containing any one of the terms, and so the "OR" operator is employed.

2. The operator "AND" (A and B). The "OR" alone tends to be too inclusive for most searches, so the librarian is likely to resort to the "AND" operator which restricts searches, causing retrieval of only documents containing the specified terms tied to each other by "AND." In the search for science materials it would now be documents with "science-courses *and* science-instruction *and* science-units," i.e., a document would have to contain all of these words or descriptors to be retrieved. The use of the logical conjunctive "AND" will narrow and clarify the search.

3. The operator "NOT" (A and not B) or (A–B). A third Boolean connector is "NOT" where it is noted a term must *not* appear anywhere in the document. Here one would say, "Give me college and library, but *not* college library circulation." The terms are limited even further. The computer is asked to locate only "college libraries," not "junior college libraries."

The vendors use the same words—"OR," "AND," and "NOT," but use various symbols or spaces as alternatives. For example, BRS will use a space to signify an "OR," which means "OR" does not have to be typed into the system. Lockheed will employ a plus sign for an "OR." This illustrates, once again, the lack of standardization and the confusion which may arise for the librarian trained with one vendor's system and then required to work on another's.

Beyond Boolean logic the searcher may use positional logic. This is involved, but essentially allows one to request terms which are adjacent to other terms in the same sentence, as within X number of words of, or in the same paragraph or field as, some other word(s). "Nesting" has reference to parentheses within parentheses, e.g., ((A or B) not C) and (D or E). This approach is used to save time and simplify search statements, and on BRS, for example, it is possible to have up to five levels of parentheses within parentheses.

How much

A great advantage to a computer search is that the librarian may ascertain quickly how many citations are available for a given term or set of terms. For example, one looks up "college libraries" and the printout shows 50 articles available in X data base for that subject.

Where the search turns up too many citations, say 150 on "college libraries," then other parameters must be introduced to limit the response. The number of citations can be restricted to certain dates or languages; employing the Boolean "AND" causes the search to be more specific. For example, the librarian might enter the keywords "college libraries AND faculty" with the result that now only material including "faculty" is retrieved.

If no citations for the subject are found, or if the number of citations is too limited, one may broaden the search by using "OR," i.e., by simply adding related, yet relevant terms.

Truncation permits searching of word stems. It is used for a variety of purposes, including the elimination of the need to think of all possible variations of a single term. A word stem may be specified and the computer will retrieve any term beginning with that stem. For example, "waste$" on the keyboard will result in retrieving "waste," "wastes," "wasted," or the multiterm "waste-material," if it is a precoordinated term. The right-hand truncation works only to the right of the word stem; i.e., it will not retrieve "nuclear waste," but will retrieve "waste-nuclear," if the latter term were precoordinated. Left-hand truncation, soon to be implemented on BRS, will retrieve "nuclear waste." Depending on the system, it may even be possible to retrieve terms from the middle of a descriptor.

In a modified approach, the user can ask the system to display (a) all entries in the dictionary file which begin with a specified set of characters (e.g., the root of "computer" would be followed by "computer-aided-learning," "computer-audits," "computer-based," etc.); and (b) the number of documents available for each term. By truncation, i.e., simply adding a dollar mark ($) after the root ("computers$"), the system will search for all terms beginning with that word or stem.

A great time-saver is the use of coding—a type of shorthand which saves the librarian from entering instructions, which might be quite lengthy in natural language, into the system. Every system has such a coding device, normally numeric or alphanumeric in nature. For example, there are codes for commands such as "begin," "expand," "print," "type," "select term," etc., which are usually symbols found on most typewriters or teletype machines. For example, BRS uses ". . . L" for "limit"; Lockheed uses "L" and suggests a whole battery of commands in abbreviated version ("E" for "expand") or in a symbol version (quotation marks for "E" or "expand").

Shortcuts and errors

While an experienced and trained librarian can usually "shortcut" most of the preliminary steps of a search (as would be done in a manual search), it is likely that there will be a certain sequence of steps before the final results are printed out. As the search progresses, most systems allow a display of intermediate results which can be checked and modified. The display is usually a citation of a basic item along with assigned descriptors and, if available, an abstract. The user may then decide if the sample is relevant before calling up additional similar citations.

The ability of the user and the searcher to examine sample citations is one of the primary advantages of the online search. It allows immediate modification of the search, just as it would were the two working with a printed source. Parenthetically, in some libraries citations are not tested because it is thought to be too expensive to print them out, or put them on the CRT. The result is often a disaster and, in the end, more expensive because the citations can be wrong.

Search failures

It is no more possible to explain causes of specific search failure when working with data bases than it is to pinpoint the source of error in standard reference searches. Because different systems have different methods for searching, only broad generalizations may be made.

The major problem areas which lead to failures or only partial successes include:

1. The searcher's lack of familiarity with the indexing vocabularies. Because each data base has its own vocabulary, the searcher's grasp must be broad. Furthermore, in technology and science where terminology is being updated constantly, failure is often due to lack of knowledge of new terms. Printed indexes tend to compensate for noncompatibility of user language with index language through *see* and *see also* references, which are often not found as easily in a data base. A thesaurus can be an aid, but only if the thesaurus is updated and in a form that can be easily used.

2. The indexer's and the searcher's typographical errors. Data-

base use results in about a 10 percent rate of error, much higher than in most printed services. An awareness of the error rate must be kept in mind, particularly when there are too many citations or too few. Terms can be cross-checked using other spellings, truncation, expansion, etc.

3. The searcher's use of too many general terms rather than specific terms. The result of multiples is often too many citations which, in turn, require numerous search revisions.

The search: An example

What follows is an abbreviated version of an actual search conducted and recounted by Sara D. Knapp:

> *A faculty member of the chemistry department presented a request for a bibliography: "Dietary fat or oil in cancer etiology; specifically effects of unsaturation in the fat or oil." The MEDLARS data base was used for the search.*
>
> *The search analyst pointed out that limiting the articles to etiology would imply the development or history of the disease in a particular patient or group of patients. She asked whether or not the patron would also like to have studies relating the presence or absence of these oils and fats to the absence of the disease in different populations with different dietary habits. The patron said that was actually what she wanted and not just articles on the etiology of cancer, as she had originally stated.*
>
> *Since the patron was interested in both saturated and unsaturated oils and fats, terms for both of them were included. The search analyst showed the patron the relevant pages of "MeSh Tree Structure" of medical subject headings for fats, oils, and fatty acids. The patron said she thought that some specific headings would be retrieved by more general terms, and the analyst explained that articles are usually indexed under the most specific headings.*
>
> *The analyst explained that MeSh terms are also retrievable through a numerical hierarchical arrangement, in which numbers are substituted for terms, known as the MeSh tree structure. More specific terms are numerical subdivisions of broader categories and thus, by truncating a broad-category "tree" number from the tree structure, it would be possible to search entire broad categories. The patron then defined the relevant subject categories which defined the fat/oil aspect of her search. Among them were dietary fats (butter, cholesterol, dietary margarine, fats, unsaturated, triolein) and fatty acids (caprylates, octanoic acids, decanoic acids, decanoates, etc.). The vast group of terms*

was simply entered into the search formulation by the use of eight truncated "tree words," e.g., fats, oils, fatty acids saturated or unsaturated, etc.

Since the patron indicated she was not interested in limiting the search to particular types of cancer, the analyst used a broad formulation which retrieved all general headings for carcinoma, neoplasms, etc. This formulation was so broad that thousands of articles on cancer were "retrieved" from the MEDLARS data base.

These citations were then limited to three aspects previously mentioned: etiology, occurrence, and prevention and control. These limitations reduced the figure to 670 citations. By entering the limitation of oils or fats the output was next reduced to a reasonable number of articles. Given this satisfactory grouping, the titles were then printed at the terminal to determine their relevance. One example will suffice: "Incidence of Stomach Cancer and Its Relation to Dietary Habits in Japan between 1900 and 1975."

After the search

The most common complaint concerning the use of the computer search is that too much irrelevant material is presented. Most people prefer a few highly relevant citations rather than all citations pertaining to the question, i.e., all citations available online. As more than one study has found, users will opt for a fast and convenient way to retrieve a few good articles rather than all the articles in the base.

Asked to evaluate one system, 45 percent of the users said there were too many irrelevant references. Here the solution lies in a finer definition of need, a definition which can be worked out by the librarian and the user.[10] The lack of enthusiasm for computer services by some people is supported by such comments as "My fields of interests are rather broad and such services would not be able to select appropriate material."[11]

There is a great danger of swamping individuals with information when a computer search is introduced, a danger which can be easily overcome by drawing a careful profile of the type of information needed by individuals in the initial phase of the process, and by monitoring the user satisfaction at the end of the process.[12]

[10]J. P. Wilson, "An SDI Experiment, . . ." *New Zealand Libraries*, no. 1, 1978, p. 6.

[11]Katherine Packer and Dagobert Soergel, "The Importance of SDI for Current Awareness in Fields with Severe Scatter of Information," *Journal of the American Society for Information Science*, May 1979, p. 133.

[12]Alastair Pilkington, "Information in Industry," *Aslib Proceedings*, January 1980, p. 15.

In view of the importance of relevance, follow-up procedures must be considered in the time frame of the search. For MEDLINE *(Index Medicus et al.)* searches in 345 libraries in 1976–1977 the average time spent interviewing the user was 9.3 minutes; 12.8 minutes was used for formulating the search; and 12.7 minutes was the actual time online. This 35-minute average does not include follow-up time, i.e., time devoted to finding what was used, what more was needed, etc.[13]

PERSONNEL

Once it is determined to employ online searches, organizational patterns for such service will differ. Many librarians believe that a full-time position, at least for the supervisor, should be established as the computer service grows. In commenting on service at the University of Utah, one critic observes: "Avoid mandating that the online service manager wear two hats. . . . Ideally the manager should have primary responsibility for the online service and secondary duties as a librarian in traditional reference service."[14]

The larger the library, the more obvious the need for a search expert—or experts. At the same time, duties should be shared, if only in a small way, with other reference librarians. Ideally the organization should include a head and an assistant, plus all of the reference librarians helping, as needed, with subject areas in which they are most familiar. This relegates command to a supervisor, yet allows everyone involved with reference to take part in the vital searches.

Actual organizational patterns differ, but a good example is found at the State University of New York at Albany where an Information Retrieval Section is a unit of the Reference and Collection Development Services Department. Ms. Knapp explains:

> There are eleven searchers, seven of whom are also members of the *Bibliographic Development Unit. Their searching is related to the subjects of their other responsibilities. Broadening the distribution of responsibilities reduces the tendency to view both of these groups as*

[13]Gloria Werner, "Use of On-Line Bibliographic Retrieval Services in Health Sciences Libraries . . ." *Bulletin of the Medical Library Association,* January 1979, p. 7.

[14]Ryan E. Hoover, "Computer Aided Reference Services in the Academic Library," *Online,* no. 4, 1979, p. 37. See, too, Marjorie Hlava, "Are You Ready for a Search Center?" *Information World,* April/May 1979, p. 5. The author considers the various aspects of just who does what in a general reference situation and asks, "Should all of the staff members be searchers or only a select few?" No answer is given.

unique. To paraphrase an old cliche, "If you can't fight them, invite them to join you."... Librarians will be interested if they perceive searching to have a meaningful relationship to their roles within the organization. It adds a zesty dimension to the job and additional skills to each person's repertoire.[15]

Each of the searchers, under the overall supervision of the coordinator of the Information Retrieval Unit, is scheduled for a minimum of four hours a week at the terminal. The library has been providing close to 2500 searches a year, and the number is higher if ready-reference queries are included in the count.

Each of the reference librarians should also be conversant with the computer search. Every reference librarian should know when, and when not, to suggest a computer-assisted search. Also, librarians must be equally familiar with the printed versions of the machine-readable records, particularly as it is often desirable to help a user with a presearch of the printed indexes before moving on to the computer. The general reference librarian must be able to follow up a computer search by helping the user locate documents cited, suggesting other sources, answering questions about the printouts, etc. The general reference librarian who knows the capabilities and the limitations of the computerized search is more likely to have an even better understanding of the more often used printed versions of the indexes.

The most important factor built into a computerized search is the one-to-one relationship between the user and the librarian. It is assumed from the beginning that a certain amount of time and close attention are required on the part of the librarian. Equal concentration is expected of the user.

The most popular location for the computer terminal is in a room within the library, usually away from the noise of the reference desk. The room assures the same quiet and comfort desirable for any reference interview but so rarely found in the day-by-day operations of manual reference searching. Still, this separation may sacrifice visibility and ease of use. Consequently a number of libraries prefer to have the terminal visible to users; thus it may or may not be in the ideal quiet space. A compromise is the mobile terminal. Many terminals may be placed on wheels and moved from place to place.[16]

[15]Sara Knapp, personal communication to author, October 1, 1980.

[16]James Kusack, "Integration of On-Line Reference Service," *RQ*, Fall 1979, pp. 64–69. This is a good discussion of the various approaches to location of online data-base search terminals and the different attitudes of librarians to such service.

Special qualifications

What are the desired qualifications of a librarian search strategist? They are much the same as for a good reference librarian. According to one study:

> Information service managers felt that a reference service, data base, or subject background was the most important characteristic. . . . Other characteristics mentioned . . . a logical, thorough, analytical mind; a willingness to learn; ease with mechanical devices; ability to deal with system failures; patience and persistence. . . . Another [qualification] believed to be of critical importance to the success of the retrieval process [is] the ability to handle the question negotiation interview with the potential search requestor.[17]

Essentially, the librarian must know the individual data bases, but it is of equal importance to know the differences between online files and their printed equivalents and when to use one rather than the other. In addition, the searcher should know the various indexing patterns of the abstract and indexing services, and have a solid knowledge of Boolean logic, the key to searching.[18]

SUGGESTED READING

Bellardo, Trudi, et al., "Education and Training for On-Line Searching: A Bibliography," *RQ,* Winter 1979, pp. 137–142. An annotated bibliography "intended to be used by searchers . . . who must plan or provide for the training and continuing education of on-line searchers."

Chen, Ching-chih, *Online Bibliographic Searching: A Learning Manual.* New York: Neal-Schuman, 1981. A "hands-on" learning manual, this includes chapters on data bases and the fundamentals of online searching. It is an example of several manuals now available, often from vendors, which assist in learning the basics of online searching at a computer terminal. See Lucy A. Tedd, "Teaching Aids Developed and Used for Education and Training for Online Searching," *Online Review,* June 1981, pp. 205–216. See, too, footnote 18 in Chapter 7, where there is a brief note about Sara Knapp's *BRS Training Workbook,* probably the best of the kind now available.

---

[17]Thomas P. Slavens and Marc Ruby, "Teaching Library Science Students to do Bibliographical Searches of Automated Data Bases," *RQ,* Fall 1978, pp. 39–40. The authors are citing several sources. See, too, Charles P. Bourne and Jo Robinson, "Education and Training for Computer-Based Reference Services: Review of Training Efforts to Date," *Journal of the American Society for Information Science,* January 1980, pp. 25–35.

[18]Dolan, op. cit., pp. 8–16. An outline of objective criteria for determining who is the best type of search analyst. See, in the same issue, Ann Van Camp, "Effective Search Analysts," pp. 18–20.

Fenichel, Carol, "The Process of Searching Online Bibliographic Databases: A Review of Research," *Library Research,* Summer 1980–1981, pp. 108–126. A detailed study of the theoretical and practical aspects of searching, based upon surveys and interviews with users.

Hawkins, Donald, and Carolyn Brown, "What Is an Online Search," *Online,* January 1980, pp. 12–18. An effort to isolate and explain an online search, primarily for the benefit of the library maintaining records and statistics on various types of reference service. Along the way the authors give some good definitions and explanations.

Knapp, Sara, and Jacquelyn Gavryck, "Computer Based Reference Service—A Course Taught by Practitioners," *Online,* April 1978, pp. 65–76. The two experienced teachers reveal a few of their secrets and, in so doing, clearly explain the basic computer search.

Marshall, Doris, "To Improve Searching, Check Search Results," *Online,* July 1980, pp. 32–47. The follow-up to a search is the primary, overlooked bit of the online quest for information. The author suggests methods of checking the search results.

McClure, Charles, "A Planning Primer for Online Reference Service in a Public Library," *Online,* April 1980, pp. 57–65. A practical, easy to understand analysis of steps necessary to establish computer searches in the general, not the specialized, situation.

Moore, Barbara, "Waiting at the Terminal," *Journal of Academic Librarianship,* January 1979, p. 443+. A short piece on some of the problems associated with the mechanics of the search, in this instance via OCLC, but equally applicable to other search patterns.

Penniman, W. D., and W. D. Dominick, "Monitoring and Evaluation of On-Line Information System Usage," *Information Processing & Management,* no. 1, 1980, pp. 17–36. A series of methods in monitoring presented to help the librarian ascertain the requirements for a successful search. In a more general way, the evaluative methods are applicable to other reference processes as well.

Raitt, D. I., "Recall and Precision Devices in Interactive Bibliographic Search . . ." *Aslib Proceedings,* July/August 1980, pp. 281–301. A clear discussion of the various methods of indexing and retrieving materials. While for online searches, much of the essay is applicable to any type of search.

CHAPTER SEVEN

Bibliographic Data Bases

 THERE ARE SOME 500 to 600 bibliographic data bases available in the United States, and their number continues to grow each year. In addition, the bibliographic data bases are supplemented by from 600 to 900 more specialized numeric and graphic data bases, many of which are privately produced and operated.[1] The actual number depends on who is making the compilation, but in practical terms there are probably no more than 150 to 165 bibliographic bases used with any consistency by a majority of people in and out of libraries. When one examines the daily use of data bases in libraries, the number can be reduced even further—to between 12 and 36.[2] Another reduction is possible when one considers only the

---

[1]The directories of data bases noted in this chapter list from 450 to 750 bases. Luedke et al. in 1977 estimated there were over 10,000 numeric data bases, although the majority are private, closely connected with business and government agencies. See too, Martha Williams (ed.), *Annual Review of Information Science,* 1977 (White Plains: New York: Knowledge Industry Publications, 1978), pp. 119–181; Nancy F. Hardy, "The World of Non-Bibliographic Information," *The Information Manager,* July/August 1979, p. 20; and a directory of services which is often updated, *Directory of NonBibliographic Data Base Services* (Santa Monica, Calif.: Cuadra Associates, 1978).

[2]As of 1981, about 170 data bases were available from the major vendors: Lockheed, Systems Development Corporation, Bibliographic Retrieval Services, National Library of Medicine, and The Times Information Bank. To these should be added European data bases, but they are not considered in this text. Lockheed, the largest of the vendors, has some 115 data bases and claims a clientele of 7000-plus users worldwide in 1981.

so-called "basic" data bases, those most often used in libraries. There is no more consensus on the "basics" here than in printed sources, but in terms of what is used most, the beginner may at least get a notion of relative popularity.

In the average public, academic, or school library the more frequently searched data bases are (pretty much in this order) (1) ERIC (Educational Resources Information Center), (2) *Psychological Abstracts,* (3) SOCIAL SCISEARCH and/or SCISEARCH (*Social Science Citation Index* and *Science Citation Index* online), (4) MEDLARS/MEDLINE (Medical Literature Analysis and Retrieval System Online), (5) NTIS (National Technical Information Service).

Others which are usually in the top 10 or 12 include: BIOSIS (Biosciences Information Service), (2) ABI/INFORM (Abstracted Business Information), (3) *Sociological Abstracts,* (4) *Chemical Abstracts,* i.e., versions thereof, (5) INSPEC (a version of *Science Abstracts*), (6) *New York Times Information Bank,* (7) *CIS Index,* (8) *American Statistics Index,* (9) AGRICOLA (Agricultural On-Line Access)[3]

Variations on the "basics" occur, to be sure, when one turns from the general to the specialized situation. For example, a survey of 345 Canadian and American libraries where MEDLINE was a first choice revealed that the next most used data bases include, in this order: CA Condensates, BIOSIS Previews, NTIS, *Psychological Abstracts,* ERIC and AGRICOLA.[4]

Frequency of use depends primarily upon subject matter but other important considerations are the availability of the data base and the familiarity of the librarian (or the user) with the base. Cost of the search must be also considered.

Familiarity and consequent ease-of-use and comfort with searching a particular base or group of data bases may be the most important factor, after subject matter, in determining the frequency of use. It is no secret that because of the current complexity of data

---

[3]John Evans, "Database Selection in an Academic Library," *Online,* April 1980, pp. 35–43. Here, at the University of South Dakota, a study showed that 11 data bases accounted for 76 percent of the searches and 29 gave almost 95 percent retrieval. New bases, of course, will change the order. See, too, Gary D. Byrd et al., "Minet at K.C.," *Library Journal,* October 1, 1979, p. 2045; Roger K. Summit, *Special Libraries,* July 1978, pp. 255–260; Amy Raedeke, "A One Month Test Period," *Online,* October 1978, pp. 56–59; Jo Robinson, "Education and Training for Computer Based Reference Services . . . " *Journal of the American Society for Information Science,* March 1980, pp. 97–104.

[4]Gloria Werner, "Use of On-Line Bibliographic Retrieval Services in Health Sciences . . . " *Bulletin of the Medical Library Association,* January 1979, p. 6.

bases, the average search analyst may be familiar with no more than a dozen different bases.[5]

Due to the inexperience of the searcher, the cost of the service, or the user's naiveté about what is available, the limited search is usually enough. As Kent points out it is "enough" because in most cases the search is relatively a simple one.

> The user's perception of the effectiveness of an online system is directly proportional to the naiveté of the system . . . .The greatest expression of user satisfaction is observed when a result is achieved by a simple search strategy with a small number of search terms and this quite independently of the quality of the result. Conversely when a user is required, either by the nature of the query, the data base or the system, to use elaborate search strategies and/or large numbers of search terms there is relative dissatisfaction.[6]

A strong argument may be made for *not* using more than a few data bases. Given a sharp perception of subject matter and user need, it is not necessary to consult more than a select number of reference works. This is equally true of online searches. Careful choices and a sophisticated search are likely to turn up more information than is needed in one or two data bases, certainly no more than a half dozen.

WHICH?

Which data base(s) is best for a given search?

It is encouraging to know there are several sources which list and explain the data bases available. Most such sources are in printed form, but all major vendors offer an online approach. Under various names, they perform much the same service.

The *Systems Development Corporation Database Index*[7] is a rapid

---

[5]This is particularly true in public situations, e.g., the Kansas City Libraries service (MINET) includes one academic, four public, and three medical libraries, and here it was found that "three-fourths of the search sessions needed only one database." Byrd, op. cit., p. 2047. Even in a relatively large library where searches comprise an important part of reference service, no more than 19 data bases were employed for 1830 searches between June 1978 and May 1979. (Statistics from the State University of New York at Albany library.)

[6]A. K. Kent, "Dial Up and Die-Can . . . " *The Information Scientist,* March 1978, p. 5.

[7]For a discussion of this, see Arthur Antony, "The Database Index," *Database,* December 1979, pp. 28–33; and *Reference Use of the Online Database Service* (Minneapolis, Minn.: Bibliographic Retrieval Services, Inc., October 18, 1979), processed, p. 5. The effort to use multifile bibliographic data bases is a major concern. See W. A. Martin, "Toward an Integral Multi-File On-Line Bibliographic Database," *Journal of Information Science,* November 1980, pp. 241–253.

method of isolating specific subjects. The file is a master index to all data bases and contains major words and/or subject terms. A first operation is to limit the search to one of four categories: science and technology, social sciences and humanities, business and economics, or multidisciplinary. A searcher enters a term. A listing of available bases is then printed out, a listing which ranks how often the term occurs in each base, e.g., "Skylab" appears in NTIS 581 times and in ERIC 29 times, with a dozen other data bases listed between the two extremes. Boolean combinations and truncation may be employed to widen or narrow the search. Cost for this type of search is $45 an hour and is economic only when working with fairly esoteric subjects. In evaluating the service, Antony points out:

> The DBI is a welcome addition to the collection of user aids for the reference librarian and online searcher. Its limitations are related to the problems of term ambiguity, and the fact that there are many abstracts, indexes, and data bases that are excluded because they are not searchable through the ORBIT system. Failure to take these limitations into account could result in costly and time-consuming searches of irrelevant or peripheral resources, or could result in missing highly relevant resources. If, on the other hand, a DBI search is used as one aid, possibly among several, in the choice of resources, it can often make a positive contribution to information retrieval performance.[8]

A similar approach is offered by **BRS/CROSS**. Here one enters the keyword(s) and then requests that the printout show all the data bases with the word(s), or perhaps only those data bases in the life science, physical sciences, or social sciences area. In addition to proving posting for a single term, the searcher may enter statements containing Boolean or positional operators.

Another system is offered by Lockheed in its **DIALINDEX**. This allows the librarian to run a search statement against data bases in any of some 25 broad subject categories. The DIALINDEX will show the exact number of citations available for that subject in each of the data bases at a cost of $35 per hour (1980).

WHAT?

After a decision is made as to which data base to search, the question becomes: What does the searcher have to know about the individual base? Essentially the searcher must have the same knowledge of the base as he or she has of a printed version, although there are more

---

[8]Antony, op. cit., p. 32.

details to remember in using the base. One, after all, can look at the printed *Psychological Abstracts* and, through trial and error, discover the pattern of presentation. Online that is not possible, so the online searcher must first know:

(1) The subjects and subtopics covered, and what related fields are likely to be a concern to the service.

(2) The type of documents included or excluded—from periodicals and reports to books and proceedings—and, to be sure, the years covered. One must know, too, what is indexed or not indexed completely.

(3) The availability of a thesaurus for a controlled vocabulary and how frequently the thesaurus or work list is updated.

(4) The types of concepts to search where there is no thesaurus and where the vocabulary is uncontrolled, and the success or failure rate of searching titles, abstracts, authors, etc.

(5) The relation of the controlled and uncontrolled vocabulary where the data base allows for both.

(6) The codes which may be used to search in addition to words and the clarity of the classification or coding search system.

The evaluation of a data base will be considered in detail here. In the next section, we will consider what one must know about a given service.

EVALUATION

Evaluative questions

The evaluation of data bases is based on standards similar to those employed for evaluating printed works. For example, one applies the same test for *Psychological Abstracts* online as in printed form. Everything—purpose, authority, and scope (as considered, often with individual titles, in the first volume of this text)—is to be tested.

However, there are additional considerations in evaluating the online version. There are some particular questions which must be asked about the computerized data base.[9] (Cost, a major factor, is considered in another section.)

(1) How complete is the coverage in the computerized data base?

[9]Basic questions searchers ask about data-base use are of an evaluative nature and may be summarized in three major areas: the level of indexing, the cost, and the availability of a thesaurus for the file. Outside of the data base itself, but a question of equal importance to the searcher: Is the material indexed or abstracted available in the library? "Bibliographic Data Base Use," *Sci-Tech News,* October 1978, p. 92.

Does it include all the major core journals, reports, documents, etc., which are indexed or abstracted in the printed version?

(2) Does the distributor/publisher clearly specify which journals are indexed in depth and which are indexed selectively? This practice is rarely followed by publishers of printed indexes and is unlikely to be taken up by data-base publishers unless users insist.

(3) Are the journals indexed listed with their abbreviations and preferably with addresses of the publishers? Is the ISSN included? If the result of a search is ever to be used to search a library's holdings records, the ISSN (or ISBN) will be the link, since these are also included in MARC records.

(4) How much does one data base overlap another in its coverage? For example, in one study it was found that in one service 29 percent of the articles cited were duplicated in another data base.

(5) How up to date is the data base? Keeping the material as current as possible is one of the most important factors, particularly since a distinct advantage of a data base over a printed version should be its currency. The data base will usually have material available for scanning weeks or even months before the printed version. Nevertheless, there should be specific information on when and how often the file is updated—as well as how much material is added.

(6) What are the retrospective capacities of the data base? One weakness of many data bases is that they do not go back in time. Most machine-readable files began in the mid-1960s or early 1970s, and the majority cover only the time span from the period of their starting date. Because of the cost involved, there is no reason to believe publishers will extend the files back. In fact, some online systems even drop older files. (The rationale is that the data bank is being used by individuals who need only current, not retrospective, materials.)

(7) Does the data base provide only citations, or does it include abstracts? Usually the data base duplicates what is offered in the hard-copy version. However, for reasons of economy most data bases allow the user to reject (or accept) the abstract printout. "Rejection" may mean only that the user decides to have the abstracts and/or the complete list of citations printed offline and sent at a later data.

(8) Where a data base indexes more than journals, is there a clear indication of the source of the nonjournal materials, preferably in the citation? Lack of full bibliographic details for such materials makes them virtually worthless. Also, policies regarding indexing of nonjournal materials should be clearly stated.

(9) What methods are used for indexing or other types of subject

analysis? The system (and/or data base) should allow the user to (a) enter a command at any time, (b) retrieve data by date, language, geographical location, or other qualifiers, (c) have unrestricted use of Boolean operators and a number of search terms, (d) link search statements and words, (e) query the base in language as natural as possible, and (f) have the use of an online thesaurus, dictionary, etc.

(10) Is there a specialized thesaurus for the data base? The thesaurus usually is required to indicate broader and narrower terms related to the primary subject term. Even with a natural language system, the thesaurus of other data bases can be useful for suggesting related terms.

(11) How effective are the access points which are provided? This is part of the previous question in that here one would like to know the best access terms (subject, titles, abstracts, keywords, codes, etc.) for a particular service. Also, one may compare similar services, although at this point the quality and type of indexing vary so much from service to service that a valid comparison is difficult.

(12) Does the publisher/vendor supply guides and manuals to assist the user with the data base(s)? Are these frequently updated? There is a related question: Does the publisher/vendor provide training courses and refresher courses—and at what intervals and at what cost? Does the publisher provide a "hot line" so searchers can call for assistance with difficult searches? Does the publisher send out a newsletter or other periodic update to inform users of changes? Does the publisher provide the means for users to suggest changes or to make complaints about features of the data bases?

Beyond these evaluative queries are ones regarding the technical aspects of the access and retrieval process from the type of terminal to the printout format. Such questions are too technical for a beginning text, but the reader should be at least aware of their importance.

The points enumerated here are to evaluate, only in a general way, the machine-readable data bases. A more meaningful evaluation would also include such criteria as the user's acceptance or rejection, the efficiency of the system within the context of the total reference situation, comparative costs, etc.[10]

---

[10]Beyond this the librarian would apply evaluative methods similar to those used with printed sources. For example, an obvious point is the quality and accuracy of the material in the reference work, i.e., data base. Searchers cannot always depend on file quality. See Nancy Norton, "Dirty Data: A Call for Quality Control," *Online*, January 1981, pp. 40–41.

Standardization

The primary difficulty in evaluating computer-linked reference sources is the lack of standardization. Everyone seems to use different procedures and systems without much regard for even minimal standardization. An analogy is the now-settled war between recording companies, who at one time were putting out recordings of various speeds and types of equipment just as diverse as now seen in the computer industry. Data-base producers are guilty of the same failure to consider the ultimate user.

Even the well-trained librarian is confused by the lack of standardization—a lack which makes it essential to learn a new set of rules for each data base (i.e., reference book) consulted. In the publishing world the situation would be considered intolerable, and now that the glow has worn off the initial delights of automated reference work, librarians are beginning to demand standardization among the various data-base publishers.

In one survey, for example, librarians were asked, "What are your worst problem areas in using online systems?" The most frequent complaints included remembering multiple retrieval languages, learning new data bases, learning the unique features of each data base—complaints all pertaining to nonstandardization among data bases.[11]

The librarian may become quite efficient with one base but be lost with another. The wide, some would say wild, variations between software commands from one vendor or system to the next forces the librarian to learn not just one system, but sometimes several.[12] For example, in comparing MEDLARS as it is searched via the National Library of Medicine and through BRS one study revealed:

> The same citations are present in the data base on both systems, but the individual elements of the citation differ in each. . . . There are many elements unique to the NLM system. . . . The major software and data-base differences . . . are mechanical, not capability.[13]

[11]"Online User Preference Survey Results," *Online,* January 1977, p. 76.

[12]Lucinda D. Conger, "Multiple System Searching . . . " *Online,* April 1980, pp. 10–21. A 20-page chart showing retrieval functions and commands of the three vendors and four other services is available from *Online.* It appeared in the October 1980 issue; see p. 67 of that number for details.

[13]Suzetta Burrows and Sylvia Kyle, "Searching the MEDLARS File on NLM and BRS: A Comparative Study," *Bulletin of the Medical Library Association,* January 1979, pp. 1–14. The authors give 5½ pages of differences—differences which are somewhat the same in number when the librarian switches from one vendor to another.

The lack of compatible software is now of national concern. But with time the vendors are tending more and more to standardization. Competition demands that each incorporate the good new features of the other. Lockheed, which originally required each term to be "selected" before combination with other terms, as was possible with BRS and SDC, now allows that convenience in its new "superselect."

Within the next decade there is likely to be more and more standardization, even simplification of searching techniques. Ideally one program may be used with all data bases, all vendors. And the ideal may eventually happen.

Late in 1980, for example, the United States Defense Department announced it had standardized the more than 1000 languages used by its various departments and sections. Now it is possible to learn a single language called ADA, which closely approximates human language, to operate all the various data bases, from payroll processing to information retrieval. The ultimate step will be the use of natural language which will allow the user to type in commands without thought of specialized, computer terms. While there are numerous experiments in this field, the success rate has been low.

Another situation which can mean trouble for the librarian is traced to the inventor of an information system who is so enamored of technology that he forgets its ultimate purpose. Many of these designers "have come to visualize some hypothetical user in a hypothetical environment." The machine is as complicated as the environment and the result makes one wonder if systems designers "have not forgotten that in any man machine system it is the machine that must be attuned to the human . . . and not the other way around."[14]

GUIDES TO DATA BASES

The best available guides to data bases currently include:

> Williams, Martha (ed.), *Computer-Readable Data Bases: A Directory and Data Sourcebook,* 1979. White Plains, N.Y.: Knowledge Industry Publications, 1979. $95.
>
> *Information Industry Market Place.* New York: R.R. Bowker Company, 1979 to date. Biennial. $32.50.
>
> *Directory of Online Databases.* Santa Monica, Calif.: Cuadra Associates, 1979 to date. Quarterly. $60.

[14]Emmanuil L. Shapiro, "The Functions of Information Work in the Scientific Communications System," *International Forum on Information and Documentation,* no. 2, 1979, p. 3.

Hall, J. L. (ed.), *Online Bibliographic Data Bases.* London: Aslib Publications, 1978 to date. Irregular. (2nd ed. 1981 $70). Distributed in U.S. by Gale Research Company.

The *Guide to Reference Books*[15] for data bases is yet to be compiled, although there are by now several good ongoing bibliographies which, at a minimum, indicate the availability of data bases in a given subject area. When, for example, the user wants to know what can be found in the way of data bases for sociology or for statistics, the Martha Williams guide and the Cuadra Associates directory are of great help. Lockheed's monthly *Chronolog* reports on additions and changes to bases available from that vendor, and other vendors publish guides and provide updating services. From a practical point of view the user is likely to turn to what is available in the library, that is, what data bases are online at a given terminal at a given moment. This, of course, varies from library to library.

Most guides list more than the 150 to 165 bibliographic data bases familiar to librarians. The guides include highly specialized bases as well as numerical bases which are not likely to be used by librarians or their patrons. Exception: special libraries. Turning first to the basic bibliographies and guides, the best retrospective source is *Computer-Readable Data Bases.* Supported by the American Society for Information Science, and edited by the capable Martha Williams, the directory includes some 500 bases.[16] The editor has given extensive detailed information about each one, descriptions based upon the Database of Databases maintained at the University of Illinois.

Specifically, each listing includes the name and producer, subject(s) covered, year of origin, number of items in the base, and availability. Subject, producer, process and data-base indexes make this an invaluable aid for quick reference.

The directory is to be totally revised about every two years, but is updated by a loose-leaf service, *Computer-Readable Bibliographic Data Bases,* published by the same organization. New pages are sent out about every six months, and of the 500 or so bases in the larger work, about 300 are kept current through this system.

---

[15]Actually the 1980 supplement to *Guide to Reference Books* does include a brief section on data bases (selected and annotated by expert Martha Williams). The best comparative guide to directories is Linda C. Smith's "Data Base Directories: A Comparative Review," *Reference Services Review,* October/December 1980, pp. 15–21.

[16]Of this number Williams lists 149 in her "Data Bases On-Line in 1979," *Bulletin of the American Society for Information Science,* December 1979, pp. 22–31. This is updated annually and is one of the best sources for a listing of "basic" data bases.

For ongoing listings, the best of the directories is the Cuadra Associates' *Directory of Online Databases*. Both bibliographic and non-bibliographic data bases are listed in one handy volume. About 770 are briefly described as to content, coverage dates, and frequency of update. (Individual cost is not given, because the publishers think the matter too complex. See introductory statement in each issue.) It is especially useful because it is issued quarterly with a complete revision every six months. (The subscription includes two editions, plus two supplements per year, i.e., it is completely updated every six months.) The directory's various indexes, including one of data bases by subject, by publisher, and by vendor are particularly useful.

For an overview of bibliographic data bases available throughout the world, with particular focus on Europe, the standard directory is the one edited by J. L. Hall. This includes 189 individual entries with a description of each base. There is a listing, too, of related data bases and an index by name and subject. Several are included here which are not found in the other directories. *The International Directory of Software* (Bournemouth: CUYB Publications, 1980 to date, biennial) includes both English and American products—over 3000 listings. The same publisher issues *The Computer Users' Yearbook* (1980 to date), a grab bag of useful data.

The three main vendors have their own guides, issued in the form of loose-leaf notebooks which allow the users to add or delete pages as the guides are updated. Arranged by file number, each of the data-base summaries includes similar information. The outline for each description includes: (a) data-base summary sheet with sample record; (b) subject searching options; (c) code searching instructions; (d) limiting capabilities, if any; (e) output formats; (f) sortability options, if any; (g) search aids available; and (h) document retrieval, if available.

Guide to Dialog Databases (Palo Alto, Calif.: Lockheed, 1978 to date, 3 vols.) is the most exhaustive of the vendors' offerings. While the *Guide* is more for the beginner than the expert, it is "replete with reminders, short cuts, caveats—details that no searcher can keep in mind at all times."[17]

The *BRS Reference Manual and Database Search Guide* (Latham, N.Y.: BRS, 1979 to date) gives basic instructions on how to use BRS, from logging-in to general searching techniques available only on BRS and different from those used in the Lockheed or SDS systems. Each data base is listed and described. A set descriptive pattern, from

[17]Celine H. Alvey, "Guide to Dialog Databases—a Review," *Online,* July 1978, p. 22.

the various citation elements to online search techniques, is used for every base. Systems Development Corporation offers its version of a user guide in its *Quick Reference Guide.*

Each vendor also has a newsletter in which information on individual data bases is included. BRS publishes the *BRS Bulletin,* as well as a "brief paper series" which considers, in five to ten pages, some developments of interest to librarians. Lockheed publishes *Chronolog.*

Given a general look at the data bases, the librarian's next need is for an exhaustive guide which tells how to use the *individual* data base.[18] Almost every publisher and/or vendor has one or more guides for each data base. But how does one find these?

The answer, at least for about 100 basic bases, will be found in the *Online Reference Aids: A Directory of Manuals, Guides and Thesauri* (San Jose, Calif.: California Library Authority for Systems and Services, 1979, 56 pp.)[19] Each entry in the loose-leaf directory includes names and addresses of the vendors and producers, bibliographic data, and the availability of subject and vendor indexes to the data bases. The vendors publish their own such guides; e.g., Lockheed has *Search Aids for Use with Dialog Databases,* which is often updated. Then, too, the various vendors' newsletters carry notes on new aids; e.g., *BRS Bulletin* has a regular feature, "Tools of the Trade."

Libraries lacking the specific guides may find some help in more general works likely to be in the reference collection. For example, brief, directory-type information on a variety of topics is included in the *Information Industry Market Place,* which lists data bases, vendors, information brokers, suppliers of hardware, and reference works in the field. There is an adequate index of subjects and services and because of its frequent updating, it is a good place to turn for current names and addresses.

For more listings on equipment one may turn to the frequently updated *Online Terminal Guide & Directory* (Weston, Conn.: Online,

[18]The primary purpose of articles in *Database, Online,* and *On-Line Review* is to describe the various search procedures with new and old data bases.

[19]A fine example of only one of these reference aids, and one of the best of its kind is Sara D. Knapp, *BRS Training Workbook,* BRS, 2d ed., 1981. As *Database,* March 1980, p. 75 notes of the first edition, "This is among the first self-paced workbooks in the online field. It is based upon the computer searching course that Ms. Knapp taught at the State University of New York at Albany. The workbook includes sections on terminal mechanics and diagnosing error messages—lessons which are particularly difficult for beginning searchers. The workbook also explains the ERIC thesaurus and the differences between controlled vocabulary and free-text searching. Although it is useful for a course in information retrieval, the book can also be used independently to learn or review the BRS system. Answers to the exercises are included."

1976 to date). Some 3000 manufacturers and dealers are included as well as a section on how to select terminals. The standard *Directory of Special Libraries and Information Centers* and *The Encyclopedia of Information Systems and Services* are useful here in that they list organizations, libraries, and publishers, many of whom produce, administer, or otherwise engage in some data-base activity.

Until 1977 there were no journals exclusively devoted to online retrieval. Today there are over a dozen, not to mention such periodicals as *Special Libraries* and *RQ* which regularly include articles on computer-assisted reference service.[20] *RQ*, also, has a regular column, "Online," devoted to developments of particular interest to reference librarians.

The three basic periodicals in the field are *Online*, which includes general material; *Database*, by the same publisher, which concentrates on specific data bases; and *On-line Review*, an English-based periodical which is more scholarly than the American counterparts, yet covers a good deal of related territory. All are good sources of current material on various data-base reference guides and bibliographies and often run both critical and noncritical reviews of such materials.

Interface Age is a periodical written for a broad audience, i.e., not confined to librarians; it has relatively basic material on developments in hardware.

Other journals of this type found in many libraries include: *Byte, Datamation,* and *Recreational Computing.*

Journals of a more specialized nature would include: *Journal of Documentation, Information Processing and Management; Journal of Library Automation, Journal of the American Society for Information Science;* and the *Journal of Information Science;* as well as the offset *The Journal of Fee Based Information Services.* While involved with broader implications of data bases and automation, *Information World,* a monthly tabloid, and *The Information Manager,* a bimonthly magazine, are both useful for learning of the information-industry viewpoint.

There are scores of newsletters published. Representative examples include: *Information and Data Base Publishing Report* (White Plains, N.Y.: Knowledge Publications Industry), a bimonthly which focuses on the information industry with special attention to new technology; and *The Information Intelligence Online Newsletter* (Phoenix, Ariz.:

[20]Complete bibliographic information will be found in the author's *Magazines for Libraries*, 3rd ed. (New York: R.R. Bowker Company, 1978). For an earlier study see Donald T. Hawkins, "Bibliometrics of the Online Information Retrieval Literature," *Online Review*, December 1978, pp. 345–352.

Information Intelligence), a monthly which is about equally divided between news of software and hardware.

The technical abstracting service is *Computers and Control Abstracts* (London: Institution of Electrical Engineers, 1966 to date, annual), which includes over 25,000 abstracts for journal literature, books, symposia, and technical reports. It is also the source of a considerable amount of information on information science and documentation. *Computer Abstracts* (St. Helier, Jersey, British Channel Islands, 1957 to date, monthly) covers the whole field of computer literature as well as technical reports and related items. It contains a special section on "information retrieval" in each issue, and the usual author, subject, and patent indexes. The third basic service, *Computing Reviews* (New York: Association for Computing Machinery, 1960 to date, monthly) has the advantage of being published in America and offers a broader sweep of nontechnical as well as technical materials. Less technical material will be found through the standard Wilson indexes, from *Library Literature* to the *General Science Index* to the *Applied Science and Technology Index.*

The two library abstracting services, *Information Science Abstracts* and *Library and Information Science Abstracts,* are standards in the field. The Machine-Assisted Reference Section (MARS) of the American Library Association Reference and Adult Services Division is the professional organization which probably best serves the general reference librarian, and its new RASD newsletter, *Update,* carries a regular news column.[21]

An organization less formal than MARS, The National Online Circuit, is an affiliation of online user groups that exchange ideas about "searching techniques and strategies." It embraces about 100 or so user groups, and the number increases each year.[22] News about the Circuit is carried in *Online* and in a column by Majorie M. K. Hlava in the *Information Manager.* That magazine also issues the Directory of Online User Groups from time to time.

GENERAL DATA BASES

In the early years of machine-readable indexes and abstracts most of the focus was on scientific and related technological areas. The reason

---

[21]*RASD Update,* 1980 to date, bimonthly. This also includes current information on RASD activities.

[22]For a history of the organization see Ms. Hlava's column, *The Information Manager,* September/October 1979, p. 26.

for such emphasis was funding. Money was relatively easy to obtain either from government agencies or from private organizations. And the specificity of the systems did not require too much consideration about ambiguous terminology.

Lower costs, more sophisticated programs, and a search for larger potential audiences have conspired to change the balance. There has been particularly rapid development in the nonscience and nontechnology bibliographic data bases. Development has been most noticable in such areas as government, legislation, health, economics and business, and the social sciences.

Several general data bases have also been developed, sources where the average user, not the specialist, may turn for information on almost every subject. The number is likely to increase, particularly when the H. W. Wilson Company puts the *Readers' Guide,* as well as its other broad subject indexes, online. The most promising aspect of these general data bases is that, as long last, they offer the large public library a wide base of information for the average user. The American Library Association in the early 1980s was making a concerted effort to establish, organize, and channel such bases for general public use.

Taken as a group, the general public constitute a major new audience for data bases, an audience matched in size only by teachers and students. But greater growth will come only when, and if, the cost for searches decreases.

The fastest growing group of nonscientific users is in the business sector, a sector that includes both businesspeople and laypeople involved in some aspect of economics and business. The reason for the potential is obvious: business has the greatest need for immediate information and the means to pay for it. The Chicago Public Library, for example, has an information program designed for business-related queries, but users are not, by any means, all in offices. Who are the users? People with personal, business, and school/university demands, Wilkens says. Her April-December (1979) statistics break down user needs this way: 311 personal, 306 business, 191 student/faculty, and 14 government agency. The subjects these users searched: 518 business, 328 social sciences, 224 sci/tech, 122 biography, 62 library science, 9 literature/philosophy, and 7 fine arts.[23]

The rapid development of general or business-oriented data bases has primarily been accomplished by such publishers as The New York Times and other news organizations which have a heavy

[23]*American Libraries,* March 1980, p. 159.

print investment in information and are seeking new methods of employing that information for profit. The plummeting costs of computer power and computerized storage and developments in telecommunication have made it impossible to consider turning daily as well as retrospective information into a commodity of value. A newspaper publisher who must maintain files for daily use now seeks to offset this overhead by enlarging the market—the more uses and users, the better.

News and current events[24]

> *The (New York Times) Information Bank.* New York: New York Times Company, 1969 to date. Various update schedule. $80–$110 an hour.
>
> *Newsearch.* Los Altos, Calif.: Information Access Corporation, 1979 to date. Daily update. $95 an hour.
> > a   *Magazine Index,* 1976 to date. Monthly. $45 an hour.
> > b   *National Newspaper Index,* 1979 to date. Monthly. $75 an hour.
>
> *Newspaper Index.* Wooster, Ohio: Bell and Howell, 1976 to date. Monthly. $80 an hour.
>
> *Dow-Jones News/Retrieval.* New York: Dow-Jones & Company, 1978 to date (90 day file). Daily. $40 to $80 an hour.
>
> NEXIS. New York: Mead Data Central, 1978 to date (magazines retrospective to 1975). Daily. $50 to $75 an hour.

Newspaper services are particularly useful, in varying degrees, for the user who up to this point has had to rely upon the printed *Readers' Guide to Periodical Literature, The New York Times Index,* and the *Newspaper Index,* among other current services, for summaries and popular and semipopular articles on general subjects. The data bases covered here now do the same thing, although much more rapidly and with considerably less energy expended. Current affairs, legislation, national and international political and economic trends, scientific and social breakthroughs, data on business and companies, book

[24]Brian Aveney, "Competition in News Databases," *Online,* April 1979, pp. 36–38. *Note: Here, and throughout the remainder of this chapter, the prices given for online hourly rates are those based on the Lockheed schedule of 1981 and may be lower/higher for other vendors and systems, and are, of course, subject to change. The basic hourly rate at least gives the beginner some notion of relative expense.*

and play reviews, and hobbies—all are covered in these services. One publisher rightfully claims that the data base *(Newsearch)* is so broad that "valuable information may be found on almost any topic which is being researched." Much the same is true of the other data bases, and, combined, they are an answer for the librarian or layperson seeking information on any of thousands of subjects. *The New York Times Information Bank* offers not only material found in the printed index, but includes indexing and some briefer abstracting of 80 other newspapers and magazines, among them: *The Wall Street Journal, The Times* (of London), *Harper's,* and *Scientific American.*[25]

Eventually, the full text of newspapers should be available online. Experiments have been and will continue to be made in this direction. For example, beginning in 1980 *The Columbus (Ohio) Dispatch* became the first "electronic newspaper" when it made its whole editorial content available to OCLC subscribers.

A tremendous advantage *The New York Times Information Bank* holds over competitors is the availability of abstracts and/or the first line of the abstract. These abstracts include: (a) those used in the printed version of *The New York Times Index* and (b) abstracts added for material from the other newspapers and journals.

> *Searching patterns are such that the index may be used online for ready reference work. For example, using Boolean and positional operators one may quickly find the earnings of American Motors for the 3rd fiscal quarter. The printout would be: "American Motors 3d fiscal quarter earnings were $15.1 million, up 147.5% from '78."*[26]

Other features of the *Information Bank* include:

(1) Currency. The main items in the late city edition of the paper are indexed and put online within 24 hours after publication. The remainder of the paper is indexed at a more leisurely pace and is online about one week after publication. The time span is the same for other material indexed, i.e., about one week after date of publication an item is indexed and online. Some titles, however, are indexed a month after publication.

[25]Donna Dolan, "Subject Searching of the New York Times Information Bank," *Online,* April 1978, pp. 26–30. For a more cursory appraisal see "The Information Bank Picture Story," *Online,* July 1980, pp. 49–50.

[26]*BRS Bulletin,* February 1980, p. 3.

(2) Availability. Initially the service was available only through the publisher, but can now be obtained via BRS.[27]

(3) Indexing. Coverage of titles, other than the *Times,* is selective in that not all of the other newspapers or periodicals are indexed. The staff determines what may be repetitive and eliminates it from consideration. The result is that one can never be sure whether a whole issue of a magazine or an index is available online.

Until the late 1970s there was no free-text word-by-word search possible, and one had to use only a controlled vocabulary (e.g., *The Information Bank Thesaurus and User Guide* which suggests over 700,000 subject, organization, geographic, and personal name descriptors).[28] This has been modified; the BRS system now allows for a combination of free-text and thesaurus term searching. The searcher may now search the abstracts and employ Boolean logic.

(4) Cost. As in all of these services, the online charges are relatively high, i.e., about $80–$110 per connect-hour. This compares with a figure of over $400 for the printed version of just *The New York Times Index.* Nevertheless, the service has captured the imagination of users and by early 1980 claimed 1300 direct customers. This figure is hardly a measure of the daily use, but it is a measure of growth—in 1973 there were 10 customers.

(5) Documents—that is, material from *The New York Times* itself—became available online in late 1981.[29] Retrospective searches may be made back to June 1, 1980. Also, the *Times* is available on microform, although other indexed materials are not furnished by the newspaper.

In an effort to find broader audiences for their services many of the publishers are experimenting with simplified subsystems which are programmed for the average user, not the experienced searcher. For example, AMI (Advertising and Marketing Intelligence) Service is a spin-off of the *New York Times Information Bank.* The search pattern is simple. The user enters keywords found in conversational English. If

[27]Taking a complicated commercial stance, the publisher makes the index available through BRS only to certain users.

[28]Lack of free-text searches proved a major drawback in that very current topics, where the thesaurus did not furnish subject headings, were difficult to search. New terms are added to the subject-heading authority file only twice a year. Descriptors assigned to an article are not available online.

[29]The publisher is working on full text storage and delivery of other materials indexed, but no date is given for this service.

no dates are given, the system calls up citations for the past 31 days. In addition to the citation, there is an abstract, or brief summary, of the information. Additional search terms are listed to help the user to search further, if so desired.

AMI is also searchable using the same program employed for the *Information Bank* at a cost of $4850 a year for 33 hours of use or $8700 for a two-year contract. This service is available only from the publisher, as is the *AP Political Databank,* another spin-off. A topical gimmick, *Databank* consists of information on political campaigns; e.g., the 1980 version of this service traced the presidential battle at both the state and national levels.

Another, perhaps obvious, spin-off of the service is the compilation of bibliographies; here the publisher has been quick to advertise scores of such titles in print form. The user simply enters a command or two at the terminal and the necessary material is printed out. This, in turn, is mass-produced and issued as a separate printed publication. Nothing is to prevent the user from getting the same thing, often at much less cost, at the terminal, but that's another matter.

Examples of such bibliographies include *Key Issues* (New York: Arno/Bowker, 1979, 257 pp., $21.95). This is little more than a brief summary (three to five pages) of ten issues. The number of abstracts is so limited that it is more efficient to use the printed version of *The New York Times Index, Facts on File,* or the *Readers' Guide to Periodical Literature.* Another example is *Health Care in America* (New York: Arno, 1979) which consists of seven reports, priced from $25 to $35 each; again, these are little more than printouts of the online abstracts. Sometimes The New York Times does add reprints of stories from the newspaper, but it seems this is done as much to fill out the work as for any other reason.

Newsearch is an online data base which offers citations to current news events. Competing directly with *The New York Times Information Bank, Newsearch* is available only through a vendor (Lockheed) and is made up to two distinct indexes *(National Newspaper Index* and *Magazine Index),* which are available both online and in another form discussed in the first volume of this text (p. 150). Beginning in 1981 it also includes articles from *Management Contents* as well as some from the *Legal Resource Index.* Essentially *Newsearch* offers the same approach as the *Times,* but differs in three important respects: (1) There are short descriptors in *Newsearch,* but it lacks abstracts of the *Times.* (2) *Newsearch* includes the *Christian Science Monitor,* but not the *Washington Post* (or English newspapers) found in the rival service;

both index *The New York Times*[30] and the *Wall Street Journal*. (3) *Newsearch,* because it includes *Magazine Index,* has close to 300 more magazine sources online than the competitor. (4) *Newsearch,* via the *National Newspaper Index,* indexes all newspapers cover to cover, not on a selective basis as the *Times* does. (5) Some claim *Newsearch* is easier to use than the *Times,* but this was prior to the addition of the free-text search to the *Times* by BRS; today the searching patterns, while they differ, seem of equal ease or complexity.

Perhaps the biggest drawback, at least to some libraries, is the *Newsearch* emphasis on currency. In order to keep the file a manageable size it is "flushed" each month so that the file includes only citations entered daily from the first day to the last day of each month, or 30 to 31 days. Tapped in midweek of the first week of the file, the number of citations will be less than if tapped the last day of the month.

The publisher compensates for this by transferring the citations, with some variation, to the *National Newspaper Index* (an online file from January 1, 1979) which provides an index to the three newspapers from 1979 to the present. The same process is used for the magazine citations which become part of the *Magazine Index* (online file from January 1, 1976). The trouble is that both of these are separate files, require separate searches, and run up separate charges of $45 an hour for the magazine file and $75 an hour for the newspaper file. The online $90 an hour *Newsearch* fee is about the same for other services, but it has numerous complications. If one subscribes to the service (at from $1860 a year for 25 hours to $7130 for 100 hours), the charge per hour is less.[31]

Newspaper Index[32] follows much the same pattern as its two rivals but differs in that: (1) It includes indexing to *The Washington Post* and to eight regional newspapers: *Chicago Sun Times, Chicago Tribune, Denver Post, Detroit News, Houston Post, Los Angeles Times, New Orleans Times Picayune,* and the *San Francisco Chronicle.* (2) There are descriptors, but no abstracts. (3) The index is retrospective to 1976 for some newspapers, but not all. Eventually all indexing will go back to 1972.

---

[30]Is it legal for a competitor to index *The New York Times?* Apparently this is not being tested and probably because the *Newsearch* uses only titles of articles, index terms, and short descriptive phrases, and makes no effort to employ the full abstracts found in the *Times* service.

[31]The offline prints vary from an additional $1250 for the 25 hours to $5000 for the 100 hours.

[32]The printed form is discussed in the first volume of this text, p. 150.

(4) The data base is updated only once a month, and no effort is made to make it as current as its two competitors. Available from SDC, the cost of $80 a connect-hour is no less than the other services and the search patterns are much the same, too. It is primarily employed in libraries for retrospective searches and is especially useful in searching the social sciences and history.

There appears to be no end of commercial interest in news, and another version, especially tailored for reception on home television via a Viewdata system (see p. 117) is the United Press International's *NewsShare*. This costs from $2.75 to $15 per connect-hour and provides national, international, sports, and financial news. However, cable television offers many of these same services on a set broadcasting at less than $10 a month.

The Canadian Newspaper Index (Toronto: Information Access, 1977 to date, monthly, $55 a connect-hour $75 for nonprint subscribers) is a single example of the same pattern in another country. Here seven newspapers are indexed, from the *Montreal Star* to the *Halifax Chronicle Herald*. Again, it has the advantage of being much more current than the printed version.

The British Broadcasting Company, among other European groups, is planning a system similar to *The New York Times Information Bank,* which will be available to Americans just as the English and the Europeans now make use of the Times effort.[33]

Full-text services

Three of the news services data bases differ from the others in one important respect. *Dow-Jones News/Retrieval* and NEXIS[34] include full texts of material. Both are purchased directly from the publisher, not through a vendor. (See p. 164 for *The New York Times* service.)

NEXIS indexes the *Washington Post,* selections from the Associated Press wire service, and material from Reuters wire service. Full texts from several Congressional Quarterly publications are included, such as *Weekly Report.* In addition, the weekly *Economist,* an English news/business magazine, is indexed, as are three other periodicals. The latter are retrospective files to 1975, the newspapers and wire services retrospective to 1977. The service is updated every 24 hours to match the schedule of the daily newspapers. Magazines are indexed one week after they are published.

[33]"Beeb's World of Information?" *The Observer,* London, March 9, 1980, p. 26.
[34]The publisher also issues the full text LEXIS for law. See p. 171.

Commands are given in what the publisher calls "plain English," which is to say the system may be used, at least at its most basic level, by the less-than-experienced searcher. However, where more sophisticated searches are required, an expert is needed.

Costs are somewhat higher than for other services. "The average customer will pay approximately $75 per hour of usage, but that figure may drop down to $50 an hour for heavy users (volume discounts) or go as high as $90 per hour for light users. In addition, a monthly access fee in the neighborhood of $300 will be assessed. . . ."[35]

Citations, as in any online bibliographic system, may be had via NEXIS. One can also call up the full text. However. as with all full-text systems, the average user is given a shortcut. By employing keywords (KWIC), the searcher commands the unit to show only those parts of the story which have the words wanted. For example, one might want material on the Chicago Public Library. The system would search a wire story, come up with a report on the Chicago city budget, but display only that section of the story which deals with the Chicago Public Library. Provision, of course, is made for the user to call for more of the story to appear on the screen. This selective use of the full text is both cost-saving and time-saving in that the system picks out precisely what is needed. It serves, in effect, as a rapid method of scanning material.

What is needed, but not now provided on many units, is a printing device. Once the material is located it is now necessary to take notes; a printing unit would overcome this problem.

The *Dow-Jones*[36] is more limited than NEXIS. In *Dow-Jones* the focus is on financial news, particularly stock quotations. Introduced in 1978, it offers full-text material from *The Wall Street Journal, Barrons's,* and the Dow-Jones News Services. It includes, too, minute-by-minute stock quotations. Data is fed into the data bank as fast as it is processed—of all the services this is the most current. The material, however, is retained for a maximum of 90 days, although beginning in 1981, elements of the service will be available via BRS back to 1979. An effort is made here, as with NEXIS, to get around the necessity of

[35]Thomas H. Hogan, "News Retrieval Services—Growing But Where Are They Headed?" *Online Review*, September 1979, p. 249. In addition a special terminal is required at a rental fee of about $175 a month with an attached printer at $95. Neither is compatible with existing systems.

[36]James H. Bement, "DJNR—What Is It? How to Use It?" *Online*, July 1978, pp. 39–40. See, too: "Dow Jones Expands Electronic Capability," *The New York Times*, May 4, 1981, p. D4.

having a trained searcher. It does not always succeed, and, in fact, where the terminal is used heavily there is usually an expert on hand for the searching. Essentially the search is a push-button system; that is, there are a number of items keyed, and one simply pushes the proper key for the desired information. But this simplicity drives out sophistication, and one cannot use Boolean logic, a thesaurus, or free-text searching. [Note: Beginning in 1981 the service became available through BRS. Here Boolean logic may be used in a modified fashion. The name, too, is changed a bit. With BRS it becomes DOW-JONES NEWS DATABASE]

All industrial and geographic information is placed in very broad categories. For example, steel industry is found under "mining, metals." In addition to the 57 broad categories, information is searched under codes for about 6000 publicly held companies and 16 major governmental divisions. These codes, plus over a dozen miscellaneous categories (the current day's news, Dow-Jones stock averages, foreign news, tax news, etc.), are listed in the operating guide for the file. The indexing is purposely kept to a minimum in order that information can be put in the file almost immediately without waiting for in-depth indexing. The list of searchable categories comprises four fields: (a) companies (about 6000 publicly held); (b) government agencies (16); (c) industries (57 broad categories); and (d) miscellaneous categories.

This type of data base is likely to develop rapidly. In Canada, for example, *Info Globe* offers full text or headlines of stories appearing in *The (Toronto) Globe and Mail*. This may be searched on a regular terminal and does not require a special system as do other services.

The availability of *Dow-Jones* on BRS is one of several moves the concern is making to bring their service to more people. It had experimental services tied to two-way cable television in the Dallas area in 1981, and made available a retrieval service for business via Radio Shack, which sells home computers. The various approaches to the data base are likely to develop in the decade ahead. There will be more marketing of these types of data bases, and competition between publishers is likely to become intense, particularly in the business, life sciences, and technology areas.

Standard & Poor's News (new York: Standard & Poor's Corporation, 1980 to date, weekly) is a more restricted type of data base, but at least rivals the *Dow-Jones* in that it includes ticker services. It also gives news on more than 9,000 companies.

In 1973 *The New York Times* was the first to offer a newspaper index online. Today there are four competitors, and each has something special to add to the reference needs of the user. Broadly compared: (1) *The New York Times* is the oldest of the lot, and its files go back further than any of the others, to 1969. It remains the best single source for politics, biography, and current events. (2) *Newsearch* has the advantage of indexing more material than any of the services and is particularly useful for citations to popular kinds of data, information most likely to be called for by laypersons and students. It has a drawback of not offering abstracts as *The New York Times* does. (3) *The Newspaper Index* has one real advantage—it includes several newspapers which are not indexed elsewhere. (4) *Dow-Jones* differs radically from the other three in that it is updated minute by minute, includes full text (not just citations), and is primarily involved with business news. (5) NEXIS, a rival to *Dow-Jones*, also focuses on business, but in offering full text and a broader base of news stories, it may develop into a serious challenge to the more general services.

A basic question bothers all publishers: Will there be a viable market for so many news-related services, particularly via an online terminal. As one expert puts it:

> *News is something we all need and use, of course. But the kind of news most of us are used to receiving is the serendipitous, unstructured kind that happens to reach our eyes and ears on a daily basis. Online searching, on the other hand, is, by its very nature, a structured, orderly procedure. One must, after all, ask the computer for* something, *not* anything. *Whether the news is searched against a profile in a current awareness mode or against a search strategy created for a special purpose, the need for this type of information must be perceived and the cost of obtaining it justified. On the other hand, maybe these doubts are near-sighted. Perhaps the news retrieval services of today are the forerunners of services which will capture the imagination and support of the general consumer population in years to come.*[37]

Full-text specialized services

Although hardly general data bases, legal bases should be mentioned as examples of what may be done with full-text retrieval. They are worth considering briefly because it is likely that in the not-too-distant future numerous data bases, including *The New York Times* may offer complete text. At this writing, three legal data bases exist—LEXIS,

[37]Thomas Hogan, "News Retrieval Services—Growing But Where Are They Headed?" *Online Review*, September 1979, p. 252.

WESTLAW, and JURIS. Discussion here will be confined to the characteristics of LEXIS.[38]

LEXIS (New York: Mead Data Central, 1965 to date, current, $150 an hour) is the legal service from the same company which produces the general data base NEXIS. LEXIS has a word-for-word duplication of cases found in print, e.g., federal and state court opinions, statutes of the United States Code, decisions of the Supreme Court, etc. Coverage dates vary and the whole file is continuously updated. The arrangement is "by library"; hence the New York Public Library would have *New York Reports* and *Consolidated Laws* among others. The Federal Tax Library would have the *Internal Revenue Code,* tax cases, etc.

Searches follow the normal pattern, and the material may be searched entirely, that is, not only by title and author, but by words found in the text of the legal material. As there is so much data online the particular problem in searching here is to limit the terminology employed, or one ends with hundreds of citations to less-than-relevant data. Another difficulty with the full-text search is that in earlier days the recorders were not that careful about how names were spelled, and searches may be incomplete because of an improper spelling.

If the cases are to be viewed, the user pushes the "cite" key. As with NEXIS, the full text, or more likely only that part of the text which has the keywords, will appear. The case is then read by pushing keys which turn the pages.

Because LEXIS is an expensive way of reading cases, it is used primarily, as are other data bases, for citations and possibly a few lines in the case itself. Its real value, of course, is where the material is so current as to be not yet in print, or where the material is simply not in the library.

READY-REFERENCE DATA BASES

Until relatively recently the emphasis on data-base content has been on bibliographic services, primarily indexes and abstracts. Some of

---

[38] As with the newspaper data bases, there are distinct differences among the services. For a comparison of the systems see the July 1980 issue of *Online*. See also Robert J. Munro, "Lexis vs. Westlaw . . .," *Law Library Journal*, February 1978, p. 475. (Since the article was written LEXIS has broadened its scope to include decisions from all states.) See, too, Ronald A. Rust, "Automated Legal Research . . . ," *Online*, July 1980, pp. 12–15; and Eric L. Welsh, "Westlaw," *Online*, July 1980, pp. 16–23.

the newspaper indexes discussed above offer an exception to this in that they are capable of broader types of information retrieval, but they do remain indexes and abstracting services. There is evidence of a gradual change as more and more standard reference works—other than indexes and abstracts—become available as machine-readable records. This trend has numerous implications; for the moment consider only what it may do for the librarian answering ready-reference queries.

The standard indexes and abstracts online, of course, may be employed for some ready-reference questions. However, there are new directories, encyclopedias, and other standard reference works available online. Given these, the librarian is able quickly to answer queries not found in the indexes or abstracts. The primary benefit, of course, is that an answer may be found (or not found) quickly and the librarian is saved the time of laboriously hunting for the elusive fact in not only one, but perhaps several, reference works.

What follows is an explanation of the ready-reference data bases most frequently used as of early 1981. It should be noted that many of these—the *American Academic Encyclopedia* and *Comprehensive Dissertation Abstracts,* to name two—are not completely limited to ready-reference questions and may be used for more extensive subject searches.

> *American Academic Encyclopedia.* Princeton, N.J.: Arete, 1980 to date. [Price to be determined]
>
> *Biography and Genealogy Master Index.* Detroit: Gale Research Company, 1980 to date, $55 an hour.
>
> *Encyclopedia of Associations.* Detroit: Gale Research Company, 1979 to date. $55 an hour.
>
> *Book Review Index.* Detroit: Gale Research Company, 1981 to date. $55 an hour.
>
> *Foundation Directory.* New York: Foundation Center, current. Semiannual. $60 an hour.
>
> *Foundation Grants Index,* 1973 to date. Bimonthly. $60 an hour.
>
> *Comprehensive Dissertation Index.* Ann Arbor, Mich.: Xerox University Microfilms, 1961 to date. Monthly. $55 an hour.
>
> *U.S. Public School Directory.* Washington, D.C.: United States Department of Education, 1978 to date. Monthly. $35 an hour.

The next set of data bases include those more often employed for ready-reference (i.e., brief facts, directory-type information, statistics, etc.) than for citation searches. At the same time, when one speaks of ready-reference service and data bases, most data bases are generally included. For example, *The New York Times Information Bank* or *Social Sciences Citation Index* or MEDLINE (*Index Medicus* et al.) may be searched for dates, names, verification of spelling, directory-type information, and other instant facts.

Almost all types of data bases are useful, too, when one has a questionable or incomplete journal title, spelling of an author's name, or date of a periodical. Because a data base can deal with small parts, bases are ideal for ready-reference searches when information is incomplete. This is particularly true of the newspaper data bases, and especially of *The New York Times,* as here one may find a faster answer in a title of an article. A question, for example, as to the cost of X legal case, finds a quick answer in a headline: "X Company Settles Damage Case for $1 Million." Given familiarity with the case, the ready-reference search may be done in a matter of seconds or minutes.

There are now several data bases which are *specifically* for ready-reference work and their number will grow. It is with these that this section is concerned.

Considering the nature of ready-reference work and the sources used, there can be a serious problem as to whether or not online services are always the better method of search. One must evaluate the service in whole and in part:

1. **Cost:** the cost of frequent or occasional online searches vs. the cost of the printed version.
2. **Currency:** whether or not the online version is more up to date and whether this really matters for most reference queries.
3. **Use:** whether one is really easier to use than the other.
4. **Depth of search:** whether the online service really does offer more depth of search than the printed version.

Time is increasingly on the side of the online ready-reference search, and most of the reservations set down here are applicable only for the present. In a decade, or possibly less, there is no doubt that numerous ready-reference queries will be best answered at a terminal.

The most ambitious ready-reference work currently which is scheduled to go online is the new *American Academic Encyclopedia.* Made available by OCLC, the system will be piped directly to the home and follows the Viewdata format discussed elsewhere (see p. 117). The experimental nature of the system at this writing is of importance in itself to reference work, for if it succeeds there is every indication that other reference-book publishers may consider an online version of their works.[39]

The Biography and Genealogy Master Index, to become available online in late 1981, lists over 3 million names, with citations to where additional information may be found for each individual name. As in the printed work considered in the first volume of this text, a typical record here includes the name of the person, date(s) of birth (and death), and name(s) of the biographical source(s) which include information on the person. It is an invaluable method of finding biographical data, as well as ready-reference facts (the spelling of names, however, is not reliably accurate).

There is no question that limited bits of data such as are available from the *Biography and Genealogy Master Index.* as well as *Book Review Index,* may be called up much faster on a data base. *The Book Review Index* holds online about 11 years' worth of information from the printed publication and corresponds to the cumulation of the set issued by Gale in 1981.

The *Encyclopedia of Associations,* as discussed in the first volume of the text, offers facts and data on about 14,000 organizations in two-volume printed form. The first volume is a subject approach, the second volume is a geographical and name index. A periodical publication updates the set, and it is thoroughly revised every two years. As of late 1979 all of this data is now available online and is updated three times a year. The cost is $55 a connect-hour, plus 15 cents per citation, whereas the total cost of the printed version is $220.

At this time it is just as easy and almost as fast to consult the printed version as the online work. In fact, because the user can scan a page of, say, sunflower associations, that user is able to pick out what is needed much faster than is possible in calling up the data on the terminal. Cost is a variable. If one uses the directory only a few times a year and has a terminal, the online cost is less than searching the printed version. However, for frequent use, the printed work is cheaper. Ideally, one might have both. In the case of the *Encyclopedia of Associations* the major factor of cost/use may be easily ascertained and a decision made as to what is the best form.

Other factors may not be so easily defined. The benefits of online service with this and other data bases come from the numerous entry points denied the user of the printed service. For example, online the user has the ability to locate organizations founded in any

[39]Stephen P. Harter and Kenneth F. Kister, "Online Encyclopedias: The Potential," *Library Journal,* September 1, 1981, pp. 1600–1602. The *Academic* publisher signed an agreement to provide it as part of the online service of the New York Times Information Bank. Other encyclopedia publishers plan to go online.

particular year or range of years, such as an association founded in New York between 1851 and 1853. The need for such definitive, specialized searches must be balanced against the need for more general ones and a conclusion reached as to whether the printed or the online service would be most economical.

All of this is applicable, too, when one considers the printed or the online version of *The Foundation Directory,* which is a state-by-state listing of some 3000 foundations and is supplemented and updated by the *Index.* Printed versions are under $100, while the online versions cost $60 a connect-hour plus 30 cents per printed citation. Here, however, the printed version is published irregularly and the *Index* annually. The publisher claims the online works are updated twice a year. This means the factor of timeliness is on the side of the online version and, where this is important, must be added to the consideration of print vs. online (cost/use/timeliness). There are several other related services, including *National Foundations,* a current, annually revised file of some 21,000 private American foundations. This one is particularly good for isolating foundations by geographical area and by subject. It, too, is issued by the *Foundation Directory.*

Many of the same considerations are applicable to the *Dissertation Index.* The online service does allow for more points of entry, a useful tool when one considers that the printed version is subdivided by subjects and relies on keywords in titles for subject divisions. The keywords can be misleading and may fail to turn up a pertinent dissertation. Though the same keywords are employed in the online search, the librarian here may narrow the quest by combining the title words with Boolean logic or positional operators so as to limit the search to specific sections. The online *Dissertation Index* is updated monthly, whereas the printed work is an annual issue. The services can be compared in other aspects: cost and convenience. The online charges are $55 per hour, but the complete bound index is over $2500 and the annual supplements come close to $500 a year. Although subdivided by discipline, numerous volumes must be consulted in the printed work unless the topic is focused on a single, narrow area.

Other types of data bases have a multiple purpose. For example, MARC (Machine Readable Cataloging) records allow the librarian to verify items, from the spelling of an author's name to the proper title of a book. And variations on this are possible via such bibliographic utilities as RLIN (discussed later), which allow the librarian to search for titles in MARC records and the recent holdings of some of the country's largest research libraries by subject.

Numerical data bases are not often used in ready-reference work, at least in the average library, although they may be the major source of information in a specialized situation. The *U.S. Public School Directory*, available from Lockheed, is one example of a statistical source which should have wide library use. It provides a variety of statistical data on public schools throughout the United States. Information is given on the number of teachers, students, the student-teacher ratio, names, addresses, regions, districts, and like data.

The most often used statistical source is the 1980 national census. And in daily searches the librarian is also likely to look for statistical data via the two basic indexes in the field, *American Statistics Index* and *Statistical Reference Index,* discussed elsewhere.

Graphic data bases, now used often in teaching, have numerous ready-reference uses.[40] Graphic bases are particularly helpful in geographic reference. Though it is not yet possible to project a map from a data base, as one librarian puts it, "Map librarians have been yammering at the U.S. Geological Survey,"[41] and they are likely to get action soon.

There are combinations of bibliographic, graphic, and numerical data bases. EDUNET, a national network of colleges and universities formed to promote the sharing of computer-based resources in higher education, represents one such combination. Members have access to some 500 sources, from interactive statistical packages and analytical research tools to advanced computer-assisted instructional materials. The resources cover such topics as agriculture, anthropology, psychology, modeling and simulation, and many more.

Inforonics offers an expanded version of *American Book Prices Current* which allows the librarian to search online for author, title, imprint, edition, and other elements (including, of course, price) for more than 100,000 titles. This is called *Bookline*. Even autographs and manuscript data are available. A similar data base for art auction records is being developed by the Research Libraries Group.

In early 1980 R. R. Bowker Company contracted with BRS to provide online access to three of their most widely used printed tools: *Books in Print, Ulrich's Periodical Directory,* and *American Men and Women of Science.* The Bowker data bases are being handled under the BRS Private Database program.[42]

---

[40]In teaching, for example, an engineering student may tell the computer the weight and structural stiffness of each floor of a building. A model of the building will appear on the screen, and through various calculations the graphic image will show the result of an earthquake.

[41]J. B. Post, "Mapping Telereference" (a letter to the editor), *American Libraries,* April 1980, p. 196.

[42]*Database,* March 1980, p. 10.

In addition to the 640,000-plus titles in *Books in Print* online, the librarian will have access to the related *Forthcoming Books in Print.* The data base is to be updated monthly—the primary selling point, at least for obtaining the latest type of information. The rate for the online service is $20 an hour, which is quite low and is an effort to encourage use. (See, too, pp. 220–221.)

Ulrich's and *American Men and Women of Science* will be available for $20 and $25 an hour respectively. These probably will be updated, but as of mid-1981 no announcement was made about how often they will be revised.

The question which these basic works may answer is whether or not librarians will pay more money for an online service than for the same service which is easily available in printed form. Currency, although not necessarily convenience, may be a selling point for the online service. Only time and experience will tell, although if these systems work as well as the publisher hopes, the librarian may look forward to numerous other standard bibliographic works online.

Parenthetically, it also remains to be seen what will happen to an earlier online version of *Books in Print*—i.e., *Booksinfo,* published by Bro-Dart. While the arrangement and information differs, as well as some of the content, essentially they are the same.

SOCIAL SCIENCES DATA BASES[43]

The most widely used data bases in the social services field currently are:

ERIC (Education Resources Information Center). 1966 to date. Monthly. $16 to $35 an hour.

Psychological Abstracts. Washington, D. C.: American Psychological Association, 1967 to date. Monthly, $65 an hour.

NIMH (*National Institute of Mental Health*). Rockville, MD: National Clearinghouse for Mental Health Information, 1969 to date. Monthly. $30 an hour.

PAIS International. New York: Public Affairs Information Ser-

[43]Sara Knapp, "Online Searching in the Behavioral and Social Sciences," *Behavioral and Social Sciences Librarian,* Fall 1979, pp. 23–36. An outline approach to available data bases with some fine introductory remarks on their use. See also Barbara A. Epstein and Jennifer J. Angier, "Multi-Database Searching in the Behavioral Sciences," a two-part series in *Database,* September and December 1980. The authors include full descriptions of basic data bases, including BIOSIS, MEDLINE and EXCERPTA MEDICA which are discussed in this text under scientific bases.

vice, 1972 to date/1976 to date. Updated monthly and quarterly. $60 an hour.

NICEM (National Information Center for Educational Media). Los Angeles: University of Southern California, 1964 to date. Irregular. $70 an hour.

SOCIAL SCISEARCH *(Social Sciences Citation Index)*. Philadelphia: Institute for Scientific Information, 1972 to date. Weekly (monthly). $65 an hour.

Sociological Abstracts. New York: Sociological Abstracts Inc., 1963 to date. Quarterly. $55 an hour.

LISA *(Library and Information Science Abstracts)*. Oxford, England: Learned Information Ltd., 1976 to date. Bimonthly. $50 an hour.

The social sciences data bases and the related government documents files are second only to the general data bases in potential all-around use. The number of data bases for the social sciences has grown over the years and many believe the social sciences will soon equal the sciences in terms of indexes and abstracts available online. This is particularly true if one adds numerical data bases such as the United States Census and the Gallup and Roper Polls, as well as some business services which sociologists employ, to their total.[44]

The bibliographic data bases listed here have been discussed in the first volume of the text and are considered again only in terms of differences between printed and online versions.

ERIC is *Resources in Education* (primarily report literature) and *Current Index to Journals in Education* (index to education and related titles) online. It is a favored data base among most librarians because:

1. It offers a wide coverage of material in almost any education-related field.
2. Many libraries have microforms copy for report literature readily at hand, so searching for documents is made easier.
3. Most importantly, ERIC tends to be the data base which

---

[44]Many of these data bases are "inhouse" university and research center systems and usually have to be used at the individual source, or, sometimes, may be made available on tapes or disks for use nationally. Examples of such centers are the National Opinion Research Center at the University of Chicago; Louis Harris Data Center at the University of North Carolina; and the Roper Center at the University of Connecticut. (For a description of this center see "Data in Past Opinion Polls . . .," *The New York Times*, April 21, 1980, p. B2.) Unfortunately, the present lack of any comprehensive union list of machine-readable files in this area makes it difficult to find the more esoteric collections.

beginners learn first; it is most often used as a training device for searchers. Reasons for this vary, not the least of which is the minimal cost.[45]

Also considered in the first volume but worth mentioning again here, *Psychological Abstracts* in machine-readable form, is, along with ERIC, one of the most heavily used data bases in a library.[46] These tapes became available in 1967.

While the abstracting service concentrates on the literature of psychology, its popularity is due to numerous citations for related fields, from retirement and aging to care of babies and children. Material on the social sciences is abundant as are subjects in education and employment. Since 1980 *Psychological Abstracts* has also included reference to book reviews.

Data in the abstracts available in machine-readable form correspond to those found in the printed version of *Psychological Abstracts*. In an online search there is the advantage of retrieval by words occurring in the title and, in some systems, by words or combinations of words occurring in the abstracts. Natural language may be used to search the titles and the abstracts. On the other hand, a thesaurus of psychological terms is available and allows the librarian to isolate the specific search items. Here is a good example of a combination of controlled- and natural-language searches. Using natural language one may look for keywords, names, and phrases in the title and the abstracts. The controlled language allows one to search by use of broader subjects. In addition, searches may be limited by classifications (which correspond to the sections of the printed *Psychological Abstracts*), codes, publication type, language, etc.

The most striking difference between the printed and online version began in 1980. Since that time the data base has included approximately 25 percent more citations than its printed counterpart. There will soon be about 6600 more abstracts online than in the printed version, and of these, monographs will be a major consideration.

The *National Institute of Mental Health* (NIMH) data base offers an index of some 1000 journals from 41 countries. While the 3500 citations each month are primarily for periodical articles, books, technical reports, and conference proceedings are also included. This data base complements *Psychological Abstracts* in that the material indexed tends to cover a wide number of topics related to mental

[45]Katherine Clay, "Searching ERIC . . .," *Database,* September 1979, pp. 46–66.

[46]Donna Dolan, "Psychological Abstracts/BRS," *Database,* September 1978, pp. 9–25.

health. For example, one may be involved in economics, political science, or art and come here to find material which is applicable to a given study of the productivity of people under stress in a noisy factory. This is another example of a data base which has more possibilities for reference service than its title would indicate.

The NICEM indexes to various types of audiovisual materials, it will be recalled, offer a subject approach to over 500,000 items. While the online version is useful in that it combines the individual listings, it still suffers from being out of date, and the variable updating is no better than in the printed version. At $70 a connect-hour and 20 cents a citation, it is a definite luxury, of limited value to most libraries. The printed version is as good, if not better, although this situation will change when, and if, the service finds a way of becoming more current online. Related to this service is NICSEM/NIMIS (1974 to date). From the same center as NICEM, NICSEM/NIMIS—the call letters are for National Information Center for Special Education Materials—includes materials, both audio-visual and printed, for handicapped children. It, too, suffers from lack of any current updating.[47]

PAIS International is the umbrella term for the *PAIS Bulletin* and the *PAIS Foreign Language Index*. The *Bulletin* goes back to 1915 in the much-used printed work, but online begins with 1976. The *PAIS Foreign Language Index* began in 1968 and is available online since 1972. The latter is updated quarterly, the former monthly—in the same way as the printed works. The online version gives one the obvious advantage of being able to search both works at once; in this way the user has access to material in about 8000 periodicals, monographs, and reports appearing each year. The service is useful to augment government document online data bases.

Closely related to PAIS is USPSD *(United States Political Science Documents)* (Pittsburgh: University of Pittsburgh Center for International Studies, 1975 to date, quarterly, $65 a connect-hour).[48] This base consists of material from about 120 publications, including periodicals from such related fields as history and sociology. Access procedures are standard with both controlled and uncontrolled index, and the online system is updated quarterly rather than

[47]Margaret G. Slusser, "NICEM," *Database,* September 1980, pp. 63–67. For a discussion of related areas and data bases see Theodore Hines et al., "The Children's Media Data Bank," *Top of the News,* Winter 1980, pp. 177–180; David H. Jonassen, "National AV Data Base . . . ," *Bulletin of the American Society for Information Science,* February 1979, pp. 17–18.

[48]David Pilachowski, "USPSD," *Database,* December 1979, pp. 68–77.

annually as for the printed volume. It should be noted, however, that, as of this writing, the actual file was several years behind.

Sociological Abstracts covers about 1300 journals—some 80 percent of them in English—in sociology and related fields. In addition to periodicals, the service selectively indexes reports and case studies. Here the vital contrast between the printed version and the online data base is that the online dates from 1963, while the printed work goes back to 1952. The material is arranged under the normal broad subject headings with an author/subject index in each issue. Searching online follows standard procedures and the system allows entry by the majority of access points. The abstracts tend to be longer than found in many services and include the bonus of cross-reference to documents previously abstracted. Currency is a problem in that the data base is updated only five times a year, but it does have a longer life span than most services, and, by going back to 1963, it offers numerous documents found nowhere else.

Sociological Abstracts publishes a related service—*Language and Language Behavior Abstracts.* Online since 1973, it is updated quarterly and includes citations which cover such areas as speech and language pathology, linguistics, language development, and human communications.

Librarians digging about in a data base will find much related to their profession in ERIC, NTIS (National Technical Information Service), and *Social Sciences Citation Index.* In addition, the traditional *Library and Information Science Abstracts* is online; produced by the English Library Association, it is available from 1969, although abstracts are included only from 1976. Fees run $50 a connect-hour. Experience indicates that for most searches in this area, however, the printed version, primarily because of the specificity of entry, is equally as quick and as satisfactory.

CITATION INDEXING

If some indexes or abstract services may be searched just as easily in the printed form as online, the typical citation index is an exception. It usually is much easier to use in the online form. But before turning to one specifically, consider the citation index form itself.

Citation indexes are unique in that they employ a different type of indexing. The three basic indexes of this type, all published by the Institute for Scientific Information, include: *Arts & Humanities Citation Index, Social Sciences Citation Index,* and *Science Citation Index.* The avenue of access here is through references cited in articles. Each issue is in three parts:

1. The "Citation Index," which lists alphabetically by author each paper cited. The title(s) of the article(s) appears under the author's name, and beneath each article is a list of those who have cited the author's work. Most of the material is abbreviated.
2. The "Source Index," which gives standard bibliographic information for each of the papers in the "Citation Index."
3. The "Permuterm Subject Index," which indexes the articles by subject, i.e., by significant words in the title.

The uniqueness of this system, as opposed to other retrieval schemes, is that it is a network of connections between authors citing the same papers during a current year. In other words, if, in searching for particular subject matter, one has a key paper or review article in the field, or even in author's name, one consults the "Citation Index" by author. Beneath the author's name will be listed in chronological order *any* of his or her publications cited during a particular year, together with the *citing* authors (source items) who have referred to the particular work. If one continues to check the citing authors in the "Citation Index," a cyclical process takes place, often with mushrooming results. The "Source Index" is then used to establish the full bibliographic reference to the citing author.

Even without a citation index, the basic process of citations is familiar. The student who knows, for example, that Collison is an expert on indexing will look in X paper by Collison. There he or she finds references to books, articles, reports, and the like. These citations, it can be safely assumed, have a certain relationship to indexing, and the searcher then chooses the citations which seem relevant and looks them up. The citations, in turn, cite other works, which the student may follow ad infinitum.

To describe the process in simple, metaphorical terms, friends attract other friends of similar disposition and background. In this case, articles attract other articles (via citations) of similar disposition and background. One friend may introduce you to five friends, who in turn will each introduce you to five friends, etc. One article will introduce you to five similar articles, each of which in turn may introduce you to five related articles, etc. This chain reaction is familiar to everyone.

A citation index has a major production advantage which makes it particularly suited for automation. Indexers do not have to be subject specialists, and there is no need to read the articles for subject headings. All the compiler must do is (1) enter the author, title, and full citation in machine-readable form and (2) list all the citations used in the primary article in order by author, title, and full citation in machine-readable form. As a consequence, a careful clerk may prepare material for the computer. This obviously speeds up indexing and also makes it possible to index considerably more material quickly.

The "Source Index" gives full bibliographic details of items listed. It is arranged by author. The "Permuterm Subject Index" is an alphabetically arranged KWIC-type index. Subjects are derived from words appearing in the titles of the source articles. Each significant word has been precoordinated with other terms to produce all possible permutations of terms.

The heart of the system is the "Citation Index," which lists authors alphabetically. It is assumed that the user (1) either knows the name of an author in the subject area of particular interest or (2) lacking the name of the author, finds the subject(s) in the "Permuterm Subject Index" and from that finds the name of the author(s) for search in the "Citation Index."

The disadvantages of the system are numerous: the high price, the reliance on type so small that it makes classified-ad-size type look gigantic, and confusing abbreviations. The most serious drawback is the lack of controlled vocabulary; where subject is an approach, there is total dependence on words in the title. This may work well enough in science, but it fails in the service of the humanities and the social sciences. For example, one critic lists some 30-plus titles which appeared on social science articles over a two-month period. There is some question that the titles would reveal content in a subject search: "The Riddle of the Sphinx," "Merry Christmas, David," and "As a Matter of Fact," for example.[49]

Conversely, the great advantage is the trade-off in timeliness. As human indexers are not needed, the material may be entered into the data base much faster than normal; citation indexes tend to be months, even years, ahead of other services. For example, a search of the *Social Sciences Citation Index* will often yield articles from one to three months old. One may search other social science indexes, such

[49]Claude Bonnelly and Gaetan Drolet, "Searching the Social Sciences Literature Online," *Database*, December 1978, pp. 14–15. Here is a long list of ambiguous titles which makes wishful thinking of a statement [p. 14] in justification of keywords in context indexing: "Every author today is very well aware that he is competing with many other authors for readers. He understands that his title must convey to the potential readers the main thrust of his work." Hah!

as *Psychological Abstracts,* and rarely find material less than a year old.

The *Social Sciences Citation Index* is available online and in printed form.[50] The latter costs $1250 which includes the basic cumulation and updates three times a year. The online version is updated monthly. About 1500 journals are indexed completely and another 2500 or so are indexed selectively. Some nonjournal material is indexed, too, making this the most comprehensive index of all those in the subject area.

Because of the small type and the natural confusion of the printed work, the online version is much easier to use, at least for a trained librarian. The search is primarily free-text from the title, because there is no controlled vocabulary or abstracts. When used only on occasion, the online index may be less expensive than the printed work.

Because the coverage is so wide, the service is particularly useful for compiling what Bonnelly and Drolet call "problem oriented needs (if they want, for example, a bibliography on all aspects of divorce, juvenile delinquency, etc.)"[51] It is particularly strong in such related fields as economics, political science, and law. And because of its timeliness the index can be used for updating ERIC, *Psychological Abstracts,* and other services. There are a growing number of online government document services, services which may be used for searches in all areas, not just in the social sciences.

GOVERNMENT DATA BASES

GPO Monthly Catalog. Alexandria, Virginia: Government Printing Office, 1976 to date. Monthly. $35 an hour.

CIS (*Congressional Information Service/Index,* i.e., CIS/Index) Washington, D.C.: Congressional Information Service, 1970 to date. Monthly, $90 an hour.

CRECORD (*Congressional Record Abstracts*). Washington, D.C.: Capital Services, Inc., 1976 to date. Weekly. $80 an hour.

FEDREG (*Federal Register*). Washington, D. C.: Capital Services, 1977 (March) to date. Weekly. $80 an hour.

Federal Index (See next section on business and economics).

NTIS (National Technical Information Service). Washington,

---

[50]Ibid., pp. 10–21. As the authors point out, the irony of the online search is that, because so much information is needed besides the author's name, other search patterns are preferable, e.g., see pp. 17–18 of the above article.

[51]Ibid., p. 20.

D.C.: NTIS, 1964 to date (some vendors, 1970). Biweekly (some vendors monthly). $35-$45 an hour.

The *GPO Monthly Catalog,* the online version of the *Monthly Catalog of United States Government Publications,* differs from the printed volumes in that it is retrospective only to July 1976, while the printed work is retrospective to 1895. It is updated monthly, as is the printed work, and about 20,000 citations are added each year. The *Catalog* lists publications of federal agencies—reports, hearings, studies, and so forth. It is the first of several steps to automate the bibliographic control of government documents, and as Barrett explains:

> The GPO cataloging is entered into the OCLC database via remote terminal; OCLC sends the GPO a magnetic tape of these entries each week. After four or five tapes are accumulated, they are run through the existing Monthly Catalog system to produce press-ready negatives for printing the Catalog. The cataloging system proposed for phase two will simply reverse this process: The GPO will create automated files and tapes of current cataloging entries. For the benefit of the library community, the GPO will continue to enter data into OCLC and make tapes available to other library networks. This system is projected for implementation in early 1981.[52]

The vendors, Lockheed and BRS, do not add any information to the tapes that they purchase from the Government Printing Office. Some information is rearranged, and the OCLC number is dropped, but material online is the same as found in the printed version. Therefore citation elements include GPO number, Superintendent of Documents classification number, personal author, corporate author, publisher, collation, item number, date, ISSN, Library of Congress and Dewey classification number, title, notes, annotation, and descriptors where applicable. All of the above fields are searchable, and the search may be limited by DIALOG accession number, English language or non-English language.

Documents listed may be purchased from the Superintendent of Documents or from another government source. Availability and price are listed as part of each citation. Unless otherwise indicated, it is assumed that publications are also available from the issuing agency.

The lack of a thesaurus, other than *LC Subject Headings,* is partially compensated for by the vendors' flexible search routine. The online version adds to the usual time- and labor-saving advantages the

[52]William J. Barrett, "The Depository Library Program," *Wilson Library Bulletin,* September 1979, p. 35.

advantage of an unusually low cost. Of course any depository library can get the printed *Monthly Catalog* free.

State Publications (Denver: Information Handling Services, 1979 to date) is available online through BRS. It is multidisciplinary and includes state agency publications from 50 states. Access is through agency, subject, author, and title. It is only infrequently updated.

The online *Congressional Information Service/Index* [CIS/Index] follows the same pattern as the monthly printed version and goes back to the same date, 1970. Providing both an index and abstracts to Congressional publications, it is one of the most heavily used of the online government document services. As is the printed version, the online work is quite complex and requires a skilled searcher; it requires more "than knowing how to deploy subject terms and witness names."[53] The file is particularly complex because CIS uses a code to designate congressional committees, there are numerous entry points, and there is an assumption that the searcher is familiar with congressional committee names, duties, and activities. Also, the sheer volume of the work—about a million pages are indexed and 14,000 to 16,000 citations are added each year—adds to the difficulty.

Furthermore, "because of the wealth of information to be abstracted and indexed, there is an occasional delay in getting the material on tape."[54] This delays both the online and printed version, although the former is rarely more than one week behind, whereas the printed version may be received one to two months after the date of issue.

Here it should be recalled that, as with any government indexes and abstracts, the material indexed is made available on microfiche. The user may order the microfiche online as needed from the vendor, SDC, via their "electronic mail box." This means the order can be on its way the same day.

The service, too, can be used for numerous ready-reference queries:

> At the reference desk, we have found that in 2 to 5 minutes we can supply answers to such questions as "What did Henry Kissinger have to say about the oil embargo?"; "Where, when, and before what committee did James Schlesinger testify on arms control?" We have found that we can approach questions from several angles, and that almost any bit of information with which we are supplied is adequate to lead us to the

---

[53]Lucinda D. Conger, "Codes and Content in the CIS Database," *Database*, September 1978, p. 42.

[54]Lynn Green, "Data Base Review: CIS Index," *Online*, January 1977, p. 47.

*answer. Citations to specific House, Senate, or Joint Committee publica-
tions are easily traced by the committee name. Bill numbers, report or
document numbers, or public laws are verifiable on the basis of numbers
alone. Date ranging or searching by Congress and session are useful
limiting devices. Limiting can also be achieved by searching only specific
document types.*[55]

The Congressional Record Abstracts (CRECORD) offers an online
index to the *Congressional Record* since 1976, and it is updated weekly.
The *Record* publishes proceedings of the Congress, a daily digest, and
speeches (i.e., "extension of remarks"). While the *Record* has its own
biweekly index, it is more likely to be searched by various other
indexes, including CRECORD. The user receives coverage of a wide
variety of legislative topics, including references to bills and resolutions, committee reports, action on the floor, and speeches. In
addition, there is a special version, printed daily, which differs
somewhat from the online work.

The Federal Register is the source of rules and regulations,
proposed rules, notices of changes, opinions, etc. The printed index is
issued monthly, but the online version has the advantage of weekly
updating. As it covers so many subject areas touched upon by the laws
and decisions of the federal government, it is used much in business.
The index to the register is FEDREG, which has many of the elements
found in CRECORD.

Reports, conference proceedings, etc.

Published material is difficult enough to find, but an even greater
challenge is to locate the work which has only limited publication
(mimeographed or duplicated) or is simply buried in another work.
This is the situation with the typical report or conference proceeding.

By now the reader is familiar with the effort of ERIC to control
report literature, but an even greater challenge is to control the vast
output of technical reports. To some degree this challenge is met by
the National Technical Information Service (NTIS). Before considering the online version of this work one should be familiar with the
printed volumes: *Government Reports Announcements* (Springfield, Va.:
National Technical Information Service, 1946 to date, semimonthly)
and *Government Reports Index* (1965 to date, semimonthly).

The two services are really one. The announcement section
includes abstracts of about 70,000 reports each year. By 1980 the total

---

[55]Ibid., p. 50.

number was well over a million. These are divided into some 26 major subject areas and then subdivided. Produced by local, state, and federal government agencies,[56] as well as by individuals and private and for-profit groups, the reports cover a wide spectrum of interests, including much material in the social sciences.[57] In fact, NTIS and ERIC interchange some report information and there is a limited amount of duplication. The *Index* includes subject, personal and corporate author, contact number, and access/report number. Annual cumulations may be purchased separately.

A weekly subject version of the service, *Weekly Government Abstracts,* is available for individuals or libraries that do not wish to subscribe to the full service or, more likely, wish advance news about reports that will appear in the service. There are some 26 subject categories in the newsletter, and one of particular interest to libraries is *Weekly Government Abstracts: Library and Information Science.*

The online *Government Reports Announcements* data base is available from 1964 and is updated semimonthly. The content is similar to the printed version.

The NTIS system is backed up by documents on microfiche, which may be on standing order selectively through the Selected Research in Microfiche program (SRIM). Standing orders are for subject, category, agency, or discriptor. The library may also order individual documents on microfiche or in printed form as needed.

An unfortunate aspect of document delivery, at least to some people, is the fact the service must pay for itself. Because of this a most useful system, the Journal Article Copy Service, has been discontinued. Begun in early 1979, the service provided automated referral of orders for photocopies from NTIS customers to publishers, libraries, and information brokers. But too few customers used the service and NTIS had to discontinue it.[58]

As more and more government agencies and departments become involved with automation there is better control over reports

---

[56]The greatest contributors of reports include the Department of Defense, NASA, Department of Commerce, Department of Health, Education and Welfare, and the Environmental Protection Agency.

[57]Rao Aluri, "Reference Sources Among NTIS Technical Reports," *Reference Services Review,* September 1977, pp. 27–32. The author lists 67 sources from the reports that are of use to librarians.

[58]There continues to be a controversy about the notion that a government information agency should make a profit. Those who argue that information, not profit, is the first consideration believe that the document service should be continued. For a broader discussion of the role of NTIS and information see a special issue of *Information Hotline,* March 1979, with a follow-up in the April 1979 number.

and allied types of information. For example, in addition to filing information on reports with NTIS, the Department of Defense has developed its own Defense Documentation Center (DDC) Research Development Test and Evaluation data-base system. There are three major data bases within the system, which is made available "to any qualified Department of Defense contractor library." There is no charge for the use of the data base, although the library, of course, must furnish the hardware and the communications equipment.[59]

Another aspect of report literature is the proceeding, or report of papers and discussions at a conference. There are now several indexes to such compliations:

Conference Papers Index (Louisville, Ky.: Data Courier, Inc., 1973 to date, monthly) is available both in printed form and online. This is a record of papers presented at over 1000 national and international scientific and technical meetings each year. The online version is updated monthly. There are numerous access points, including author, title, subject, conference title, and meeting place.[60]

Index to Scientific and Technical Proceedings (Philadelphia: Institute for Scientific Information, 1978 to date, monthly) identifies papers by the main topic of the meeting, by region, and by sponsor. There is an author and keyword subject index. The publisher claims 3000 proceedings and over 90,000 individual papers are indexed each year. The price is high: $500 a year.[61]

Smithsonian Science Information Exchange (SSIE) (Washington, D.C.: Smithsonian, 1975 to date, monthly $90-$110 an hour) is a related service. It does not provide reports per se, but rather gives information on projects and research that will become reports or proceeding papers. Primarily, the file monitors about 9000 studies a month in the life sciences and physical sciences, with a nod to the social and behavioral sciences. The entries are abstracted. A record is maintained for only three years.[62]

Despite the numerous aids, there might come a time when the librarian seeking a conference report or paper is baffled. This is just

---

[59]Larry Chasen, "An On-Line System with the Department of Defense," *Special Libraries,* January 1980, p. 20.

[60]Betty Unruh, "Conference Papers Index," *Online,* July 1978, pp. 54–60.

[61]There are several other titles, but these index only the conference or meeting as a whole, and are more limited in scope, e.g., *Proceedings in Print,* Mattapan, Massachusetts: Special Libraries Association, 1964 to date, bimonthly. This is widely used but does not list individual papers; only the proceedings themselves are listed.

[62]Actually, there are two files, and one goes back to 1965–1974, but is of relatively little value for ongoing research.

as true for private organizations seeking information for users. For example, the firm Information on Demand:

> . . . has often been faced with the dilemma of finding what appears to be an impossible-to-locate publication. One of our last resort methods has been to verify an earlier conference or meeting. For example, we are trying to find the Proceedings of the 1st Annual Conference on Electrolysis. However, all of our usual verification tools can only identify the 2nd and 3rd conferences, ecah of which has a different sponsor, editor and publisher. What can we do now? IOD's next step would be to turn to one of our most useful tools—the telephone. Sponsors, editors, or publishers of conferences can often lead you to locations of proceedings from earlier (or later) conferences. They may also be able to give you the name of the sponsor or publisher of the material you are trying to verify.[63]

SCORPIO[64]

An example of maximum reference service and the imaginative use of government documents and related works is offered by SCORPIO (an ancronym for Subject Content Oriented Retrieval for Processing Information Online). After that unfortunate title it is comforting to know the mission of the online service is to provide answers to a wide variety of questions by elected officials and, to a lesser extent, the public at large. [At this writing the data bases are not generally available, although the major vendors have been trying to get them for the public use. How successful the wider use of SCORPIO will be depends upon numerous political and economic considerations.]

There are some 13 different collections of information available to SCORPIO, and of these the most important, or at least the most nonspecialized, include:

(1) *Bibliographic information files* contain full citations and numerous annotations of periodical articles, pamphlets, GPO publications, UN documents, and other pieces of information judged of value to Congress. As Congress deals with almost all aspects of the passing scene, the file is a marvelous source of both specific and general information on thousands of topics for almost anyone. Available to all users, the file has citations only for the three most recent years.

---

[63]Antoinette Colbert, "Document Delivery," *Online*, January 1980, p. 68.

[64]*Scorpio Overview*, rev. ed., Washington, D.C.: Library of Congress, 1979. A 17-page explanation of the system. See, too, Sarah M. Pritchard, "Online Reference at the Library of Congress," *North Carolina Libraries,* Winter 1980, pp. 6–11.

(2) *Major issues file* is a collection of more than 300 briefs on topics of public interest. "Specialists in the Congressional Research Service write the briefs, each of which includes a definition of the issue, background and policy analysis statements, references to Congressional action on the issue, historical chronology, references to current literature dealing with the topic and . . . topical descriptors."[65]

(3) *Legislative information files* provide bill content, bill numers, revised texts, etc. Popularly known as the *Bill Digest,* this is a method of tracing the history of any bill.

(4) *Congressional Record Abstracts* are part of another major file. Other standard indexing services are available through the Library of Congress.

(5) *The MARC data base* is the Library of Congress catalog online since 1968.

(6) *National referral center master file* differs from the others in that the focus is not on information, but on organizations where information may be found. The file lists over 12,000 libraries, networks, information brokers, etc., qualified and willing to provide information on a large number of scientific and technological topics, including some in the social sciences. In a sense, this is a national I&R service, particularly as additional follow-up often is provided.[66]

The file is the major tool of another organization within the Library of Congress—the National Referral Center for Science and Technology. The purpose of the center is to locate libraries and individuals who can answer the queries. The file is available not only to SCORPIO but to the wider public through other libraries.

(7) *General Accounting Office files,* known as the *Congressional Sourcebook,* are somewhat similar to the referral center file in that here are descriptions of over 2000 recurring reports required by Congress, as well as descriptions of about 1400 federal systems and sources maintained by 91 agencies. In addition, there is a mass of other relevant information on budgets and programs.

Meanwhile, the Library of Congress is working on other information systems to augment SCORPIO. And the Western nations are developing systems of their own, systems such as the British Library's MERLIN.

Given this array of online sources, plus the standard online and

---

[65]Scorpio, *op. cit.,* p. iv.

[66]Available in printed form as *A Directory of Information Resources in the United States,* Washington, D.C.: The Library of Congress, various dates, irregular update.

printed works available in a large research library, the SCORPIO staff may offer complete, and detailed answers to queries. There is no question here of user education or half-citation measures. Where needed, briefs are even presented to the user attempting to gather data on a given subject. And, to be sure, the SCORPIO file may be used by itself as any standard data base.

LEGIS, closely related to SCORPIO, offers information on the status of every bill and resolution currently before Congress. Sponsored by the House of Representatives, it became open to the public in mid-1979. Unlike SCORPIO, this service (one of several) is operated by the computer center in the House Information System (HIS).[67]

BUSINESS AND ECONOMICS DATA BASES

Information about business or economics is not limited to standard reference sources. In fact, as in all research, there are three source categories.

> *Primary information is obtained from the direct observations and recordings of business activity. It may consist of reports, surveys, and statistical records. Secondary information is developed from primary information and includes journal articles, news stories, published reports, and monographs. It is usually collected for periodic or on-demand dissemination. Tertiary information is developed from primary and secondary information which is collected, condensed, and organized into more easily referenced abstracts and indexes.[68]*

Tertiary sources are employed to tap the secondary information sources and, to a more limited extent, those in the first category. There are scores of business and economic data bases, particularly if one considers the nonbibliographic base such as EXRATE, a running account of exchange rates and price and production indices for 15 countries.

As in other subject areas, searches for material on economics and business are not limited to specific business data bases. For example, numerous nonbusiness bases have reference to company names, to names of officials, and to products.

The number of business bibliographic data bases increases by

---

[67]Robert S. Willard, "Legis Goes Public," *Information World,* August 1979, p. 10+. A brief discussion of the history of the service.

[68]Goeffrey Sharp, "Online Business Information," *Online,* January 1978, p. 33.

four to ten per year, and the number is likely to grow larger. Only a few of the more prominent and heavily used bases are briefly discussed in this section.

Basic business bases

ABI/INFORM. Louisville, Ky.: Data Courier, August, 1971 to date. Monthly. $75 an hour.

American Statistics Index. Washington, D. C.: Congressional Information Service, 1973 to date. Monthly. $90 an hour.

Canadian Business Periodicals Index. Information Access, 1975 to date. Monthly. $75 an hour.

Predicasts. Cleveland, Ohio: Predicasts, various dates and service charges.

    a   *F&S Index of Corporations and Industries.* 1972 to date. Monthly. $90 an hour.

    b   *Federal Index.* 1976 (October) to date. Monthly. $90 an hour.

See, too, discussion of *Dow-Jones News/Retrieval* on p. 162.

One of the most frequently used data bases is ABI/INFORM,[69] an index to about 400 periodicals. Material is selectively indexed for the use of businesspeople, administrators, and those in sales and marketing. Each citation has a detailed abstract and the file may be searched with both a thesaurus and free text. It is updated monthly with about 1600 citations and abstracts. There is no print equivalent. And, as is the case with most of these services, the publisher offers a document-delivery service.

It might be instructive here to consider some of the elements that go into what is known as *selective* indexing. Some basic considerations are followed by many services in their selective indexing.

Articles are selected on the basis of subject, scope, and content. The definition of a subject is that it must be (1) some matter having to do with management and (2) something that will have an impact on how a person can fulfill the duties within an organization. The scope includes articles that should be relevant to one or more of the functional areas of management. . . . The content should be usable by more than one specific function within one specific organization and should contain one or

[69]Robert Wagers, "ABI/INFORM and Management Contents on Dialog," *Database,* March 1980, pp. 12–37. See, too: Loene Trubkin, "Auto-Indexing of the 1971–77 ABI/Inform Database," *Database,* June 1979, pp. 56–61.

more of the following characteristics: present a new idea, discuss variations of an idea or developing trend, reinforce an existing technique, discuss alternatives to or critize an existing method or technique, present an application of a method or process, etc. Articles are generally more than one page in length. If the article is less than one page, the editors take a close look at it to see if it fits with the concepts of the database. . . . A rule of thumb is that they are not looking for the short or news type item but want a discussion or presentation of management ideas, which generally takes longer than one page. Of course, there are the exceptions.[70]

In subject coverage and in types of materials indexed, *Management Contents* (Skokie, Ill: Management Contents, 1974 to date, weekly, $35–$75 an hour) is somewhat similar to INFORM. It indexes some 200 American and foreign periodicals, as well as selected proceedings and reports in the area of business and management, including accounting, finance, marketing, public administration, and the like. Only business material is indexed; book reviews, editorials, and digests are excluded. There are no detailed abstracts, but there are two- or three-sentence annotations. There is a print variation, *Management Contents,* a biweekly current-awareness service which includes tables of contents of the journals and proceedings.[71]

The CBPI *(Canadian Business Periodicals Index)* is a subject and corporate and personal name approach to about 150 Canadian business and economics periodicals, all in English. While of primary use to the business community, it can be used for related areas, from the social sciences to biography. It is updated monthly and is often used with the publisher's other index, *Canadian Newspaper Index.* The business service is available, too, in printed form. Unfortunately, *Business Periodicals Index,* the H.W. Wilson company equivalent, is not available online at this writing.

The ASI *(American Statistics Index)* previously discussed in the first volume is available from 1973 and is updated monthly.[72] An almost complete index to governmental statistical publications, it is an invaluable aid online because it is somewhat easier to search than the printed version. Both free-text and controlled-vocabulary terms may be used.

PTS or Predicasts system is really a collection of several data

---

[70]Charles Popoich, "Business Data Bases . . .," *RQ,* Fall 1978, p. 7. (The report is given by Jo Susa, representing the publisher.)

[71]For a comparison of this data base with ABI/Inform see Wagers, *op. cit.*

[72]Lynn Green, "American Statistics Index," *Online,* April 1978, pp. 36–40.

bases, each of which serves a specific purpose. The data bases are tapped by well-defined thesauri for products, organizations, events, and geographical locations.[73]

The various services index over 5000 domestic and foreign trade journals, business periodicals, government documents, reports, statistical publications, bank letters, long-range forecasts, and a variety of other materials. While the focus is on business, the subject matter covers millions of records in related areas, from agriculture to education and the social sciences.

Coverage is generally from the late 1960s, although this varies with the different data bases. Each base must be searched separately and some files are used for both retrieval and computation; i.e., it is possible to perform algebraic, statistical, and forecasting routines, as well as to enter data.[74]

Both controlled and free searching are possible, but most of the files use the Standard Industrial Classification (SIC) System. This is a numerical hierarchical system established by the United States government to classify the total economy into different industrial segments. Using specific numbers one may retrieve a "needle" from millions of records.[75]

One of the basic indexes of Predicasts, *F&S Index of Corporations and Industries,* was discussed in the first volume of this text. The data base version is a combination of this weekly domestic index with *F&S Index International* (1967 to date, monthly) and *F&S Europe* (1967 to date, monthly). Combined, they offer an index to periodical articles, monographs, and other financial and corporation reports from both American and foreign publishers. Approximately 1000 sources are searched and about 12,500 new records are added per month—which is roughly equivalent to the additions to the printed versions. The base, like the printed versions, may be searched via product, industry, country, company, or specific subject. Whereas the printed volumes of the *F&S Index of Corporations and Industries* go back to 1960, the data base begins only with 1972.

The actual search may be done either by a code or by almost the

---

[73]For a discussion of the basic thesauri see Geoffrey Sharp, "Online Business Information," *Online,* January 1978, pp. 35–36. See, too: Joanne Tyzenhouse, "The Pleasures and Pitfalls of the Predicasts Computational System," *Online,* January, 1980. pp. 26–29. [Note: In 1981 the service was purchased by Information Handling Services, who bought out BRS.]

[74]Joanne Tyzenhouse, "Econometric and Statistical Bases for the Non-econometrician," *Online,* April 1978, pp. 48–54.

[75]The SIC Classification is found in *Predicasts Terminal System Users Manual,* among other places.

same vocabulary used in the printed versions. And the printout, like the printed index, usually includes brief comments or abstracts.

The *Federal Index,* while it is used by other than those in business, is part of the Predicasts system because "business decisions must reflect legislation (proposed or enacted), regulations, procedures, etc., which emanate from the federal government."[76] The primary indexing is of material found in congressional bills, the *U.S. Code, Code of Federal Regulations,* the *Congressional Record,* and other publications. In addition it includes material from the *Washington Post* and the business newspaper, *Commerce Business Daily.* The basic index is updated once a month, but there is a weekly version, *Federal Index Weekly,* which after four weeks becomes the monthly update. The service is available in printed form (both weekly and monthly) and is published monthly for a subscription of $400 as compared with the online charges of $90 a connect-hour.

The system includes a number of other data bases such as PROMT *(Predicasts Overview of Markets and Technology,* 1972 to date, weekly, $90 a connect-hour); International Time Series (1972 to date, quarterly, $90); PTS/US Statistical Abstracts (1972 to date, quarterly, $90 an hour) which draws upon the *Census of Manufacturers* and other data for forecasting materials; and related specialized works which are relevant to business and economics research.

There are numerous other business data bases, including an impressive number of numerical, nonbibliographic types. For example, for media advertising there are bases of survey data about readers of magazines, viewers of television, and other audience statistics. For magazines some of the files come from Simmons, Market Research Bureau, and Mediamark Research, Inc. For television the familiar names are Nielsen Data and the Arbitron Radio and TV Data.

Lockheed's *Foreign Traders Index* is an interesting example of another type of nonbibliographic data base. Here one may search for importers, exporters, or distributors of products by SIC code and by country. The *Index* is used by manufacturers looking for out-of-the-way and not-so-obvious outlets for their products.

HUMANITIES AND HISTORY

Some commonly used data bases in the field of the humanities and history include:

[76]Charles J. Popoich, "Business Data Bases: The Policies and Practices of Indexing," *RQ,* Fall 1978, p. 11.

Three from American Bibliographic Center (ABC), Clio Press, Santa Barbara, Calif.:

    a *America: History and Life.* 1964 to date. Three/year. $65 an hour.

    b *Historical Abstracts.* 1973 to date. Three/year. $65 an hour.

    c *Art Bibliographies Modern.* 1974 to date. Three/year. $65 an hour.

Modern Language Association (MLA) International Bibliography. New York: Modern Language Association, 1976 to date. Annual. $55 an hour.

Philosopher's Index. Bowling Green State University, 1940 to date. Quarterly. $55 an hour.

Religion Index. Chicago: American Theological Library Association, 1974 to date. Semiannual and annual parts. Price to be determined.

RILM Abstracts (Répertoire International de Littérature Musicale). New York: RILM Center, 1972 to date. Three/year. $65 an hour.

Arts & Humanities Citation Index. Philadelphia: Institute for Scientific Information, 1977 to date. Price to be determined.

Online data bases in the humanities and history have been relatively scarce but will increase in numbers as more and more of the general public is involved with online services. Those listed here are representative of the better-known ones, although there are—as of mid-1981—very few others. That having been said, it should be obvious that anyone working in these fields will find much material in the aforementioned data bases in general topics, news, and the social sciences. For example, *Magazine Index* will furnish considerable data on authors, current art shows, developments in historic research, etc.

The three online versions of the services from the American Bibliographic Center are essentially the same as the printed works. They are indexes to the periodical literature of history and art, both international and in the United States and Canada. Monographs are also considered, though in a more limited way. *Historical Abstracts* online is available only from 1973, while the printed volumes go back to 1955; but *America: History and Life* and *ArtBibliographies Modern* correspond with the printed titles. The three parts in *America: History and Life* (i.e., articles, abstracts, and citations; index to book reviews; and the bibliography) are repeated online. The machine-readable files generaly follow similar patterns for the other two works.

The publisher does not have hard copies or microforms of the indexed material available. This is particularly unfortunate as some indexed works are difficult to find in a less-than-specialized library.

In discussing *ArtBibliographies Modern,* a trained searcher makes the point applicable to all data bases: there are subject areas which are not self evident in the normal use of the data base. For example, while one would automatically turn to *ArtBibliographies Modern* for modern art and design since 1800, the index can be useful for such related subjects as ecology, feminism, language, music, literature, nature, occultism, philosophy, photography, politics, psychology, science, time, education, and therapy.[77]

One of the potentially more useful data bases in the humanities, and particularly in literature, the *Modern Language Association Bibliography* has the drawback of going back only to 1976.[78] The printed work, with variations on content and approach, dates from 1921. Since most work in literature and linguistics requires extensive retrospective searches, the data base version is of limited value other than as a current-awareness service.

The printed form, the *MLA International Bibliography,* is divided into multiple volumes. The work is organized by national literatures and by periods with author subdivisions and, in some years, author indexes. For the data base the same 3000 basic sources are searched, and this includes both books and periodical articles. Neither the printed nor online version is current, that is the 1978 record was published in 1980 and made available online at the same time. This means that, as of 1981, there are only three years of the service online, i.e., 1976, 1977, and 1978. Needless to add, the publisher is considering more frequent updates.

A guide to the literature of philosophy in some 200 journals and books, the *Philosopher's Index* offers citations from American journals from 1940 to date and from foreign publishers from 1967 to date.[79] While the basic index did not go online until relatively recently [1978], the publisher has chosen to take part of the base back to an even earlier date than found in the printed version, which dates from 1967. Good abstracts are included.

An interesting aspect of this data base is that, despite the subject matter, it is "a fairly simple, straight-forward database to search. There are no codes or complicated subject headings, in fact, free text searching. . . . should produce satisfactory results."[80]

[77]Katherine K. Sheng, "Art Modern/Dialog," *Database,* June 1979, p. 31.

[78]Eileen M. Mackesy, "MLA Bibliography Online . . . ," *Database,* September 1979, pp. 36–45.

[79]Mary E. Sievert, "The Philosopher's Index," *Database,* March 1980, pp. 50–62.

[80]Ibid., p. 56.

The *Religion Index* is in two sections, as is its printed counterpart. "Index one" is an abstracting service covering periodical literature. "Index two," which comes out annually, as contrasted with the semiannual schedule of the first part, is an index to material in collections. About 275 to 300 books are analyzed each year. The online service is similar in that over 200 journals are indexed and about 12,000 citations are added each year. Coverage is not limited to any particular religious group, which is to say, "religion" is broadly interpreted to embrace ethics, church history, theology, philosophy, and the like. The index is a fine place to begin a search which may end with the *Philosopher's Index.*

The *RILM Abstracts* began in 1968, but is available online only from 1972. The work is updated quarterly, and an effort is made to abstract all significant literature that appears about music in books, articles, essays, reviews, dissertations, etc. Major publications in 43 countries are searched. With automation the time lapse between the appearance of the article abstracted and the index entry has been considerably shortened. This has meant faster production, too, of the printed version.

Certainly the most ambitious data base and the one with the widest scope is *Arts & Humanities Citation Index.* Since this citation form has been discussed previously, suffice it to say here that 1000 national and international journals are covered, from architecture and art to theater and theology. Beginning in 1979 books were also included, and most of the 250 to 300 items indexed are collections of essays and papers. There is an overlap, although not a serious one, between this index and the publications of the *American Bibliographic Center* (viz., history and art), the *MLA Bibliography,* the *Philosopher's Index,* and *RILM Abstracts.* However, in any extensive search, all the titles must be consulted because most of them consider not only journals, but monographs, dissertations, and reports.

The index is useful for book reviews; in 1978 of the 85,000 source items indexed, 38,000 were book reviews. It should be noted also that the work covers poems, short stories, and other literary works.

In the printed version, the *Arts & Humanities Citation Index* appears three times a year, with the last issue serving as a cumulation. The data base is updated in a similar fashion. [Note: According to the publisher the data base is to be online in the first part of 1982.]

Tear sheets of most of the articles cited may be had from the publisher via the OATS (Original Article Tear Sheet) system.

Eugene Garfield, in a discussion of the citation indexes he published, makes some fascinating points about the various citation approaches:

(1) The humanities are involved with the history of ideas, the sciences primarily with the past five years. In science 60 percent of the citations are to work published within the past five years. For the humanities this hovers around 38 percent for the same period.

(2) Of the 300 scientific authors most cited, the oldest person on the list was born in 1899. In the humanities, of the 300 most-cited authors, nearly 60 percent were born before 1900.

(3) There is a preeminence of books over journals in the humanities, and the tendency to cite is not as strong as in the sciences. For example, a literary critic will not cite Shapespeare each time his work is considered.[81]

The publisher also issues *Current Contents,* which lists the title pages of over 1000 journals. This is published weekly and follows the same format of the *Current Contents* titles for the sciences and the social sciences. *Journal Citation Reports,* which will show, among other things, the journals cited most often, is soon to be published for the humanities.

SCIENCE DATA BASES

Data bases most frequently used to search scientific topics include:

CA Search *(Chemical Abstracts Search).* Columbus, Ohio: Chemical Abstracts Service, 1967 to date. Biweekly. $50 to $70 an hour.

MEDLINE (MEDLARS, i.e., Medical Literature Analysis and Retrieval System, online). Bethesda, Md.: National Library of Medicine, 1966 to date. Monthly. $10 to $15 an hour.

BIOSIS Previews (BioSciences Information Services Previews). Philadelphia: BioSciences Information Service, 1969 to date. Monthly. $30 to $45 an hour.

SCISEARCH *(Science Citation Index).* Philadelphia: Institute for Scientific Information, 1974 to date. Monthly. $30 to $120 an hour.[82]

AGRICOLA (Agricultural On-Line Access). Beltsville, Md.: United States Department of Agriculture, 1970 to date. Monthly. $10 to $25 an hour.

---

[81]Eugene Garfield, "Is Information Retrieval in the Arts and Humanities Inherently Different . . . ," *Library Quarterly,* January 1980, pp. 40–57.

[82]The $30 is for subscribers to the printed service, the $120 for nonsubscribers. Retrospective searches for 1974–77 are $40 to $130.

Early and ready funding, narrow subject areas which are easier to program than are the more general areas for the humanities and social sciences, and a significant built-in audience in terms of ability to pay—all of these factors gave the science data bases an early, often commanding, lead over other subject areas. The lead is now much shorter and, in terms of number of users, may actually dwindle in comparison to other fields.

Scientific data bases tend to be more sophisticated, more complex, and certainly more difficult to search than other bases. The possible exception is MEDLINE, which is one of the best and has a broader base in medicine than in chemistry or agriculature. In an earlier form it was the training ground for many of today's veterans of computer searches.

Produced by the National Library of Medicine, MEDLINE[83] (MEDLARS online) is one of the four or five most heavily used data bases in the academic or public library.[84] It is available directly from the National Library of Medicine or through a vendor. Either the online or the printed version of *Index Medicus* (1960 to date, monthly) is popular because it, like other data bases such as ERIC, *Psychological Abstracts,* and *Science Citation Index,* has a broad potential use beyond its primary focus. Thanks to a file of close to 3 million citations, MEDLARS may be used to find data on such related fields as psychology, education, anthropology, sociology, technology, agriculture, and almost any other area—including politics—which is connected in any way with medicine.[85]

The National Library of Medicine backs up MEDLINE with an efficient interlibrary loan procedure. About 1500 requests for materials are received each day. Before requests for material reach the NLM they are filtered through three other possible sources of supply. The librarian may send the request to a local library (say, one which is larger or has medical journals); to a resource library, usually at a medical school; to one of 11 regional medical libraries which cover

[83]Suzetta Burrows and Sylvia Kyle, "Searching the MEDLARS File on NLM and BRS: A Comparative Study," *Bulletin of the Medical Library Association,* January 1979, pp. 15–24. See, too: Stuart J. Kolner, "Improving the MEDLARS Search Interview: A Checklist Approach," *Bulletin of the Medical Library Association,* January 1981, pp. 26–33.

[84]More particularly the online version not only includes *Index Medicus* (the heart of the system), but related titles: *International Index to Nursing Literature, Index to Dental Literature,* and since 1977, *Population Sciences.* These are *not* part of the printed *Index Medicus.*

[85]There are some dozen separate, but related data bases in addition to MEDLARS, among them: *CANCERLINE, EPILEPSY, History of Medicine, TOXLINE,* and several others usually employed in medical libraries.

well-defined geographic regions; or finally, when none of these are possible sources, to the National Library of Medicine. In other words, the NLM serves as the final resource after requests are unsatisfied at three previous levels of processing.

The library can fill from 80 to 85 percent of the requests received. The unfilled requests are transmitted by computer to the British Lending Library in Boston Spa, England, and quickly accessed by the British Lending Library, thus making it possible to receive materials often more quickly from England than from another part of the United States or Canada.

PRE-MED represents an effort to make MEDLARS more current. PRE-MED now makes it possible to access 125 key journals within 10 days of their publication when normally the citations would not be online until 5 to 12 weeks after publication. Produced by BRS, the file is an example of an effort to speed up what is essentially laborious manual indexing. The file is the tables of contents of the 125 journals, not the articles themselves. The vendor points out: "A number of special problems are encountered when keying records directly from the table of contents pages of a journal. For example, author names are not included in full for some journals . . . and title page print is often unusually small and difficult for keyers to read. Pagination cannot always be exact because the full body of the journal is not available for verification."[86]

As with numerous data bases with a controlled vocabulary, there is a difference between the printed and the online work. Drawing from MeSH (Medical Subject Headings) for manual searching, the indexer, using the four to six major descriptors under which an item will appear in the printed work, assigns both the major and minor descriptors—an average of about 12—by which the item may be retrieved online.

Medical Subject Headings comes in several different forms, from an annotated alphabetic list to the tree structures. The latter, which is very useful for online searching, is a hierarchical arrangement of subject headings. In this case, the headings are grouped, in relation one to the other, under 15 broad categories, including geographic terms.

Europe has the equally well-known *Excerpta Medica* (Amsterdam, The Netherlands: Excerpta Medica, 1975 to date, weekly, $55 an hour), which indexes 3600 journals from more than 110 countries. Again, the coverage is so wide that the service is often used by

[86]*BRS Bulletin*, June 1980.

researchers in related fields. It is particularly valuable for information on drugs and public health.

Science Citation Index (SCISEARCH) is another of the most frequently used data bases. The first of the three citation services, it follows the citation indexing pattern. It is updated monthly and lists about 500,000 references a year, references drawn from the over 3000 journals scanned. The publisher claims the tapes are fed new material no later than two weeks after a journal arrives at the firm. As a result, material may be as recent as two weeks and is seldom older than eight weeks before it is indexed.[87]

BIOSIS Previews corresponds to the printed *Biological Abstracts* and *Biological Abstracts/RRM* (formerly called *BioResearch Index*). The system is one of the most sophisticated of the sciences and regularly examines over 8000 periodicals as well as books, monographs, research papers, and conference proceedings. The title suggests the topic, but the material covers a wide range of related areas from medicine and biochemistry to ecology. Because of its wide scope, BIOSIS is frequently used to answer many scientific and even social science queries.

The printed version is updated twice a month, while the online work is updated by vendors monthly, but the publisher claims the online tapes are "available approximately five weeks before the printed version." The printed volumes and the online version employ a keyword-in-context subject index, though they may be searched as well by broad subject concepts, by genus-species and organism names, by broad taxonomic categories, and by author. The online service offers a master index of keywords; the other search elements are much the same, but with considerably more variation, as is true in most online systems. However, there is no controlled vocabulary. Abstracts are to be available online in the near future and will be updated 24 times a year. For earlier abstraces the printed work must be consulted. The price of the printed abstracts is $1300, plus $650 for BA/RRM, plus about another $800 for the cumulated indexes. The online search fee is $30 to $45 per hour. The publisher offers numerous other printed publications and the printed work is available on microform.

Developed by the National Agricultural Library, and formerly known as CAIN, the AGRICOLA data base provides worldwide coverage of agricultural materials, as well as allied sciences, from rural sociology and forestry to entomology and pollution. In printed

---

[87]Gretchen S. Savage, "SciSearch on Dialog," *Database*, September 1978, p. 64.

form it is the familiar *Bibliography of Agriculture and National Agricultural Library Catalog,* plus several other sources.[88] Emphasis here is on journal material, but the data base does include some monographs, government documents, and special reports.

About 150,000 citations are fed into the system each year. By the early 1980s the citation file had some 2 million entries, primarily from over 6500 journals.

In Europe there are over 22 agriculture-oriented data bases, but closely related to the American effort is the CAB *Abstracts* (Commonwealth Agricultural Bureau, Slough, Berks, England, 1972 to date, monthly, $35 and available through Lockheed), made up of similar types of material from the British Commonwealth countries and others around the world.[89] There are some 8500 journals examined, journals which represent 37 different languages. Actually, the system is divided (as is ERIC) into separate main abstracting subject areas, now over 24, and it may be searched online by more discrete subject areas than the overall title suggests.

CA Search is a highly technical, equally involved data base of many parts. Its counterpart is found in the printed work, *Chemical Abstracts* (1907 to date, weekly).[90] Suffice it to say here that the service is the most comprehensive of any and indexes close to 15,000 periodicals and other materials. The coverage is international and the abstracts are in more than 50 languages. There is both a keyword and a detailed subject index, as well as author, numerical patent, and patent concordance indexing. There are numerous aids, parts, and sections, including the better known *Chemical Titles* (1960 to date, biweekly) which indexes chemical research papers. A major difference between the online and printed version is that there are *no* abstracts available online. The lack of such service was corrected by *Biological Abstracts,* but to date this has not been corrected in *Chemical Abstracts*—many believe, for good reason, that this lack persists because it assures purchase of the printed set by libraries.

The system is so complicated and in so many different parts that a good case can be made for a search only by a subject expert or by a

---

[88]The same system generates a number of other data bases, including CRIS (Current Research Information System), an abstracting service which follows current research projects. For a discussion of the base see Jeffrey R. Peters, "Agricola," *Database,* March 1981, pp. 13–27.

[89]David E. Wood et al., "CAB Abstracts on Dialog," *Database,* December 1978, pp. 68–79.

[90]There are major differences, but the file may include *CA Condensates;* CASIA (Chemical Abstracts Subject Index Alert); *CA Patent Concordance;* CIN (Chemical Industry Notes); and CHEMLINE (Chemical Dictionary on Line).

librarian who is thoroughly familiar with the literature of chemistry and related areas.[91]

Another giant in the science field is INSPEC (International Information Services for the Physics and Engineering Communities). This online version corresponds to the printed version of *Physics Abstracts, Electrical and Electronic Abstracts,* and *Computer and Control Abstracts,* usually described as *Science Abstracts A, B,* and *C.* Updated monthly, this is an index to over 2000 journals. The file now has well over 2 million citations and is available online from 1969 to date.

SUGGESTED READINGS

Barlow, D.H., "Some Conditions for Successful Commercial Information Operations," *Aslib Proceedings,* January 1980, pp. 34–40. The view of a publisher as to whether or not to develop a data base, this is of value to librarians because it shows the "host of difficult and interrelated decisions," including probable costs and markets, of developing a data base for information use.

Herlach, Gertrude, "Can Retrieval of Information from Citation Indexes Be Simplified?" *Journal of the American Society for Information Science,* November 1978, pp. 308–310. A critical discussion of citation indexing which relies upon statistical analyses. Primarily for someone quite familiar with the process. For a detailed study of the system by the man who brought it to its present state, see Eugene Garfield, *Citation Indexing.* New York: Wiley, 1979. A good overview, although the author tends to sidestep most of the criticism of the system.

Hoffman, Herbert H., and Alice B. Grisby, "Online Access to the Embedded Literature of 'Literature.' " *Database,* March 1981, pp. 55–63. The authors discuss *MLA Bibliography* and *Magazine Index* and demonstrate, through test searches, how each may be used for ready-reference work. They admit online searching for literary texts and critiques is more difficult than finding an author's single work, and make several recommendations to improve data-base availability.

Keller, Michael, and Carol Lawrence, "Music Literature Indexes in Review," *Notes,* March 1980. A thoroughly detailed and easy to follow discussion of *RILM* and *Arts and Humanities Citation Index* online, as well as three other printed music indexes and reference sources. The discussion of data bases is applicable for other fields.

Lancaster, F. W., "The Evaluation of Machine Readable Data Bases and Information Services Derived from These Data Bases," in F. W. Lancaster and C. W. Cleverdon, *Evaluation and Scientific Management of Libraries and Information Centers.* Leyden: Noordhoff, 1977, pp. 73–100. Although somewhat dated, this is useful for its clear explanation of primary points of evaluation.

Usdane, Bernice S., "U.S. Government Publications: Their Value, Online Accessibility . . . ," *Online Review,* no. 2, 1980, pp. 143–151. A clear description of the basic online data bases which are useful in most libraries.

---

[91]David M. Krentz, "On-Line Searching–Specialist Required," *Journal of Chemical Information and Computer Sciences,* February 1978, pp. 4–8.

CHAPTER EIGHT

Networks and Interlibrary Loan

T HE TERM "NETWORK" is used in many different ways, but essentially it refers to "any kind of formal cooperative arrangement where people agree to exchange information or resources."[1] There are two basic forms of library networks. One, the earliest, is built upon agreements to allow free access to information via interlibrary loan, joint acquisition policies (to avoid, for example, duplication of expensive materials), and cooperative bibliographic control (from union lists to informal meetings of staff about cataloging to reference problems). The other is built upon the modern electronic systems which link libraries of various types and sizes for rapid access to resources; this form of network is broader in scope and geographical area than the first. This chapter discusses, first, networks that exist within a nationwide system: bibliographic utilities; regional, state, and local networks; and the national library network. Next, it examines interlibrary loan. Finally, the chapter examines international networks.

Nothing so revolutionized the working concept of networks as the computer. Online processing now makes it possible to have centralized information facilities serving distant, decentralized librar-

---

[1]Martha Williams, "Networks for On-Line Data Base Access," *Journal of the American Society for Information Science,* September 1977, p. 247. A good overview of networks is provided in the May 1980 issue of *American Libraries,* pp. 264–279.

ies. Networking online, that is, connecting one library with another through use of electronics, is a fairly new development. For the most part it supersedes, although it does not replace, the older definition of a network as a limited cooperative procedure between libraries, normally within a fairly well-defined area or region, a consortia.

In tracing the history of online networking, one might begin in the mid-1960s with such projects as shared cataloging between the Columbia, Harvard, and Yale medical libraries. Then in April 1968 came the creation of the weekly MARC (machine-readable cataloging) tape service at the Library of Congress. In 1971 OCLC went online, followed by BALLOTS (later RLIN) in 1972, and the Washington Library Network in 1975. Emphasis during these years was on obtaining libraries to join the networks.

By the late 1970s the major online networks, assured of library support, began to develop new services and modify older ones. For example, in less than a year the OCLC interlibrary loan subsystem (which began in early 1979) was in operation and an acquisitions subsystem was planned for the early 1980s. In reviewing the history of networks, one expert concludes:

> *Online library networking now seems to be emerging as a specialty in its own right, which requires knowledge of, and draws from, library and information science, computing, telecommunications, information technology, economics, marketing business, public service administration, and the behavioral sciences. Thre are examples of this formalization. One example is the formal corporate establishment of the Council for Computerized Library Networks (CCLN). It is a professional society that draws together networks, libraries that participate in networks, suppliers of components of network services (including data bases), and the educational arm of library and information science. Its program includes a publication and newsletter series, clearinghouse services, annual colloquia and regular program meetings, and other member services.[2]*

Other terms used to indicate cooperation and sharing: (1) "Cooperative" usually refers to a group of libraries which offer common service to members bound together by informal or formal ccontracts. (2) "Consortium" is generally used to designate a formal agreement of two or more libraries for joint activities to improve

[2]Glyn Evans, "On-Line Networking: A Bibliographic Essay," *Bulletin of the American Society for Information Science,* June 1979, p. 12. This, as the title suggests, concludes with a useful bibliography, particularly for those interested in the past and future development of networking. Networks have developed new positions, too. See Nancy Melin's "Professional Without Portfolio: The Network Librarian," *Wilson Library Bulletin,* January 1980, pp. 308–310.

service. It is a favored word among academic libraries where the term "cooperative" seems to be out of fashion. The difference between the two terms is negligible. "Network" is similar to both, but suggests more complexity.

TYPES OF NETWORKS

There are four basic types of networks. Most fit losely into a nationwide system, although there is yet to be realized a fully functional national network which connects the various types.

(1) *Data-base vendors.* The first type of network is the search-service network which provides data bases for bibliographic and numerical searches. Such networks are often described as "data base vendors" or "information retrieval facilities." They are primarily commercial, operated by such companies as Lockheed, SDC, and BRS, and are discussed in Chapter 5.

(2) *Bibliographic utilities.* The second type is the bibliographic utility, often referred to as a "customized service network," or "library processing facility." Nonprofit organizations supply libraries with a variety of services, from remote cataloging access to circulation control and interlibrary loan. The records are held by a central organization, which makes them available to individual libraries or sublets the records to regional and state libraries. There are three large operations of this type today: OCLC,[3] by far the most ambitious in terms of number of members: RLIN (Research Libraries Information Network); and the Washington Library Network (WLN). In Canada the University of Toronto Library Automated Systems (UTLAS) has close to 100 Canadian libraries as customers.

(3) *National library network.* While the elements are in place for such a network (see pp. 228–236 in this chapter), none now exists as such.

(4) *Regional, state, and local networks.* The fourth basic type of network is the regional system, sometimes called a "user network," "broker network," "library service center," or "affiliated network." The regional network channels data from the other three types of networks to the individual libraries. There are about 20 or so such systems, but among the larger are NELINET (New England Library Information Network), SOLINET (Southeastern Library Network), and MIDLNET (Midwest Regional Library Network).

[3]The acronym originally meant Ohio College Library Center, but today has no meaning and is simply OCLC, period.

There are variations of the four basic types of networks, variations such as the Library of Congress and the National Library of Medicine and their services, which are fed into the networks, and international systems such as the British Library Lending Division and EURONET (European Online Information Network). At the other extreme are the state and local networks which may consist of no more than two or three libraries working together for interlibrary loans and/or acquisition of materials.

No matter the size of the networks, as they exist today they offer essentially either one of two basic services. The first service allows the librarian to search for citations in machine-readable indexing and abstracting files. Here we have Lockheed, BRS, and SDC acting as vendors to publishers who produce the indexes and abstracts.

The second service has little or nothing to do with indexes or abstracts. Here the network operates as the familiar bibliographical aid for the librarian searching for a particular book, serial, even film or recording. (However, most emphasis today is on books and serials.) These services are operated by nonprofit organizations at the national level and channeled by the third type of network at the local, regional, or state levels.

These services today are mutually exclusive. Both systems are entirely separate. Different keyboards, different signals, different systems are operational in each one. The dream, which is bound to come true, is that the librarian should be able to sit at one terminal and search all types of networks. Here, for example, one might look for articles on modern painters or the common cold and be able to call up not only citations to articles, but specific books, individual periodicals, government documents, films, etc. Furthermore, at the same terminal the librarian should be able to ascertain if the item is in the library, and if not, where it may be obtained. Ideally, too, sample pages of the item could be examined.

Still in the developmental stage, networks continue to change almost every day, both in organization and in membership, but essentially they link the library with the outside world, or as one observer puts it:

> With the single exception of awkward and often slow and limited resources available through interlibrary loan, users have been restricted to local collections with their weaknesses and lacunae. A user might have to do without even a fundamental text in an area of interest or might find that an exhaustive study of an area is impossible in his local library. Patrons who are situated near the largest academic, public, or sometimes special libraries have had the best chance of locating materials. . . . Now we may have entered an era when the accident of location may be less important in the equation of access to information. Advancing tech-

nology may offer the tools through which a solution is realized.
Computers coupled with new forms of communication have given library
users access to the materials and indexes of remote collections. . . .[4]

Today, the question for most librarians is no longer "Should we
join a network?" but "Which network(s) should we join?" In order to
determine the answer to that, Kent suggests several questions:

What criteria should be used in deciding?

How are competing networks (e.g., OCLC vs. RLIN, DIALOG
vs. Orbit) to be evaluated?

Which functions of a network should be used?

What is the likelihood of system failure?

What quality-control standards does the network enforce?

What is the cost?

The answers to such questions are not easy to come by, and
many library administrators are understandably confused by the
mélange of seemingly impenetrable choices.[5]

BIBLIOGRAPHIC UTILITIES

There are three major bibliographic utilities now operating in the
United States. The first, and oldest, is OCLC, located at Columbus,
Ohio. The second is RLIN, which is a network for research libraries
and is based in California. The third is the Washington Library
Network (WLN). Another bibliographic utility, UTLAS, operates in
Canada.

The bibliographic utility networks offer a variety of services,
although they tend to provide a basic six:

1. Shared cataloging, which allows the members to catalog most
   of their ongoing collection at a terminal. This has made it
   possible for from 80 to 98 percent of all cataloging to be
   performed through the network and its cataloging data
   bases.[6]

2. An online union catalog, made possible by the shared catalog-

[4]Charles H. Stevens, "Emerging Network Services," *Bulletin of the American Society for Information Science,* June 1979, p 26.

[5]Allen Kent, "The On-Line Revolution . . . ," *American Libraries,* June 1979, p. 341.

[6]Catalog service is not limited to networks. Several private firms sell such services. Baker & Taylor, for example, offers what they call LIBRIS, which is a data base providing 2 million titles in MARC II format and is supported by a computer-output microfilm catalog. The firm also has online acquisitions.

ing, and which, in itself, makes it possible to initiate interlibrary loans at the terminal.

3. Serials control is now part of many systems.

4. Acquisitions and record keeping of holdings is possible.

5. Circulation control and remote catalog access is often provided.

6. Reference searches are made possible by seeking material by author, title, and a variety of other entry points, including classification numbers and, in some systems, subjects.

Thus, the systems provide individual libraries with individual means for such things as circulation control, serials control, acquisitions, and the library's own catalog online.[7] In a study of public and community college libraries in Southern California it was found that all those who were members of a network (in this case OCLC) used most of the potential services to the limit.

Given access to millions of records, the services are invaluable to reference librarians who are hunting for an elusive book, serial, or other type of material. For example, one may type in an abbreviated author and title and find necessary bibliographic data from a publisher's name to date of publication.

OCLC With close to 2000 members and over 2600 terminals in operation, OCLC is the best known and the most heavily used of the major bibliographic utility networks. By the early 1980s the member libraries were cataloging some 30,000 new items each week, for which OCLC produces about 1.4 million catalog cards. Within the system there are over 5.6 million separate entries with some 40 million locations, or about eight locations for each entry. The size of the file is important because the larger the number of entries, the more likely a member library is to find the necessary bibliographic information for interlibrary loan, reference, or cataloging.

To catalog, the searcher looks for a Library of Congress record on the MARC tape (see pp. 219–220 of this chapter for a discussion of MARC) or a shared cataloging record from another library. If a record exists, in either form, it appears on the operator's CRT screen. Once an item is located the operator may edit the existing catalog

---

[7]Actually, most of the networks do not produce printed or computer-output microfilm (a favored form) individual library catalogs. But they do so indirectly in that the tapes received from libraries are processed by a commercial firm. Also, some data-base vendors are offering individual library catalogs.

information to comply with local cataloging requirements. The record thus produced by the modification is given a new identity by the searcher who adds the library symbol to the OCLC records. Other librarians, then, may be able to trace the work through the OCLC system for interlibrary loan or other purposes.

The master entry is not altered, but at the same time the local operator may order catalog cards. Cataloging records in MARC format are also available on magnetic tape for other systems or libraries with their own computers. At the same time OCLC is exploring the possibility of making the records available as computer-output microfilm.

> All libraries employed the terminals for the primary purpose of cataloging their new acquisitions, and to a lesser degree for interlibrary loan transactions and for pre-order searching. All of the OCLC libraries received pre-sorted and alphabetized printed cataloging cards which were ready for interfiling into the card catalogs. All of these libraries were pleased with the cataloging results of their data base. . . . All OCLC members praised the rapid delivery rates of their printed catalog cards. All of the libraries said that they were receiving the cards within seven to ten days. All OCLC members received a complete set of cards prepared to local content and format specifications. All cards are pre-sorted and alphabetized by machine logic and are ready to be interfiled.[8]

OCLC has become a valued link in the fight to control serials; it now provides these records, as well as those for monographs. Serials may be searched in the same way as a book, and the system improves with each year.[9]

CONSER (CONservation of SERials)[10] is a part of OCLC. An automated serials data base, CONSER makes it possible for the librarian to find information on more than 200,000 titles via the computer keyboard. Bibliographic records are authenticated by the Library of Congress, the National Library of Canada, and other cooperating libraries, and information is constantly being fed into the system by various libraries. While complicated in organization and planning, the end result is simple enough. When the librarian wants to know basic information about a periodical, the query is typed on

[8]Klaus Musmann, "The Southern California Experience with OCLC and BALLOTS," *California Librarian,* April 1978, p. 33, p. 35. See too, C. M. Bell, "The Applicability of OCLC and Inforonics in Special Libraries," *Special Libraries,* September 1980, pp. 398–404.

[9]This has some use for reference work. See too, Tom D. Kilton, "OCLC and the Pre-Order Verification of New Serials," *The Serials Librarian,* Fall 1979, pp. 61–64.

[10]Monica Pittman, "Conversion of Serials Project," *Newspaper and Gazette Reporter,* April 1978, p. 8+. This is a clear explanation of the project.

the terminal, the computer searches the file, and the answer(s) are either typed out or shown on a television screen. The system has numerous other possible uses, from speeding interlibrary loan requests to cooperative purchase of periodicals. These uses are now being refined.[11]

RLIN   RLIN was organized in the early 1970s at Stanford University. Originally called BALLOTS, it differs from OCLC in several major respects. The first is the composition of its membership. RLIN was formed to meet the unique needs of large research libraries, and its mission is to assist faculty, scholars, and students, not necessarily the public at large. The Research Libraries Group (RLG) is composed of university centers, major law libraries, and several large art institutes from the membership of RLIN. The members and affiliates read like a Who's Who of libraries and include, among others: the New York Public Library; the libraries of the University of Michigan, the University of Pennsylvania, Princeton, Yale, Columbia, Stanford, and Dartmouth; and affiliates such as the Metropolitan Museum of Art, the Boston Museum of Fine Art, and New York University. There are a total of about 70 members. In an effort to widen support, the group may induct other member types in the 1980s, but this remains speculative.

The four primary programs of RLG are (1) cooperative collection development; (2) shared access to collections; (3) preservation of research materials; and (4) creation and operation of sophisticated bibliographic tools.[12]

Looking to the future, RLIN plans to develop alternative catalog forms, such as computer-output microfilm and book catalogs; an acquisitions system which will facilitate better records as well as shared collection development; and more effective public access. The latter is of particular interest to reference librarians. There will be a "low-cost, synchronous-compatible printer and/or video display terminal for use by reference staff and library patrons, to be used with a simplified user query system to access records in the data base.[13]

A serious criticism of RLIN is that it is limited to a small group

---

[11]For a study of how CONSER is used in practical reference work see Kilton, *op. cit.*, and Michael Roughton, "OCLC Serials Records . . . ," *The Journal of Academic Librarianship,* January 1980, pp. 316–321. See too, Carol C. Davis, "OCLC's Role in the CONSER Project," *Serials Review,* October/December 1980, pp. 75–77.

[12]Jan Thomson and Jennifer Hartzell, "RLG's Research Libraries Information Network: Bibliographic and Information Services," *Online Review,* no. 3, 1979, p. 281. See too, David McDonald et al., "The Research Libraries Information Network . . .," *Reference Services Review,* January/March 1981, pp. 33–37.

[13]Thomson and Hartzell, p. 294.

of libraries and their users. This is perpetuating, or so the critics argue, an elitist situation beneficial only to the few fortunate enough to have some relationship with the members' research libraries. Financial limitations seem to make it even less desirable to concentrate funds in an organization with limited users.

> *RLG is building an image as a prestigious research library club taking responsibility for national network services to all research libraries, and therein lies some of its appeal. But some academic libraries have remained fiercely loyal to OCLC, claiming it to be a proven system, improving every day, and far less expensive than its unproven competitor. But the exodus of OCLC members to RLG raised fears that OCLC could lose major sources of shared cataloging, and with its volume of business reduced, would be forced to hike its prices.*[14]

WLN   WLN is much smaller, having about 40 members, and less ambitious than either OCLC or RLIN, yet it is likely to play an important part in the national network scheme because it has a rather sophisticated system in operation—a system which can be used by other networks, local regional organizations, and, of course, individual libraries. It has service alliances with RLIN, for example, and is striking out for other partnerships.

Participants in the WLN system include libraries in Washington, Alaska, Idaho, Oregon, and parts of British Columbia. WLN offers much the same basic services as the other major bibliographic utilities; for example, it has five subsystems: bibliographic, acquisitions, circulation, detailed holdings, and serials control. The data base, as of early 1980, contains about 1.4 million bibliographic records and about 1.3 million holding locations.

WLN was among the first of the networks to develop an online authority file, which now contains over 1.8 million records. The file holds "the authorized forms of author headings (including uniform titles), author/title series and title series (traced form only) headings, and subject headings used in bibliographic records, and also cross references and notes."[15] This is particularly useful and necessary to standardize the records which are fed into the system by members.

UTLAS   UTLAS (the University of Toronto Library Automation Systems) focuses on Canada, but offers services to other countries. Drawing upon a data base with close to 8 million records,

---

[14]Noel Savage, "News Report, 1979," *Library Journal*, January 15, 1980, p. 173.

[15]Richard Woods, "The Reality and the Dream for WLN Reference Librarians," *RQ*, Fall 1979, p. 33.

customers enjoy the usual services, from offline production of catalog cards to checking and verification. There is a much-praised authority file and an interlibrary loan program.

Looking abroad for customers, the system offers a "minicomputer package that allows for online inventory controls, including searching and circulation."[16] There is reason to believe that in the years to come UTLAS will be a strong competitor for library attention not only in America but in other countries as well.

Differences

The bibliographic utilities do differ in particulars, some of which are noted throughout the chapter. An overall notion of the differences can be illustrated by a comparison of OCLC and WLN. As of early 1980, OCLC had a larger number of records, a greater selection of catalog-card printout options, and a logical cost effectiveness. On the other hand, WLN had superior data-base records, which may be searched in a greater number of ways, i.e., much more of each record is actually indexed and made searchable; in serial searching the availability of keywords in titles and in corporate authors is "most useful"; and for reference purposes "WLN's subject search and keyword approach was judged quite attractive and well used."[17]

The primary competition, however, is between the two major utilities, OCLC and RLIN. The latter claims to offer better reference service potential. As of 1980 this was true, because RLIN "provides access to member holdings through title and author entry keywords as well as subject access features."[18] The subject approach is by far the most useful for reference librarians and allows a much wider use of the files. OCLC, however, plans a subject capability in the early 1980s.

Another advantage of the RLIN system is that it provides a considerable amount of nonbook cataloging information, the type of

[16]UTLAS, *American Libraries,* May 1980, p. 277.

[17]*Library Journal,* October 15, 1979, p. 2148. By far the best comparative guide, updated from time to time, is the one edited by Susan Martin in which OCLC, WLN and RLIN are compared side-by-side, i.e., in parallel columns. See *Online Resources Sharing II* (California Library Authority for Systems and Services, January, 1979). For a practical explanation of what it means to change from one system to another, and differences in the systems see: Susan Kallenbach and Susan Jacobson, "Staff Response to Changing Systems: From Manual to OCLC to RLIN" *Journal of Academic Librarianship,* November 1980, pp. 264–267.

[18]"OCLC & RLIN Backers Cross Swords," *Library Journal,* November 15, 1979, p. 2389. Obviously conditions change, and this quote may no longer be applicable. What is applicable, however, is the fact that the two networks do compete with each other. See Susan Martin, "OCLC and RLG: Living Together," *American Libraries,* May 1980, pp. 270–271; plus articles on RLIN, OCLC, WLN and UTLAS in following pages.

data most needed, in fact, by large research or specialized libraries. In addition to films, maps, and music via MARC tapes, the system holds these same forms from other libraries and eventually plans to include manuscript holdings. The search for these terms is facilitated by an even greater variety of approaches than available for book searches. Approaches can be made via a Superintendent of Documents number, the International Standard Serial Number, title phrases, and subject words and phrases. Catalog cards, as in the book records, can be manipulated online and then produced as required.

The various bibliographic networks provide varying degrees of success for the librarian seeking a particular record. Experiments continue, and systems will be modified over time, but in a general way MARC records tend to provide the greatest number of records— from 50 to 65 percent or more. Beyond the MARC records, which are available in the various networks, OCLC "produced by far the highest number of hits." And where a library is testing in the same state or region as the network, the hit rate is close to that of OCLC. Failure is usually no more than 3 to 6 percent, thus requiring original cataloging. However, there are so many variables, including the size and the needs of the library, that such success-ratio tests can only be approximate. "Other factors," too, "must be evaluated . . . quality of the non-MARC records; opportunity for, and cost of, joining the networks; other features available (e.g., acquisition systems, interlibrary loan capability).[19]

Bibliographic utilities and data bases[20]

Use   While originally tailored for catalogers, the bibliographic utilities are of increasing value to reference librarians, most particularly when someone wants information on a book or an author, or, with some networks, on a subject. For example, one may search for all the work published since, say, 1972 by poet John Ashbery or novelist John LeCarré. In effect, one would use the terminal to verify data (from exact titles and dates of publication to the spelling of the author's first name), to compile a bibliography of works by that writer

[19]Joan Tracy and Barbara Remmerde, "Availability of Machine-Readable Cataloging," *Library Research,* no. 1, 1979, p. 281. Here the sample was of OCLC, RLIN, BNA (Blackwell North America), and WLN. In another study at Illinois it was found that "55 percent of records for current Western European language books used by Illinois came from the Library of Congress, the remaining 45 percent from 205 other institutions." *American Libraries,* January 1980, p. 50.

[20]Capacities differ from bibliographic utility to utility or other type of network, and what is described here may vary from one situation to the next. Eventually, however, all utilities and related networks should provide the described reference capacities.

(at least after about 1970), etc. Where subject access is granted, one may run a search for almost anything, just as one would look in the local catalog or other bibliographic aid. All of this, of course, has the advantage of being done at a terminal, rather than by dashing about the library looking for individual reference works, and, in the end, having a printout of the results.

More importantly, the search may be done both in the traditional fashion—author, title, subject—and by techniques available only via a machine-readable record. One may use Boolean operators to narrow or broaden the search. For example, "after a list is obtained of titles in the data base authored by Isaac Asimov, that list can be combined with a search for all titles that contain the keyword Mars to result in a list of all titles authored by Isaac Asimov that contain the keyword Mars in the title."[21] Furthermore, in the Washington Library Network (WLN) one may search only the local library catalog, the network catalog (except those on Library of Congress MARC records), or the whole bibliographic data base.

Preparation of bibliographies, by author or by subject, tends to dominate the reference use of the networks. While often the request is for no more than monographs by this or that writer, it is just as likely to be a subject inquiry. Here the searcher employs the normal searching techniques, from truncation to Boolean logic to call numbers. For example:

> In search for information on equipment leasing, we combined equipment and leasing (in its truncated form to also pick up lease and leases) in the title field, then further combined it using Boolean "OR" logic with the LC subject heading "Industrial equipment leases," again truncated to give the highest number of responses. . . . Another form of subject searching is to use the call number rather than the subject heading. If the topic has a fairly definite place in a cataloging scheme, it may make more sense to search under the call number [which . . . may serve to reduce some of the problems inherent in subject headings using a controlled vocabulary. It makes no sense, however, if the call number and subject are likely to coincide. Every book, for example, classified under HD2745 also had the subject heading of Directors of corporations. The subject search alone turned out to be more efficient. A call number search is in order when a searcher feels the need to browse in the stacks of a large research library or to riffle through their shelf list.[22]

[21]Woods, op. cit., p. 35.

[22]Mary P. Ojala, "Using BALLOTS (RLIN) as a Reference Tool," *Online,* October 1978, pp. 13–14.

When is a search by a terminal more appropriate than a manual search? This depends on many variables, but generally both are used. For example, "Our pattern is to first check our own catalog, then look in the subject volumes of *Books in Print,* and then turn to [RLIN]."[23] This method is particularly good for garbled requests.

> *Library users coming in with garbled citations for books they want us to order have long been the bane of our existence. Someone has a reasonable sounding title and author, only we can't find it in* Books in Print. *By searching on the most distinctive word in the title, we can often discover that the title given us is actually a subtitle and that the spelling of the author's name is mangled beyond all recognition. Because RLIN searches on every word in the title, as well as added entries, series added entries and the title portion of author-title added entries, user-supplied information can be quite spotty and not ruin a search's results.*[24]

The success of this type of search depends upon a large record store, and by far the best known, most widely used store—particularly by the bibliographic utilities—is MARC.

MARC and Other Bibliographic Records   MARC (Machine Readable Cataloging) is distributed by the Library of Congress. Magnetic tapes are sent out each week, not only to individual libraries, but to local and national systems such as OCLC. Corresponding to the *National Union Catalog,* the data base covers materials (including films, 1972; maps, 1973; and serials, 1973) from 1968 to the present.

While originally the access points were limited, and thus MARC tapes for reference service were limited, lately most of the networks offer, or are in the process of offering, subject and numerous other access points.[25] This is particularly important as the online data base can be a major method of finally conquering the faults of the typical catalog. Here Swanson summarizes the possibilities:

---

[23]Ibid., p. 14.

[24]*Ibid.*

[25]In March 1980, *Database* (p. 73) reported: "BRS is conducting pilot projects with two academic libraries to test the feasibility of using online searching techniques to access cataloging records. Online catalogs have been developed for the Rochester Institute of Technology and Dartmouth College, including titles previously cataloged by the libraries via Blackwell/North America and OCLC respectively. When searching catalogs on the BRS system, many different access points are available because of the flexible free text subject approach. Searchable elements include title words, main entry, subject headings, local call number, LC card and call numbers, and language codes and publication dates. The goal of both projects is to develop a user interface which will enable the patron to interact directly with the online catalog."

The importance of non-traditional access points is underscored by the essential role that guesswork often plays in the process of searching for recorded information. . . . One may assume that a library should respond helpfully to a user's request even—or perhaps especially—when the request is fragmentary or inaccurate. . . . Conventional library card catalogs provide only a limited number of entry points (essentially author, exact title, and a few subject headings) to each catalog record. . . . In principle any element of a machine readable catalog record can serve as a point of access for purposes of retrieval.[26]

LIBCON (Library of Congress) is primarily another version of the MARC records online, but with some additional access points. It is updated weekly and has been operational since 1968. Distributed by 3-M Library Systems, it includes most of the material found via the MARC records. SDC makes it available online (for $2 a minute) and the user can search title, subject headings, added entries, series notes, etc.[27]

Books in Print online includes 640,000 books from about 7000 publishers. As one may use a free-text search, the librarian can identify titles, even when given only one or two correct words or phrases. It may be searched, too, by author, publisher, and LC or Dewey call number. Updated monthly, it has the advantage of being current, particularly in terms of prices, out-of-print titles, verification, etc.—the type of information needed for ordering. Also, it has more information on the bindings and publishing schedules—from "not yet published" to "publication cancelled"—than found in the printed *Books in Print.*

Another version of this is *Books Information.* Here the service is provided by a book jobber. One may sit at the terminal and place an order directly with Brodart. The order is modified by a system which indicates what is available in the company's inventory and what may have to be ordered. Similar systems are offered by other dealers such as Baker and Taylor.

R. R. Bowker, which offers *Books in Print* online via BRS, also has the same service for *Ulrich's International Periodicals Directory* and *Forthcoming Books.* This is not tied to an inventory and cannot be used directly for purchase, but it does provide an online system with pertinent up-to-date bibliographic information.

In the early 1980s, RLIN and other networks began, or were

[26]Don Swanson, "MARC . . . ," *Journal of Education for Librarianship,* Fall 1979, p. 93.

[27]Online catalogs are a major breakthrough of the 1980s and there is much written about them. An excellent summary of an actual project is Robert M. Hayes, "On-Line Microfiche Catalogs," *Journal of Micrographics,* March/April 1980, pp. 15–33, 58–63.

experimenting with, automated acquisitions systems in cooperation with Blackwell North American, R.R. Bowker, and Brodart, to name three private concerns involved with the systems. The network plays the role of the middleperson, allowing the library to order the books by computer. Filling the order is left to the vendor of the library's choice.

Eventually networks will allow libraries to perform several acquisitions functions including the ability to share on-order information. The latter ability will allow one library to have immediate knowledge of the collection development decisions of another library in a comparable area, by an author, or in a language. Given this information it will be easier for a librarian to deterine whether to buy X title or to build extensively in Y area, particularly when a neighboring library also has the source.

A quicker, more efficient library loan system supports the joint acquisition decisions. Not only will the librarian in one institution be able to discover the specific buying patterns of another, but he or she will also be able to ascertain whether a library close by has the desired item and, if available, can order that item for the user via the network. This kind of backup for reference service will make the service much more current and viable than is possible with the present practice where it is necessary to buy as much as possible because, while X document may be available on interlibrary loan, one cannot be sure that: (a) it really was purchased by a neighboring library, or if purchased (b) it will be readily available for interlibrary loan.

Thanks to relatively easy commands, the bibliographic utility terminal may become readily available to the public. Anyone looking for a particular book or serial or trying to verify a title might use the terminal. Public access is already a success. "Reports from (Illinois) libraries having such terminals indicate acceptance on the part of the library patron for their use. Some libraries have even reported long lines of patrons awaiting their use."[28]

A major result of national, regional, and local bibliographical networks is the serious question concerning the future of professional librarians in technical services. Some have even called for the abandonment of "the sweatshop cataloging department," pointing out that:

> *Automation has already reached the point at which one can conceive of a central automated processing system for the ordering, receipt, rapid cataloging, and routing of library materials with little or no professional*

[28]"OCLC Services . . . ," *Illinois Libraries*, September 1979, p. 574.

involvement. Staffed by nonprofessionals . . . the centralized processing unit will free professional librarians (for specialized work) . . . around services or subjects or language or combinations of the three.[29]

Needless to say, catalogers are not very likely to accept this summation.

REGIONAL, STATE, AND LOCAL NETWORKS[30]

The regional system of networks includes those networks, such as SOLINET (Southeastern Library Information Network), NELINET (New England Library Information Network),[31] and MIDLNET (Midwest Regional Library Network), comprising individual libraries in a given region; or it includes networks such as WILCO (Western Interstate Library Cooperative), AMIGOS (a Texan operation with more than 120 members), CLASS (California Library Authority for Systems and Services), and numerous others comprising state or regional libraries organized as a multistate system.

Whatever the concept of organization, the general activities of a regional system include: "identification of products needed by the region, the state, and the local library; establishment of a clearinghouse for library automation and network activities; identification of political issues involved in regionwide cooperation; the pinpointing of funding sources; the development of a regional data base to be loaded on regional hardware; [and] development of system specifications for interfacing with other networks."[32]

Services of the regional networks vary, but in general they include: (1) arranging contracts with the major bibliographic utilities,

[29]Michael Gorman, "On Doing Away with Technical Services Departments," *American Libraries,* July/August 1979, p. 436. The author points out that "at least 80 percent of cataloging" can be done by clerks who learn how to tap OCLC. The writer sees the professional librarians free to do necessary original cataloging and "selection, collection development, reader advisory and reference services . . .and bibliographic instruction." Actually, the new systems necessitate revision of cataloging organization. For a clear article on this see Sally Braden et al., "Utilization of Personnel and Bibliographic Resources for Cataloging by OCLC Participating Libraries," *Library Resources & Technical Services,* Spring 1980, pp. 135–154.

[30]For a list of these, with the inevitable acronyms, see the *Bulletin of the American Society for Information Science,* June 1979, pp. 22–23.

[31]Rodger S. Harris, "Is Another National Network the Best Answer," *North Carolina Libraries,* Winter 1979, pp. 7–12. While a comparison of relationships of SOLINET with OCLC, this gives some insight into how a major regional network operates.

[32]*Library Journal,* October 15, 1979, p. 2150.

and in so doing, acting as director in negotiating terms between the utilities and the individual members of the regional network; (2) holding down the cost of services because of a large membership base; (3) providing for the training of librarians and consulting with libraries which wish to modify existing data-base services; (4) arranging new services for members developing those services at the local, regional, and national levels; (5) determining the authority control of records for the members and improving circulation and acquisitions data bases; and (6) helping members to change or even drop bibliographic brokers who serve the local system.

In working out a 1980 contract with OCLC, the local network (SOLINET) had enough strength to ensure better and more specific services from the larger network. As a result of SOLINET's mediation, "performance requirements now include deadlines for delivery of catalog cards, processing profiles and profile changes, and giving notices of times the system will not be operating. . . . SOLINET claims to have gained ground in its efforts to become more than an OCLC middleman, winning OCLC cooperation to help it develop the capability to provide new services for its own members."[33]

The local/regional network serves as an efficient method of concentrating skills in a central place. The centralized, specialized staff advises individual libraries on new technologies and the need for continual planning and development. As the salaries of such specialists increase, it becomes obvious that there is a need for a central service rather than a single specialist in each library. For example, "a library using OCLC supports about one-fifth of an OCLC staff member's time a year and obtains skills, such as electrical engineering, cost accounting, programming, computer operation, telecommunication planning, and systems analysis. Few libraries can acquire even some of these specialists on their local staffs."[34]

Another aspect of regional control is that new technology is making it possible for more libraries to have individual systems which can compete with the national networks. The so-called "stand-alone" systems can be interactive, one with the other, and these form the subnetworks which are the regional system.

Subnetworks are now becoming more common as the individual circulation or acquisitions systems can be connected to employ both large mainframe and minicomputers. For example, a library may have its own circulation file stored at a commercial vendor. Each day's local

[33]*Library Journal*, February 1, 1980, p. 340.
[34]Barbara Markuson, "Cooperation and Library Network Development," *College & Research Libraries*, March 1979, p. 128.

results are collected on a minicomputer and then transmitted to the central computer. "In most cases the cost to the library will be on a per-transaction basis, eliminating the need for the library to purchase costly stand-alone equipment."[35] Also, over a period of time the acquisitions and circulation records develop into additional access points for interlibrary loan.

Statewide networks

The earliest, and still the most successful, networks originated at the state level. Today some networks operate directly under the jurisdiction of the state library—Maryland, Michigan, and Washington are examples—but some have established separate ruling bodies outside the state library. In the latter situation are such organizations as CLASS (California Library Authority for Systems and Services).

The New York State Interlibrary Loan (NYSILL)[36] is one of the larger state systems. Designed to provide access to research-level materials, it is composed of over a dozen libraries. The New York State Library serves as the head of the network. Where materials or answers cannot be fielded from the state, the query is passed to one of a dozen referral libraries.

A common pattern of state reference/networking is connecting the smaller libraries in a state to a central library. When a person has a question the local librarian cannot answer, usually for lack of materials, the request is sent to the central network headquarters by teletype, telephone, and/or in writing.[37] Where the request is not clear the central service may talk with the librarian and/or the user. The

[35]Harold Epstein, "The Networking of Networks," *Bulletin of the American Society for Information Science,* June 1979, p. 15.

[36]Activities concerning NYSILL, as well as related networks such as the 3R's program and METRO, will be found in quarterly issues of *Bookmark,* the official publication of The New York State Library.

[37]Why not give the user direct access to the central system? This may happen in time, but for the moment one answer is that it should not be done because "giving patrons direct access allows no opportunity for the local library to know what user needs it is not able to meet; it prevents screening before referral to the network; and, of most importance, denies patrons the opportunity for direct service from the librarian." Andrea C. Honebrink, "Quality Control," *RQ,* Summer 1979, p. 362. Actually this is highly debatable, although it is a real situation and one which often threatens network plans. Institutional jealousy can wreck a scheme, particularly when individual librarians think the "system" is taking over their reference service. For comments on this situation, see *Library Journal,* August 1979, p. 1523. For the viewpoint from the school media center, see Dawn Heller, "So What About Networks," *School Library Journal,* December 1978, p. 38.

service may consist of no more than supplying needed materials via interlibrary loan, but today it is more likely to involve, as well, a computerized service giving access to data bases. Thus the individual may receive (a) simple citations, (b) citations and annotations, and (c) in rarer cases the documents and articles themselves.

Where data bases are employed and the person making the request is not present, it is necessary that the librarian who channels the inquiry to the central library be at least aware of what is involved in such a search. Almost every librarian today must have a basic knowledge of data-base searching and, of course, be skilled in the reference interview.[38]

Local cooperative networks

Sometimes in the confusion of computers, data bases, and managerial pronouncements it is forgotten that much of the daily cooperation between libraries, networking, if you will, is carried on at the grass-roots level. This situation will continue, even as sophisticated regional and national networks grow. Briefly, then, what does a local cooperative system do? More particularly, what type of cooperative activities is the reader likely to find, say, in a school media situation? Most of the activities, as in public and academic libraries, occur via informal arrangements, usually at the local levels, without any sharing on a regional or statewide basis. Examples include:

1. Informal meetings between public and school librarians to address mutual concerns.
2. Exchanging lists of collection holdings.
3. Joint compilation of community resources.
4. Joint material evaluation, selection, acquisitions, and processing programs.
5. Placement of public-library book catalogs in school libraries.
6. Reciprocal borrowing and lending of materials.
7. Providing the public library with curriculum guides and units of instruction.
8. In-service programs designed around topics of mutual interest and concern.

---

[38]For a discussion of the situation of the local librarian and the dialogue between that librarian, the patron, and the search analyst, see Susan Snow, "Computerized Cooperative Reference," *RQ,* Summer 1979, pp. 364–366.

9. Production facilities for materials.
10. Preparation of union lists or catalogs.
11. Access to specialized and computerized data bases.
12. Joint film cooperatives.

I am certain that, collectively, we could expand this list and provide numerous examples relating to each of the items. However, the success and continuation of these activities rests with the individual commitment of staff members who are willing and eager to engage in inter-institutional activities.[39]

An example of a local network is CAL (Central Association of Libraries), which includes various types of libraries in seven California counties. Several of those libraries, in turn, belong to other networks such as the California State University and Colleges, and interlibrary loans are often made between the two networks. The advantages of belonging to a local-regional intertype library network such as CAL are (1) better service to library users, (2) savings on purchase of materials through the holdings of other network libraries, and (3) easy search, including subject search, of holdings. "Other important benefits of cooperation flow from choice, including de-selection of serials, consolidation of holdings, cooperative selection, and improved bibliographic control. In summary, a library that is poor in library resources has, through regional cooperation, become rich in library services without overburdening its neighbors or the major research libraries.[40]

The Metropolitan Inter-Library Cooperative System (MILCS) is an example of an urban network, although a larger one than found in most situations. The size is understandable, as the base for the network is the New York Public Library.

The MILCS data base currently (i.e., 1979) contains approximately 300,000 NYPL Branch Libraries cataloging records showing 1.7 million locations for these items within the NYPL Branch Library System, and, as a result of LSCA supported projects, an additional one million locations within the Brooklyn, Queens Borough, and Westchester systems, bringing the total up to 2.7 million location identifiers. The on-line MILCS data base is augmented with LC MARC monograph records.[41]

[39]David R. Bender, "Networking & School Library Media Programs," *School Library Journal*, November 1979, p. 31. Some of Bender's points are deleted.

[40]R. D. Galloway, "Library Cooperation at the Grass Roots . . . ," *The Journal of Academic Librarianship*, January 1979, p. 433.

[41]S. M. Malinconico, "Machine-Readable Bibliographic Data Bases," *The Bookmark*, Summer 1979, p. 191.

Numerous versions of the local-to-central reference service will grow in the future, and service is likely to become more personalized as minicomputers become widely available. For exmple, the Fairfax County Public Library in Springfield, Virginia, proposes a central data-base search for smaller libraries, but with a difference.

> *Each library, large or small, would have a display terminal linked to a central searching facility where an expert searcher (or searchers) would respond to a call for service by interacting with the seeker of information —both by phone conversation and by displaying on the remote user's screen the search progress as it developed at the central facility. A library, however small, could get hooked up with a terminal for about $1,000. And although it (or the patron) would have to pay for service consumed, there would be a price range related to depth of service chosen. Fairfax sees two desirable outcomes: people would find the service so effective that it would help the local library to start making its own searches.[42]*

Bell Laboratories[43]

Networks are not limited to publicly supported libraries or government organizations, but are evident in the private industrial and commercial sectors. One example is the Bell Laboratories Library Network, which serves employees of American Telephone and Telegraph and Western Electric whose laboratories have over 17,000 employees involved with technical research. They form, in effect, a large technical university and rival MIT in personnel and activities, although in a limited fashion. At any rate, the analogy explains the need for a sophisticated library system. In this case 20 libraries scattered throughout the United States are focused in the main library at Murray Hill, New Jersey.

Acquisitions, current-awareness services, translation services, technical report searching—these and many other activities are carried on in the central library. Most importantly, the library provides all literature searching services, employing both machine-readable records and printed works, and compilation of bibliographies as needed. Needless to say, the various libraries are connected by telephone and other telecommunication systems. Data bases, as, for example, MERCURY, which is a method of disseminating data from technical reports and seminars, are generated from the main library.

---

[42]*Library Journal,* August 1979, p. 1523.

[43]There are numerous articles on what has come to be a model of its kind; e.g., see articles by D. T. Hawkins, Eileen English, and Robert Kennedy, who frequently discuss some aspect of the Bell system in *Special Libraries* and elsewhere.

Then, too, the system has access to major national and international data bases, the use of which increased some 700 percent from 1975 to 1977 and continues to grow.

NATIONAL LIBRARY NETWORK

The next step is a national library network, or the networking of networks. This will mean that the librarian will be able to use the same terminal to search for bibliographic data, index and abstract citations, and for cataloging information. In effect a national network will combine the data-base vendor, the bibliographic utilities, and the regional, state, and local networks. This is the plan for the 1980s. The combination will have numerous advantages, not the least of which is lower cost. Beyond that:

> The greatest unmet need in library networking is the creation of implemented network standards for network message traffic. Successful implementation of the library network line and message protocols will allow any network to communicate with any other network. One of the major goals of the national network is to provide the capabilities for any terminal to access any network host or data base through the local terminal connection, request any available service, and receive the results on the local terminal and in the local file. Some of the preliminary design work to develop the protocols has been completed through committees of network developers, coordinated by the Library of Congress. What remains is to complete the detailed design and to implement the network protocols on various network hosts, including cataloging, circulation, ILL, and any other type of network vendor that wishes to offer on-line services to U.S. libraries.[44]

Lacking a national system, there is the possibility of massive duplication of effort, but also the possibiliy of healthy competition. It depends upon one's viewpoint.

Some data-base vendors now offer online cataloging, as well as employing those same catalog records for reference work. This seems repetitive of OCLC, RLIN, and WLN, but there are modifications. For example, BRS offers users online individual library catalogs, a service available, in different form, for RLIN members. The BRS system allows the library to use the sophisticated BRS program to

---

[44]Epstein, op. cit., p. 15. A study released early in 1981 urged the development of linkage between the various bibliographic utilities. See "Bibliographic Utilities Urged to Link," *Library Journal*, February 1, 1981, p. 290.

retrieve information in its own catalog. This means that once the library catalog is in machine-readable form, the user at a library terminal may (1) search the catalog by subject, author, and title, and, in addition, search for terms used not only by the assigned subject heading but in the title or notes, (2) search by manipulation of two or more units (such as subject and publication date) to produce a select group of citations; (3) search by other fields such as call number, publisher's name, location, and publication date; and (4) if a printer is available, print out the citations rapidly.

National network elements

There are at least three elements which most people agree should exist in a national or international network: (1) A periodicals/serials center with a large collection from which specific periodicals or, more likely, copies of specific articles are available for loan. (2) A collection of books and related materials available for loan in the same fashion. (3) A centralized collection of other information materials—films, recordings, and whatever may be of value for informational purposes.

These central resource capacities do exist, at least in part, through such elements as the National Union Catalog, OCLC, and the British Library Lending division. However, there is no single place, at least at this writing, which provides all such resources.

Why isn't there a national network, and why is it unlikely to come about in the next few years? Answers vary, although a nice summary is provided by Joseph Matthews, a consultant in the field:

> [None of the utilities] started out with a national perspective. OCLC originally was the Ohio College Library Center, a statewide network in Ohio, and planned on having its system replaced by other networks. RLIN (formerly BALLOTS) was developed specifically to meet the needs of the Stanford libraries. WLN was intended to be only a statewide network. . . . The second major factor that has prevented the establishment of a national network is that the utilities have already been pushing the current technology to its limits, consistent with good reliability of the systems, and up to this point the technology for supporting a national network has not existed. Third, all the systems were started and evolved in the same general time frame with modest funding and equally modest goals, although, not surprisingly, with success has come raised expectations. Fourth, growth to date has been governed by geographic proximity and state or national boundaries, rather than by an "open market" situation in which the utilities are striving to meet the needs of one or

more of the library markets based on type of library rather than geographical location. . . . Finally, some argue that competition in any field is healthy and good, and that a single, noncompetitive network would not necessarily be a good thing. They believe that competition means that each type of library is likely to have most of its bibliographic information retrieval and manipulation needs met sooner and at a more cost-effective price than if there were only one utility building a "national network."[45]

In 1979 a bill (National Library Act S1124) was introduced in Congress to establish a national agency as well as to provide funds for public library programs. The proposed agency would not exercise direct control over operations and policies of local libraries, but would oversee federal library aid programs, plan and coordinate a national library and information network, and work on a network for federal agencies. But the bill itself emphasizes the opposition to the idea of centralization, and it is unlikely there will be a national information program per se. "Nothing in this Act," the bill states, "shall be construed to interfere with state and local responsibility in the conduct of library services."[46]

Some believe that within the next few years the previously mentioned "stand-alone" systems will effectively compete with national network systems. Possibly one version will be the stand-alone system as subnetwork, which, in turn, will be part of national networks. Those who believe this tend to favor grass-roots network development, i.e., evolution from the bottom up rather than via an organized, perscriptive, "top down approach that necessarily involves a national coordinating organization."[47]

---

[45]"Understanding the Utilities," *American Libraries,* May 1980, pp. 262–263.

[46]"National Library Act . . . ," *Library Journal,* August 1979, pp. 1504–1505. At the late-1979 White House Conference on Library and Information Services, delegates praised the network concept, but voted that "control of these networks should remain with state and regions, although coordination would be handled by whatever library authority is built in the new Department of Education. An attempt to give coordination responsibility to the Library of Congress was defeated." "Cadres or the Library Future," *Library Journal,* January 15, 1980, p. 162. There is some coordination of effort at the national level; e.g., the National Commission on Libraries and Information (NCLIS) was created in 1970 and has been actively engaged in numerous projects to improve information channels. Charles Benton, "The National Commission," *Library Journal,* September 15, 1979, pp. 1976–1979. This is a brief discussion of the Commission and its activities. An independent agency, the NCLIS advises the government regarding development of library and information services. In 1977 it published a survey of library resources and plans for the future, *Toward a National Program for Library and Information Services.* Equally a power center is the much older Council on Library Resources and, of course, the Library of Congress.

[47]"Key Network Issues Aired . . . ," *Library Journal,* September 1, 1979, p. 1607.

The so-called "grass roots" argument takes many forms. Some favor or oppose a national program; some believe the state library, not the state or regional networks, should direct network development. Network development has in some areas been encouraged by the state library and in others by various libraries within a multistate region, usually with a separate governing mechanism.

The situation is interesting here because it touches some basic problems in networking. In order to be financially viable a network must have a given number of members, and the larger the network, the greater the need for more members. Given this situation, can a large network such as OCLC continue if its membership drops away to join RLIN, WLN, or, for that matter, regional systems such as SOLINET? And if regional networks are desirable, and they seem to be, how can they afford to operate if their major role (and funds) is assumed by larger operations such as OCLC?

Both queries are part of a larger question:

> Is it desirable that there be a number of networks in the country, or would it be preferable to permit or even encourage OCLC, Inc. to turn its present commanding lead into a permanent monopoly? To permit one strong network like OCLC to dominate the field may seem expedient now because it avoids unpleasant confrontations, but how will it look to us five or ten years hence? Will OCLC more nearly resemble the telephone company or the U.S. Postal Service?
>
> It is too early to answer these questions, but it is not too early to begin asking them. Library networking is confronted by a number of critical issues: they should be faced squarely and discussed openly.[48]

Looking to the future it is probable that RLIN and OCLC will continue to operate independently, although they may work out a method to use each other's files. It is unlikely that there will be a master national online service, primarily because most politicians and many librarians prefer the regional and local systems.

At the same time there is a need for an overall organizational pattern to eliminate duplication of effort between the major services. Methods of figuring costs, determining relationships with individual libraries and regional networks, and the like will require some central organizational planning. Equally important is the need for standardization of hardware and software and quality control over the bibliographic data.

After outlining the benefits of a national network system, one expert asks, "Where are we toward this end?" And her reply is as applicable today as the day it was uttered.

[48]Richard DeGennaro, "From Monopoly to Competition," *Library Journal*, June 1, 1979, p. 1217.

Where are we toward this end? To build a nationwide network is to assemble organizations and individuals into a mutually beneficial relationship while maintaining a high degree of autonomy for those organizations and individuals—which is a very large order. This process will take place over many years, with many activities proceeding in parallel. It is not simple to categorize or assign names to these many activities, which, unfortunately, do not fit into nice, neat little black-and-white boxes. Individuals involved with complex systems work in that wonderful gray world where ideas can be proven to be neither right nor wrong until tried, and then there is high praise for success and high price for failure. There is no well-defined map to follow that will guarantee arrival at the destination, but one thing is for sure—we are on our way.[49]

Network problems

There are numerous administrative, organizational, and financial problems faced by all networks, no matter what type or size. An intensive investigation of several metropolitan consortia revealed that basic problems existed in almost every situation. The first was the "fear of undue dominance or loss of political or fiscal autonomy" by the individual libraries, more particularly, the smaller libraries. Once the fears are overcome there is almost always a need for a "full-time coordinator" and "some budget or financial support." Equally essential are "standardization of routine procedures and policies" and frequent meetings of those involved in the consortia.[50]

Fears and biases of librarians often block more than just local planning for networks. For example, if school media libraries are linked to academic and public libraries, there may be an intolerable drain on the latter's resources. Second, school librarians are reluctant to give up local policy and power. The fears are not entirely goundless, and must be considered. Meanwhile, one report put particular stress on the need for effective planning.

What is needed is the establishment, at the state level, of a network coordinating unit responsible for network planning. This unit should include state education agencies and state libraries, and representation of school library media programs should be "mandat-

[49]Henriette D. Avram, "Toward a Nationwide Library Network," *Journal of Library Automation,* December 1978, p. 286.

[50]Ellis Hodgin, "Metropolitan Consortia: Some Observations," *South Carolina Librarian,* Fall 1978, p. 9.

ed." [The report also urged] the development of plans for adequate compensation to libraries that bear a special burden in serving other networks and the preparation of planning tools; a manual for network planners; guidelines specifying minimal and optimal level of school library service; a directory of consultants; and empirical data regarding the cost of interlibrary cooperation. And the state level coordinating unit should establish standards for admission to the network and identify responsibilities for governance and participation.[51]

Governance

How does a network operate and who is in charge? This is the question of governance.[52] It is solved by traditional private corporate structures, such as Lockheed, which act as vendors of data bases, but it remains a touchy problem for nonprofit networks such as OCLC, RLIN, and local service networks. Normally the procedure is to have a board of directors, and/or council made up of representative members of the system. There is, then, a network executive.

This is an extremely rough summary of an extremely complex matter. Numerous states have laws which must be assessed before tackling problems of multistate funding and governance. In addition, when one network begins cooperation with another or with a series of networks, there are other governance problems. The outline of the administrative procedures, particularly on a national level, has been drawn, but there is no agreement as to details.

Funding

Finance is a related problem. Beyond the discussion of costs and fees, considered elsewhere, it is certain that the costs "of creating and maintaining networks cannot be met from currently available local sources of support, and that more federal and state aid will be required."[53]

Networks are a marvelous tool for library service, but they do

---

[51]*Library Journal,* March 15, 1979, p. 665.

[52]Charles Stevens, "Solinet," *The Southeastern Librarian,* Summer 1978, pp. 98–99. This explains the governance of OCLC and how individual networks and libraries fit into that administrative pattern. For what can only be called the mercurial governance patterns of the various networks, see the opening news section of almost any issue of *Library Journal* or *American Libraries.*

[53]Thomas J. Galvin, "The Structure, Governance and Funding of Library Networks," *Information Reports and Bibliographies,* no. 3, 1979, pp. 3–7.

impose added costs. Some libraries simply cannot afford even what many consider minor costs.

> *The principal charge for using the OCLC online shared cataloging system is the first-time-use charge, to which reference has already been made. OCLC invokes this charge the first time a participating library uses a record already in the online catalog for catalog production, whether in the form of catalog cards or magnetic tape. OCLC does not make a charge the second or subsequent times an institution uses an existing record, and never makes a charge when the institution puts the record into the online catalog. Beginning in July 1979, the first-time-use charge will be $1.25, with a 6% discount, or $1.17 if paid annually in advance. The charge for catalog cards is 3.6ᶜ, with a 6% discount, or 3.4ᶜ, if paid annually in advance. OCLC's marketing stance has been simply to make the system available, but OCLC expects to initiate more aggressive marketing policies in the immediate future.[54]*

The network concept stems from impressive capital investment and high operational costs. OCLC, in the early 1980s, had a budget of over $30 million, or about $23,000 per individual library sharing in the OCLC network.

> *It seems reasonably clear that only large firms, the federal government, a few large states, and large library networks will be able to undertake the capital investment needed to support complex, large-scale on-line networks and to provide the continuing research and development needed to mount new services. In the library community the network provides the structure required to concentrate needed capital. Networks can also employ various entrepreneurial strategies, such as indebtedness, that are unavailable to many libraries. It is important that network organizations have a legal basis which allows maximum flexibility in funding strategies and that member libraries honor contractual commitments which the network has incurred on their behalf.[55]*

---

[54]F. G. Kilgour, "Shared Cataloging at OCLC," *Online Review*, no. 3, 1979, p. 278. Comparative costs between RLIN and OCLC are of understandable interest to libraries, but there are many difficulties in making such comparisons. Charges for RLIN differ, and, as of 1979, were from 3.8 cents to 4 cents per catalog per card, from $1.60 to 1.70 per copy of an existing record in the data base. Catalog cards on magnetic tape (i.e., 500 records) vary from $37.50 to $40 with about a 5 cent charge for each record beyond the 500. Efficiency, however, is a factor and in one study it was found "that it cost Cornell (about $3 per item) to bring OCLC cataloging up to Cornell standards." *Library Journal*, August 1979, p. 1505. Whether it would improve with RLIN is another matter.

[55]Markuson, op. cit., p. 127.

Standardization

The need for standards in hardware and software compatibility is the same for bibliographic networks as for the various data-base publishers and vendors. While many librarians argue that there should be limited federal control of networks, most would agree that some national standards must be applied to allow coordination of the various network plans.

Consider, for example, the question of authority files. In all networks, regardless of size or form, there is necessity for a uniformity which will assure that libraries are employing similar bibliographic methods. Where this is not the case, two libraries may enter the same book title under different main entries, even different subject headings. The resulting catalog file is likely to be a modern-day Babel.

The phrase "authority file" is common in almost any discussion of networks and data bases. "Authentication of bibliographic records by an automated authority control system will serve to maintain network bibliographic standards, and to ensure consistency of the data base. It can be expected that this facility will serve to limit the addition of duplicate and variant records to the union catalog, which if permitted to proliferate would severely degrade the effectiveness of such an instrument."[56]

Standardization of cataloging (i.e., the bibliographic data used by reference librarians to search for an item) is the major headache for the network members. While England has a national bibliographic service in the British Library, there is no such facility in the United States. The Library of Congress comes close, but not close enough, for as more than one critic has pointed out about MARC cataloging:

> The cataloging information contained in LC records may or may not adhere to nationally accepted cataloging codes; the LC classification is avowedly tailored to the exigencies of LC's collection and may or may not meet the needs of other libraries; the Decimal Classification numbers are not accompanied by Cutter numbers and hence cannot be used automatically by the many thousands of libraries using DDC; the subject headings are in many uses known to be unacceptable and in some cases manifestly absurd, yet LC will not accept the responsibility of a thorough overhaul of the system; and finally, the MARC format (LC version) is outdated and unsuited to some of the requirements of modern machine systems.[57]

[56]Malinconico, op. cit., p. 193.
[57]Michael Gorman, "A Modest Proposal for a Future National Bibliographic System," *American Libraries*, March 1978, p. 147.

One solution is built into the larger bibliographic utilities where individual libraries can modify the cataloging as necessary for the use of that library. The ideal system might be one whereby there could be a standard set of bibliographic records for all libraries, i.e., a reference librarian might search by subject heading, number, and main entry without being concerned that one or all three may be different in different systems.[58] Steps toward standardization are seen in authority files worked out by the bibliographic utilities, more particularly in the detailed authority file of the Washington Library Network. But a national, even international system of standardization is desirable.

INTERLIBRARY LOAN

Among the first methods, if not the first method, of cooperation between libraries was the interlibrary loan. Before the advent of networks and computers, it was an established system of sharing between libraries, and it continues as such today.

Interlibrary loan has two complementary purposes. The first is to aid the researcher in acquiring specialized material from other libraries. The second is to assist the general reader in borrowing material otherwise inaccessible because of lack of proper library facilities. The interlibrary loan as research aid is almost exclusively the charge of college and university libraries. The interlibrary loan as boon to popular reading, and to a lesser extent, as reference tool is seen as primarily a service of public libraries, in cooperation with one another or with a state library.

Almost all libraries employ a standard form and follow rules and regulations set forth in the ALA National Interlibrary Loan Code.[59] But the code is subject to individual library loan policies—some libraries, for example, will loan theses and dissertations, others will not—and the resources of the particular library. On the whole, library practices are such that materials may be borrowed from the majority of federal libraries, including the Library of Congress, and research

[58]The problem wtih standardization is that there are various types and sizes of libraries, as well as different publics and goals to serve. It simply is not possible to have one set of rules applicable to all situations, or so the argument goes. For an intelligent, clear presentation of the justification for diversion, see Maurice J. Freedman, "Public Libraries, the Library of Congress, and the National Bibliographic Network," *Library Journal,* November 1, 1977, pp. 2211–2215.

[59]The code was revised in 1979, and approved in 1980. For a draft see *RQ,* Summer 1979, pp. 387–390.

and reference libraries whose holdings are identified through a national or regional union catalog or book catalog. There is a considerable amount of cooperation among all types of libraries, but this does not guarantee an unrestricted flow of materials. Certain kinds of resources, such as manuscript material, rare books, current periodicals, and audiovisual materials are usually not available for loan. Instead photocopies or microfilm of the restricted materials are sent.

While restriction of certain types of materials is understandable, in an interlibrary loan system, a check on types of users served is somewhat questionable. Borrowing limitations often exist for students, both at the university level and at the high school media center.

Conversely, consider the Universal Availability of Publications (UAP) movement sponsored by the world's libraries. As the title suggests, UAP hopes to make interlibrary loan an international aspect of librarianship, to make it possible to borrow and lend materials from almost any library in the world. A given amount of traffic now exists via such services as the British Library Lending Division and cooperative efforts between American libraries and libraries in Mexico and South America, but UAP plans call for much wider interlibrary loan systems.[60] All of this is tied, to be sure, to the increased sophistication of the related Universal Availability of Bibliographic Records (UBC). By listing the world's literature and making it available via a massive union catalog, probably online, UBC may become a base for worldwide interlibrary loan.

The tradition

In many libraries the reference librarian is responsible for interlibrary loans; hence the great amount of attention given this procedure in the literature of reference service.[61] Larger libraries have separate offices, units, or operations which handle only interlibrary loan and

---

[60]See almost any issue of the *IFLA Journal* for comments, articles, and notes on UAP, e.g., Maurice Line, "Universal Availability of Publications," *IFLA Journal*, no. 4, 1978, pp. 345–346.

[61]Interlibrary loan is part of the responsibility of the American Library Association's Reference and Adult Division, and it is here that a special committee worked on the version of the *ILL Code*. Not all librarians agree that interlibrary loan should not be a reference process. As one reader of this manuscript put it: "Good reference interviewing often reveals that ILL can be avoided because the information needed is available in the collection in another title or format. [Kay Murray, personal communication.] This is a valid point.

have little to do directly with reference service (other than by referral).

Ideally the routine interlibrary loan procedures would not be part of the reference librarian's work. The librarian has too many other duties to be involved with what is essentially routine procedure. This is particularly true in view of the development of online interlibrary loan and its expected growth in the next few years.

At the same time the average reference librarian will certainly help an individual to locate material outside of the library—by indicating what is available and by showing the user precisely what may be obtained via the loan system. The librarian, too, will verify citations and assist, where necessary, in filling out request forms. And, to be sure, the librarian will try to find substitutes if a loan is likely to take too long.

In filling requests for interlibrary loans, the librarian usually follows a well-established pattern—and a printed form.[62] The librarian is careful to:

1. Give an accurate bibliographical description of the title or material needed. Users normally fail to do this, and it is absolutely necessary to double-check. The check also serves the purpose of ascertaining whether the needed material is really in the library and has simply been overlooked by the person making the request.

2. Follow the individual coding methods of the particular system.

3. Screen the user's request. This is important because it should uncover the user who is in a rush for material, who could use something else, who really does not even know what he or she wants, or who simply does not want to walk to another library where the material may be handy.

4. Notify the user promptly when the material comes in and give a clear signal as to how long this material may be kept.

Once steps have been taken to create a common bibliographic system, union lists, and necessary forms, and after a myraid of other details hve been worked out to ensure knowing who has what in an interlibrary loan system, the next crucial consideration is how fast an

[62]Under revision, but still useful: Sarah Thomson, *Interlibrary Loan Proecdures* (Chicago: American Library Association, 1970). This is the basic guide to detailed procedures to follow, and all librarians involved with interlibrary loan should be familiar with the work.

interlibrary loan can be negotiated. The actual processing of the request may take from one to two days, but how the request is sent to the interlibrary center is of equal importance timewise. Lacking a computer terminal access point, the usual procedure is by mail, by a daily—or more or less frequent—courier service, or by telephone or teletypewriter (TWX). The material itself may be sent back by first-class mail, parcel post (particularly if the material is a book), courier, or, if it is an answer to a question, transmitted by telefacsimile.

There are numerous studies, but essentially the systems may be evaluated in terms of (1) the time it takes to submit the actual request, which usually means time for verification of bibliographic information by the requesting library, (2) the time needed to search for the material at the point of the interlibrary loan, which can mean rechecking the verification or even sending the request back to the original library for clarification, and (3) the response time, or the actual time the user has to wait for a reply.

Enter the network

Confidence has improved in interlibrary loan somewhat over the past few years because of the linking of some interlibrary loan systems to national bibliographic utilities and networks. The best-known subsystem for interlibrary loan is that operated by OCLC. Somewhat similar service is offered by the other bibliographic utilities.

Interlibrary loan is a byproduct of OCLC shared cataloging; that is to say, the subsystem offers an online union catalog which is built up by the libraries that are constantly feeding their holdings into the system. There are now about 5 million entries, many with locations listed. The OCLC system does not search for titles not in the machine-readable data base. On the other hand, regular interlibrary loan systems such as NYSILL accept requests of any type. The difference here is important.

When one is searching OCLC, or related systems, for a desired item for interlibrary loan, the entry is provided by numerous methods, from title and author to Library of Congress card number and ISBN. Usually a record is found of the title wanted, but even where no record exists the user may initiate a request for the item. The request is then sent to as many as five OCLC member libraries, chosen by the borrowing library because they are close and potential lenders.

The request remains with a potential lender until either a response is made by the lender or a predetermined number of days—presently four on-line system working days—elapses. If that lender fails to respond or cannot supply the item, the subsystem automatically refers the request to the next potential lender. Borrowers and lenders update the on-line transactions record from the time the request is initiated until it is completed.[63]

Before online union catalogs, the normal interlibrary loan strategy, despite claims to the contrary, was for the library with need of X item to contact the largest library, on the premise that it would be most likely to lend X item. This process created an imbalance in sharing of costs, not to mention less than efficient service.

The online system has resulted in a change in this small-to-largest chain in interlibrary loans. Now more and more libraries of all sizes are taking part in the process. With specific nearby locations listed online, the smaller and medium-sized libraries are now lending materials; East Texas State University, for example, notes that with the OCLC interlibrary loan system the number of loans it made to other libraries jumped from an annual average of 180 to over 500.[64] This often means the library requesting a loan can ask for an item from a much closer library than before and, in effect, can vastly improve service. Service within the state of New York, for example, "has improved to the point where about 90 percent of the local requests can be satisfied regionally.[65]

The subsystem does not deliver the documents needed. Delivery is made in the traditional way via the mails, courier, etc. However, because the record keeping is so much better, the actual point-to-point service is speeded up. In one test library a request was entered at 12:30 p.m., and the item was shipped by the lender three hours later. This is becoming increasingly normal as the networks and computers become more efficient.

Various other forms of online interlibrary loan will be developed in the decade ahead. For example, in early 1981 the new commerically developed LOAN system was available, along with a companion ACCESS operation. The hardware is no more than a commercial minicomputer with a memory unit. The software consists of records of local and regional holdings, and, while not quite as simple as it sounds, the system does allow automation of what have heretofore been printed local interlibrary loan union lists.

[63]Mary Jacob, "A National Interlibrary Loan Network: The OCLC Approach," *Bulletin of the American Society for Information Science,* June 1979, p. 24.

[64]*Library Journal,* November 15, 1979, p. 2400.

[65]Epstein, op. cit., p. 15.

Interlibrary costs of loans

How much do interlibrary loans cost? No specific figures may be given for each situation, but in the early 1980s the average cost per transaction via OCLC was about $2.75. (This, to be sure, is a simplification of a complicated analysis, e.g., borrowing unit costs may run $5 to $6, while lending costs per unit may be no more than $3 to $3.50) These costs will invariably increase, if not for particular items loaned, in terms of gross use of interlibrary loan.[66]

The better delivery effectuated by interlibrary loan, the more often it is likely to be used. Add to this an efficient online search of data bases with resulting citations for material not in the library, and the total use of inerlibrary loan will increase dramatically. For example, after a study of a research library it was concluded that:

> *Any library manager who plans to initiate computerized on-line search services should be prepared to handle a 50% higher increase in ILL requests. Naturally, the effect on ILL activity depends on such factors as size of periodical collection, ease of access to more extensive collections, and experience of research staff in computer literature searching. A marked increase in interlibrary loan activity affects many aspects of library operations, especially staffing and budgeting.[67]*

Given the expected volume and the increase in costs, DeGennaro, among others, sees the time when "librarians will finally have to put a realistic price on it." According to this argument libraries have a moral obligation to share their resources, "but borrowing libraries will have to assume a moral obligation to pay the costs involved."[68]

The problem is hardly new and discussions of charges for interlibrary loan have gone on almost as long as the system itself. The

---

[66]Interlibrary loan costs are a major consideration, and much is written on the subject. For example: Jo E. Herstand, "Interlibrary Loan Cost Study and Comparison," *RQ*, Spring 1981, pp. 249–256. For a model see William Arms, "Models for Interlibrary Lending," *Interlending Review*, October 1979, pp. 130–136. The real question is how to figure costs. Where this has been done with other systems, the range is from about $2 to over $7, and often for precisely the same type of costs.

[67]Jean K. Martin, "Computer-Based Literature Searching," *Special Libraries*, January 1978, p. 5. Other studies show much the same result, e.g., *Annual Report* (Branford, Conn.: Research Libraries Group, 1976), p. 6. Four member libraries in the original Research Libraries Group borrowed about 200 items a year from one another. After organization of more efficient interlibrary loan, the figure went to 5423 items for the same period of time. See, too, Dennis J. Reynolds, "Regional Alternatives for Interlibrary Loan . . . ," *College & Research Libraries*, January 1980, pp. 33–42.

[68]Richard DeGennaro, "Research Libraries Enter the Information Age," *Library Journal*, November 15, 1979, p. 2408. Beginning in midsummer 1979, Columbia University began to charge $10 per title loaned, and $5 per title searched but not found.

difficulties are many. Which costs can be figured? Who should pay what part of the cost? Is it more costly to collect fees than to absorb them in the system? If fees are collected, will this eliminate the use of the system by everyone except the well-off middle classes? Should the costs be absorbed by the library? And if so, what other services are to be cut? Perhaps the increased use of interlibrary loan and better technology will actually cut costs, but that remains to be seen.

Document delivery: Other avenues

Despite the marvels of the computer search, the results can be a dramatic let-down. Once the search is complete, the user is given a list of citations, normally to articles and/or books. Now the user is back to the point where he left the manual search—he is still in quest of an elusive document. The quest for the document may take much longer than the actual search for citations and can be a serious block in an otherwise sophisticated system.

Search analysts call this "closing the loop."

> *A list of 50 relevant references can be printed online in a matter of minutes, but delivery of the original documents may require days, often weeks, and sometimes months. With this long time lag, how well is the end user served by online access? "Closing the loop" means supplying the original document (most frequently journal articles) with no more delay than a few days.*[69]

There are several basic approaches to the solution of document delivery. The first, and most often used, is the interlibrary loan system.[70] Other approaches include use of commercial services which sell reprints of tear sheets of articles; microform; facsimile transmission of documents; teletext and related systems; and full-text data bases.

The librarian may sit at the same terminal where the search was made and order the documents from one of the data base vendors. The vendor, in turn, passes the order to the publisher and/or a commercial document supplier.[71] There are now several private

---

[69]Leone Trubkin, "Closing the Loop," *The Information Manager,* September/October 1979, p. 6.

[70]Jean K. Martin, op.cit., p. 5. Studies in this area report that online searching will increase interlibrary loan activity by 50 to 70 percent.

[71]Lockheed, SDC, and BRS offer variations of this system. Lockheed's DIALORDER, for example, offers a simple direct method of ordering documents at the terminal. The vendor lists and explains the services available for documents from some 30 publishers and organizations. The list is frequently updated and found as part of the three-volume

organizations which are specifically in the business of selling tear sheets or photocopies of needed material. Rush orders (for which there is an added fee) may take no more than 48 hours to fill, but even with the computer terminal there can be a delay. Given the order, the publisher or specialized service must depend upon the mails. The result is often five days to a week for delivery.

The ability to order materials at the terminal is referred to as "electronic mailbox." Another favored descriptor is "electronic mail drop." Whatever the name, it includes numerous other services.

> *Electronic mail enables messages, correspondence, orders, queries, all types of information to be sent at low cost, at "high speed" to any single location, or to multiple destinations for coordinated action. Storage can be arranged in multiple locations with maximum flexibility for retrieval, and dynamic interrelationships can be developed between information elements previously lost in filing cabinets. When backed up by tele-conferencing facilities, electronic mail enables meetings to be arranged at short notice but with optimum preparation and minimum disruption of either working routine or domestic life. The access to information and to the opinions and judgment embodied in people, which these developments give, can only improve yet further the efficiency and productivity.[72]*

Common sources of documents which may be tapped at the terminal or by letter or phone include:

(1) OATS (Original Article Tear Sheet), a service offered by the publisher of the various citation indexes, Institute for Scientific Information. More than 6500 periodicals are available, and where a tear sheet is not possible the publisher will send a photocopy. The tear sheets average from $5.50 to $6.50 per article—by far the lowest of all rates available.

(2) ABI/INFORM, a data base, offers copies of articles from "selected journals" as part of its service. *The Magazine Index* "provides a document copy and delivery service," and these are typical of the numerous publishers who are following the lead of OATS.

(3) A number of firms specialize in document delivery. ADS (Articles Delivery Service) is a system available from the Information Specialists in Cleveland Heights, Ohio. The company claims access to

---

Lockheed *Guide to Dialog Databases.* Other vendors follow much the same pattern. A regular feature in *Online* is "Document Delivery" which gives names, addresses, and services of private and public organizations in this area. See Mary Gibbs, "Ordering Through Lockheed's Dialog . . . ," *Online,* October 1980, pp. 31–37.

[72]G. P. Sweeney, "Microprocessors in Communications," *Journal of Information Science,* May 1979, pp. 102–103.

some 40,000 journal titles, charges $7.50 per article up to 20 pages and $5 for each additional 20 pages "for easily accessible items." More-difficult-to-find articles may run as high as $20. The service is available through Lockheed and, of course, via the computer terminal.

(4) Government agencies and departments with data bases, such as the National Library of Medicine, supply copies of materials, both on interlibrary loan and for a fee.

The cost, the delay even for a rush order, and the problem of copyright[73] all militate against what is essentially an antiquated delivery system. There should be a substitute for the printed version, and here there are numerous existing and promising solutions:

(1) The most common solution is to have the document available on microform. One simply goes from the citation in the index or abstract to a file where the cited journal article, report, proceeding, or even book is available on microform. It will be recalled that such a service is offered by ERIC, several publishers of government indexes, and newspapers.

(2) Variations on the microform approach are called by the familiar umbrella term, CAR (computer-assisted retrieval). Many systems exist, although no matter what the system, basically one finds the required citation via computer search. The citation indicates the 16 mm cartridge in which the record is housed. The microfilm cartridge is loaded into a fast reader/printer and the required document is automatically located on the film.[74] While primarily used in bank and credit card transactions, the system can be applicable to standard bibliographic data-base searches.

(3) Facsimile transmission is an aspect of the electronic mail system, but to date has been less than satisfactory for library use. Here one sends a copy of a page or article via a facsimile machine from one library to another. There have been problems: the high cost of the method—$1 to $3 a page, exclusive of equipment; speed—up to six minutes per page; faulty copies; and less-than-enthusiastic attention

---

[73]Copyright may be the biggest problem for document delivery. Five copies of any material per year from the same journal is the maximum allowed. The problem comes when more than five copies are needed. And while it may not be often, the multiple-copy situation defies solution other than added payment.

[74]Much of this is done manually, although more sophisticated systems allow the computer not only to designate the frame number but to drive the film to the specific frame via an interface with a separate microfilm reader. See Albert Tauber, "Computer-Assisted Retrieval Comes of Age," *Information & Records Management,* May 1980, p. 42.

to the process. To a certain degree these difficulties have been overcome with such systems as the much-advertised "Qwip System," which can "transmit full pages internationally in two to three minutes." Also, Xerox is in the field with impressive equipment; e.g., their 5700 electronic printing system, costing about $67,000, can send or receive a full page of text in three seconds. Xerox, too, offers less expensive versions. The problem, at least for libraries, is the initial cost of the equipment and the cost of transmission.

(4) In the Teletext system, the television station provides textual data on demand from the viewer. However, this is quite limited and dependent solely upon what is fed into the system. Teletext is not meant to be as complete as the back-up needed for a large abstracting or indexing service.

(5) Full-text data bases may be the ultimate answer, and here not only the citation but the full article is available online and offline. Examples include LEXIS which produces legal citations and the full cases. The New York Times has developed methods of making its *Information Bank* available in full text. The vendor BRS, in cooperation with the American Chemical Society, will soon offer full text of approximately 1000 articles from the *Journal of Medicinal Chemistry* (1976–1978) online. Not only will the articles be available, but they will be directly searchable. The search "provides not only the standard result indicating the number of articles containing the entry term(s) but also an in-context result display indicating the exact location (paragraph, sentence, and word numbers) of the term(s) within the article. The searcher can then browse within the text, requesting only those paragraphs that contain the terms.[75] The added bonus of the word-by-word search indicates the probable direction, cost aside, of free-text searching in the future. Not only will the title or abstract be searched, but every word in the text itself.

Paranthetically, one should distinguish between the terms "free text" and "full text." The difference is not always apparent in writings on the subject. "Free text" is a term which indicates the searcher is able to look for the needed subject via any searchable paragraph, such as titles or abstracts in the data base. Conversely, "full text" is a term used for a search which allows a search of words in the entire document. Hence, a full-text capacity of a data base not only means the whole document is available, but the complete document may be searched. It is necessary to note that there are some exceptions. (See p. 167 in Chapter 7 for treatment of full-text data bases.)

[75]*BRS Bulletin,* April 1980, p. 1.

National periodicals center

One major aspect of a proposed national interlibrary loan network is a national periodicals center. A plan for such a center was completed in late 1978, but is still to be formalized.

The purpose of the center, which eventually would house about 60,000 current periodicals, is to provide an effective, economical way for people to obtain copies of needed articles and even whole issues of journals. Instead of each local library maintaining its own 30,000-plus collection, the Center will provide the warehouse. The focus will be on lesser-used journals. Periodicals used frequently, of course, would still be part of each library's holdings.

Given the support of the government and nonprofit libraries, the Center will be able to cut costs because no profit is involved. Equally important, it is seen as a way of speeding up interlibrary loan procedures and solving at least part of the document delivery problem. The Center's other objectives are to assure publishers that copyright fees will be paid on copied articles, to act as an innovator of new publishing methods, to promote local and regional networks, and to offer a place for the preservation of periodical materials.

The Center would be only one part in the interlibrary network and would not handle all, or even a majority of, interlibrary loans for periodical articles. State and regional systems would continue to operate local networks. "It is important to keep the NPC in perspective. It is not something that will replace libraries and networks, and copyright, and destroy the publishing and information industries. It is just another library, only instead of serving users who walk in off the street, it will function like a mail-order house for other libraries."[76]

As a clearinghouse, the Center would channel requests for titles it did not hold, particularly retrospective works. And it is proposed that

> . . . the NPC become a kind of service and fulfillment outlet for at least some publishers. Thus the NPC might provide a back-issue service (probably in microfilm), an article sales service (so long as the article remained protected by copyright), an outlet for on-demand publishing, and/or a source for the full text of material published in synoptic form. All of these services would generate some income for publishers while providing the access to material that library users need.[77]

[76]DeGennaro, op. cit., p. 2407.

[77]William J. Welsh, "Progress in the United States Toward a National Periodicals System," *IFLA Journal,* no. 4, 1979, p. 290.

Opposition to the center built in the early 1980s from numerous sources, including private data-base publishers and vendors who now supply articles from periodicals and see the Center as unfair competition. In addition, hostility towards a national network has carried over to the plans for the Center. For example, such regional networks as the Pacific Northwest Bibliographic Center are opposed to a centralized service because it is repetitious of services now being offered. The PNBC endorses "a strong regional resource sharing approach to the planning of a national periodicals system . . . [because] the majority of requests for periodicals are satisfied within the region."[78] Also, PNBC questions that the needed funding for a national center would be available from already tightly pressed library budgets.

The British Library Lending Division

A model for national interlibrary loan systems (and for the proposed American Center), the British Library Lending Division was founded in and provides a supporting system not only for British libraries, but for libraries in other countries, including the United Sttates.[79] The library expedites the loan of both periodicals and books, but it is not just a switching center. It has its own basic collection of some 145,000 serial titles and over 2 million volumes. The serials, which include primarily journals, include about 52,000 current subscriptions; some 100,000 monographs are acquired each year.

The focus is on technical and scholarly academic titles. For example, fiction is not included because it is not considered—wrongly some believe—material for research and industrial purposes. Among the 52,000 serials, the majority (40,000) are technical and scientific. The remainder (6500) are in the social sciences and in the humanities (4500). In addition, the library collects reports, some technical newspapers. etc.[80]

"Its success rate is fulfilling requests is currently 83% from its own stock and 11% from other libraries, including other parts of the British Library, used as a backup, i.e., an overall success rate of 94%."[81]

---

[78]*Library Journal*, February 15, 1980, p. 466.

[79]J. S. Davey and E. S. Smith, "The Overseas Service of the British Lending Library Division," *Unesco Bulletin for Libraries*, September/October 1975, pp. 259–269.

[80]David N. Wood, "Acquisition Policy and Practices at the British Library Lending Division," *Interlibrary Review*, no. 4, 1979, pp. 111–118. This is a detailed explanation of acquisition procedures.

[81]*Online Review*, September 1979, p. 274.

Copyright

The question of copyright is a stumbling block for a national center of materials and, indeed, for any interlibrary loan system. Despite the 1976 revision of the 1909 law, the new regulations are still far from clear, and scores of articles, books, and even legal decisions have evolved out of the revised law. To this day, librarians are not certain about the effect of copyright on interlibrary loan, and it may be years before the question is resolved in the courts.[82]

The rule, which is little more than an interpretation and not a binding legal decision, is that "fair use"—another way of saying that the copyright is not infringed and royalties do not have to be paid—pertains when, within any calendar year, no more than five copies are made of any articles or other material appearing within the periodical. This means one might make five separate copies of a single article, or five copies of five different articles in the same periodical. There is much more to the law than that, but that simplified rule is at least a guide at the copy machine.

Various studies indicate that the fuss over copyright is more fiction than fact, at least in terms of interlibrary loan. Interestingly enough, the average library is not likely to request an article, book, or report more than once. The chance of X item being requested on interlibrary loan more than once is largely accidental. One of numerous studies found that requests for one article per periodical accounted for 68.7 percent of the total requests in one library for the first quarter of 1978. (A similar study at the National Bureau of Standards Library showed nearly the same figure, 66 percent.) Most requests involved five or fewer requests per periodical per year. There is a chance, yet to be seen, that the increased use of computerized bibliographic retrieval and online requests for material may alter these figures.[83]

If most requests continue to follow past patterns the lending library—and this might include even a National Periodicals Center— is unlikely to face more than infrequent difficulty with copyright. On

---

[82]John Steuben, "Interlibrary Loan of Photocopies of Articles Under the New Copyright Law," *Special Libraries*, May/June 1979, pp. 227–232. Here the reader will find the text of the "Guidelines for Interlibrary Arrangements," which is of some assistance.

[83]Ibid., p. 231. The library is NOAA (National Oceanic and Atmospheric Administration) Library in Boulder, Colorado. The basic study here is E. E. Graziano's "Interlibrary Loan Analysis . . . ," *Special Libraries*, no. 5, 1962, pp. 251–257. Various reports and studies from the British Library Lending Division confirm the lack of repetition patterns in interlibrary loans. See *Publishers Weekly*, August 9, 1976, p. 35. Chicago Public Library reported in 1980 that "they had never exceeded the limit of five copies from the same journal." *Library Journal*, March 15, 1980, p. 675.

very few occasions will any single periodical (no more than five years old) be copied more than five times in a given year. And even when this is done, given proper methods of royalty payment to author and publisher, it should hardly constitute a problem. Entering the 1980s there is every reason to believe DeGennaro is right when he said several years ago that the copyright law would have a minimum effect on most libraries. The reason is that material simply is not copied that much, at least via the interlibrary loan system.[84]

Actually most of the fuss is made over the expected needs of a specialist, not the average user. For example, it is true that in some medical libraries "one researcher might need a number of issues of a given journal for a given search, and thus use up the five-copy limit all at once.[85] There is the library situation where a student or a teacher copies coutless pages of a textbook or an article and distributes them in class. This is a rank infringement of the law, and in 1980 was the focus of a court case.[86]

INTERNATIONAL NETWORKS

Because of new technologies, from videodisks and satellites[87] to laser and improved telephone connections, it is not uncommon for libraries throughout much of the world to use data bases located in California, or for Californians to tap data bases in Europe. In both cases messages are relayed with the same speed and efficiency as a national tie-in.

But there is more to an international information network, or, to be more precise, to a system of interconnected networks, than technology. A few of the problems which have arisen include: (a) standardized bibliographic control; (b) the needs of potential users, which tend to vary from area to area; (c) the availability of existing resources and the potential to develop new ones; (d) administrative and financial control; (e) the problem of copyright in the relation of

[84]Richard DeGennaro, "Copyright, Resource Sharing and Hard Times," *American Libraries,* September 1977, pp. 431–432.

[85]"Seven Publishers Sue Copier as Infringer of Copyright," *The New York Times,* February 6, 1980, p. C19.

[86]*Library Journal,* March 15, 1980, p. 675. In 1983 the Copyright Office will hold a five-year review of the law and at that time more may be known about the five-copy rule.

[87]Rosa Liu, "Telelibrary: Library Service Via Satellite," *Special Libraries,* September 1979, pp. 363–366. Not only a discussion of satellites but of other technologies used to link libraries nationally and internationally.

data exchange; (f) the variety of languages; (g) the need for some type of authority control. And there is the basic question, still to be resolved in this country: What degree of centralization should an international network strive to achieve?

Canada[88]

Canadian libraries use the American networks but they have also developed their own systems. The largest bibliographic utility is UTLAS (University of Toronto Library Automation Systems), which provides online cataloging service for over 500 libraries in the provinces and ranks second only to OCLC in size.[89] As in the United States, there are subuser groups such as OULCS (Ontario Universities' Library Cooperative System.)

In Canada the major online bibliographic vendor is the government-sponsored CAN-OLE (Canadian Online Enquiry), which offers a service similar to BRS and Lockheed. Essentially the notion is to have some control over Canadian-produced data bases, but the system has made it possible to develop technological knowledge "to avoid any extensive duplicate effort, should access to the U.S. files be barred for some political reason." To this end the system has purchased several non-Canadian scientific files, such as BIOSIS and *Chemical Abstracts,* and "has become another competing force to U.S. processors."[90]

At the same time, most Canadian libraries receive online data bases from one or all of the three major American vendors and/or government distributors. "Indeed, a Canadian profit-making operation, Infomart, "actually markets the U.S. files in competition with its own government files in the case where U.S. data bases such as *Chemical Abstracts* are duplicated."[91]

The Canada Institute for Scientific and Technical Information, along with the National Research Council Computation Centre, the joint developer of CAN/OLE, has a program called CAN/SDI (Cana-

---

[88]Margaret Beckman, "Automated Cataloguing Systems and Networks in Canada," *Canadian Library Journal,* June 1978, pp. 173–180.

[89]Among other systems: BNQ (Bibliothèque Nationale du Quebec); and NLC (National Library of Canada), both of which are primarily involved with production and distribution of Canadian MARC records. Another large system is the Ontario Universities' Library Cooperative System (OULCS).

[90]Everett H. Brenner, "Opinion Paper: Euronet and Its Effect on the U.S. Information Market." *Journal of the American Society for Information Science,* January 1979, p. 6.

[91]Ibid.

dian Selective Dissemination of Information). This program provides current-awareness searches of the sciences and the social sciences, and the data bases include numerous bibliographic services from ERIC and MARC.[92]

EURONET/DIANE[93]

EURONET (European Online Information Network)/DIANE (Direct Information Access Network for Europe) makes approximately 150 to 200 data bases available to its users, and other services raise the number to over 500.[94] Until the 1980s many of the data bases were American, but in the decade ahead the Europeans are confident that they will develop their own unique sources and will put many currently printed indexes and abstracts online.

Operational since April 1980, EURONET includes service to France, Germany, the Netherlands, Belgium, Denmark, Italy, Ireland, and England. Other countries are expected to join, particularly those who are members of the European Economic Community, which sponsors the system. A feature of the European situation is that there is virtually an absence of private, for-profit organizations involved in networks and many of the data bases.

Linkage to American data bases and vendors has been possible, albeit expensive, for several years. However, general access to the European system by Americans and vice versa is unlikely in the near future. Suggestions have been made to make London a "gateway" to the Americas and provide a satellite link between EURONET/DIANE and one of the United States vendors. The problem lies in serious difficulties in maintaining unified tariff, copyright, and language systems. As of the early 1980s it appears that the European system

[92]Elizabeth Curley, "On-Line Reference Services . . . ," *Herein,* October 1979, pp. 271–273.

[93]Actually DIANE (Direct Information Access Network for Europe) is the name for the system, with EURONET used only for the telecommunications network. However, EURONET is still better known and used here. For a list of data bases as of early 1980 see Garth Davies, "EURONET/DIANE," *International Forum on Information and Documentation,* no. 1, 1980, pp. 29–34.

[94]Marshall Clinton and Sally Grenville, "Using European Systems from a North American Library," *Online,* April 1980, pp. 22–27. See, too, Michael Casey, "Euronet-DIANE . . . ," *Online Review,* March 1980, pp. 33–40. And just about any issue of this English-based journal. See, too, Lucy A. Todd, "Report on a Visit to European Computer Based Information Centres," *Program,* April 1979, pp. 47–57. A brief discussion of various information centers from Norway and France to England.

and systems in countries in other parts of the world—from Japan to Australia—will continue to develop independently until such systems are sufficiently commonplace to allow international linkage.

The European Documentation and Information System for Education (EUDISED) began as a project in the late 1960s and went into operation in the mid-1970s. It is somewhat similar to ERIC for Europe and even includes a multilingual thesaurus for English, French, and German users. Nine member states feed material on research, both completed and ongoing, into the system, as well as articles from periodicals and nonbook materials suitable for educational use. This is tapped via the Co-operative Abstracting Service (Geneva: International Bureau of Education, 1968 to date), a looseleaf service which is arranged alphabetically by country.

This network is only one of several, and the International Bureau of Education is actively engaged in formally and informally bringing the world's various educational information centers together in a network.[95]

As information becomes an increasingly valuable and equally expensive commodity, the development of international networks will become even more necessary. If nothing else, this will eliminate a good deal of duplication of effort, develop necessary competition between European and American firms, and ensure more rapid growth of both library and home information systems. Another important result may be increased understanding between countries that are working together to gather information and make it readily available to all.

BLAISE[96] (British Library Automated Information Service), primarily used as a cataloging data base by librarians, consists of machine-readable records and books. The primary source of the data base is the British National Bibliography, but it does include material from MARC. It is also a vendor for a half-dozen bibliographic data bases, including MEDLINE. The base may be searched by the standard procedures, as well as by subject—an added plus as it includes those employed by the PRECIS system. And, of course, as in any search of a data base using the hierarchical structure and Boolean logic, there is no limit to the number of search terms which can be defined to isolate an item. The cumulation of various files totals

[95]"International Information Networks and Their Role in the Transfer of Educational Experience," *Unesco Bulletin for Libraries,* July/August 1978, pp. 237–251. The article gives a detailed description of the IBE networking.

[96]Brian Collinge, "BLAISE," *Aslib Proceedings,* October/November 1978, pp. 394–402. While somewhat dated, this is an excellent overview.

something like 1.7 million records a year. In addition, the service eventually will provide information from an eighteenth-century short title catalog,[97] data from some 40 other libraries, and serials data.

BLAISE be used in reference work just as are most other such services, but with the added feature of being able to prepare bibliographies not only by author and title, but by subject and other topics. Connected to the British Lending Library, the system makes it possible to expedite interlibrary loans.

SUGGESTED READING

"Application of OCLC in a Multitype System," *Illinois Libraries,* September 1979, pp. 585–588. A series of evaluative questions concerning various OCLC services, this is an ideal outline for determining objectives and goals of almost any network. At a minimum the questions (which are to be answered at the completion of a half-million dollar project) indicate to the novice the problems involved with networking.

Corbin, John, *Developing Computer and Network Based Library Systems.* Phoenix, Ariz.: Oryx Press, 1980. A general survey of various systems which may be applied to individual library situations. Includes a good section on networking.

Galvin, Thomas, and Allen Kent (eds.), *The Structure and Governance of Library Networks.* New York: Marcel Dekker, 1979. A basic collection of articles and reports which add up to a fine summary of the administrative aspects of networks. See, too, Galvin's "Library Networks . . . ," *Illinois Libraries,* April 1980, pp. 289–291. for a lucid overview of the subject.

Malinconico, S. M., "The National Bibliographic Network: A Patrician Pursuit," *Library Journal,* September 15, 1980. One of the few arguments opposed to a national bibliographic network, which the author in his brief summary sees as "quite simply a phantasmagoria." For a somewhat counter argument see the equally thoughtful and articulate Michael Gorman, "Network or I'm Rational as Hell and I'm Not Going to Take it Anymore," *American Libarries,* January 1, 1980, pp. 48–50.

Manheimer, Martha L., *OCLC: An Introduction to Searching and Input.* New York: Neal-Schuman Publishers, 1980. A better-than-average workbook which takes the novice through the various steps of using OCLC services. There are such manuals for other networks and subsystems, but this is an example of one of the best—particularly for clarity of presentation.

Markuson, Barbara, and Blanche Woolls (eds.), *Networks for Networkers: Critical Issues in Cooperative Library Development.* New York: Neal-Schuman Publishers, 1980. A collection of papers from a 1979 conference, this is notable for the variety of practical and pragmatic suggestions on networks.

Martin, Susan, *Library Networks.* White Plains, N.Y.: Knowledge Industry Publications,

[97]Terry Belanger and Stephen Davis, "Rare Book Cataloguing and Computers," *AB Bookman's Weekly,* January 14, 1980, pp. 187–203, and February 5, 1979, pp. 955–966. A detailed discussion of the *Eighteenth Century Short Title Catalogue,* as well as the American imprints program which will be part of the end result.

1980. A descriptive account of networks and implications for individual libraries as well as an explanation of current network practices. An appendix includes a listing of 30 networks in existence at the time of publication. See, too: Richard DeGennaro, "Libraries & Networks in Transition . . . " *Library Journal*, May 15, 1981, pp. 1045–1049.

"Networks." *American Library Association Yearbook*. Chicago: American Library Association, 1976 to date. The annual summary of network activity, often written by Al Trezza, is comprehensive and easy to understand. It is a good place to find an overview of the current network situation.

The Report on Library Cooperation. Chicago: Association of Specialized and Cooperative Library Agencies, 1980. The third edition of this standard work offers a state-by-state report on current library cooperative activities. The editors claim this is "the only single source available for such a broad coverage of current library cooperative activities." It is updated approximately every two years.

Savage, Noel, "Challenges and Pitfalls of Networking Sketched in N.Y.," *Library Journal*, May 1, 1980, pp. 1022–1026. A vivid account of the practical problems of networks, this is a report on a congress on library networking attended by 130 public and academic librarians involved daily in this area.

Thompson, D. M., "The Correct Use of Library Data Bases Can Improve Interlibrary Loan Efficiency," *The Journal of Academic Librarianship*, May 1980, pp. 83–86. The author "shows that proper use of location information in the NUC and OCLC data bases can reduce costs and can dramatically improve interlibrary loan efficiency." Costs and other data are clearly given.

"Understanding the Utilities," *American Libraries*, May 1980. Almost the entire issue is devoted to a description of the major utilities, from OCLC to WLN. Particularly useful for "a utility user's glossary," pp. 264–268.

EVALUATION OF REFERENCE SERVICES

CHAPTER NINE

Methods of Evaluating
Reference Service[1]

T HE METHODS OF EVALUATING REFERENCE SERVICE vary
from the intuitive sense of the librarian that all is well
to the objective statistical analysis of reference works
and how they are used, or not used, by individuals.
Techniques and scope will differ from situation to
situation, but the extent of the evaluation will always
depend upon two factors. The first is the attitude of the staff toward
the evaluation. And the second is the skills, money, and time available
for it.

The evaluation might be undertaken (1) to check the current
status of the service; (2) to discover methods for immediate and
long-range improvement; and, often, (3) to determine the need for
modification of goals and philosophy of service. In practical terms the
analysis may be necessary to justify current budget requests, to
determine requirements for added staff, or to support changes in

[1]While there is still no single text to help the beginner with reference evaluation
problems, there are basic aids which suggest solid beginnings and point the way to
methods useful in evaluation. Aside from articles, see F. W. Lancaster, *The Measurement
and Evaluation of Library Services* (Washington, D.C.: Information Resources Press,
1977). This is the best general guide to evaluation, not only of statistics, but of other
methods touched on throughout this chapter. Another useful guide is M. G. Beeler
(ed.), *Measuring the Quality of Library Service* (Metuchen, N.J.: Scarecrow Press, 1977).
Somewhat dated: Ernest R. DeProspo et al., *Performance Measures for Public Libraries*
(Chicago: American Library Association, 1973). Examination of almost any issue of
Library Research will turn up articles of value in particular aspects of evaluation.

physical surroundings, operation of data bases, or membership in a network.

Most reference librarians are involved with two basic types of evaluative studies. The first, *indirect* evaluation, concerns budget, personnel, and, among other things, the size, age, and value of the reference collection, including all types of materials in and outside the library which may be employed for reference service. The second, *direct* evaluation, concerns the efficiency and effectiveness of the reference service in terms of the individual user.

Ideally, the librarian combines both direct and indirect evaluation in any study; it is, in fact, hard to separate them entirely for the obvious reason that one can hardly answer questions well (direct) without proper resources (indirect).

Lancaster blends the two types in suggesting five points which, included in a survey, will give back data needed for a reasonably accurate estimate of the quality of reference service.

1. The total number of questions received during a specified period.
2. The proportion of these questions the staff makes some attempt to answer.
3. The proportion of the "attempted" questions for which the staff provides an answer.
4. The proportion of the "answered" questions that are answered completely and correctly.
5. The average time it takes to answer a user's question.[2]

In concluding one of the best relatively current surveys of reference evaluation, Charles Bunge observes:

> *The main obstacle to the successful evaluation of library reference services is the inability or unwillingness of reference staff, and especially managers, to assign enough time to it. . . . The planning and execution of an evaluation program requires substantial staff time. When reference librarians speak of the difficulty or impossibility of measuring reference service they are often indicating that they are not convinced that the potential for payoff in improved service is high enough to risk the investment of time that is necessary.*[3]

A tone of pessimism pervades the literature on the subject.

[2]Lancaster, op. cit., p. 74.

[3]Charles A. Bunge, "Approaches to the Evaluation of Library Reference Services," in F. W. Lancaster, *Evaluation and Scientific Management* . . . (Leyden: Nordhoff, 1977), p. 66. This work is an excellent survey and includes reference to over 100 studies, articles, books, etc. It is dated, however, to the mid-1970s.

"Since it is statistically evident that what is now being reported does not provide any useful information . . . " is a typical conclusion in many analyses.[4]

Those who believe in the value of reference evaluation systems would argue that while reference service methods are highly personal and difficult to isolate and measure, the economics of information management forces such evaluations. Administrators, who must justify expenses and service require cost estimates, without which reference work may be curtailed. Others who argue for evaluation will rest their case, not so much on the economic factor, which most believe important, but on the necessity of determining (a) the public served (or not served) by the library, and how service to that public may be improved; (b) the types of materials and resources needed for that particular public—both in numbers and by subject interest; and (c) the type of organizational pattern that will best deliver the maximum service. And there are countless other reasons to justify evaluation.

EVALUATION TECHNIQUES

Before considering specific methods of evaluating reference collections and reference service, a broad overview of standard evaluation techniques must be considered. Presupposing the librarian knows the objective of the evaluation and has a well-constructed, well-thought-out plan of action, he or she may try one of several methods—or all of them in combination:

Interview

As a tool of evaluation, the interview is usually held with the reference librarian and with the users of reference service. Others, of course, can be questioned, from the head librarian to the nonuser. Interviews hold tremendous advantages as an evaluating technique, particularly when the interviewer has training and is able clearly to differentiate fact from fiction, opinion, and bias. The difficulty lies in the possible variables which enter into any interview: the respondent and the interviewer might be at odds; the respondent might be inhibited by the questions asked orally; the respondent might be trying to make a good impression. Still, if handled skillfully, an interview will often reveal information which can be obtained in no other way.

[4]Stella Bentley, "Academic Library Statistics: A Search for a Meaningful Evaluative Tool," *Library Research*, no. 1, 1979, p. 150. The author, though she believes in a statistical approach to evaluation, pleads for more useful data.

The guides to evaluation published by the American Colleges and Research Libraries describe a rather traditional interview methodology:

1. Ask a sampling of students about their ease in obtaining sources.
2. Talk with a sampling of students and faculty to gain insight into their satisfaction with services.
3. Talk with a few staff members at major service points to gain a sense of the public image of the library.[5]

Direct observations

Presupposing the observer has knowledge of what to look for, he or she may sit at a reference desk, or in the vicinity of the desk, and simply watch and listen. This method is often used to double-check information gained from an interview or other methods. For example, the librarian may claim in an interview that he or she always tries to help the user find materials. An observer can soon test the validity of this, particularly if the observer is not the same person who posed the original interview question. The problem with this approach is that an observer is supposed to have rather exact ways of measuring and recording what is seen, but "measurements of human actions introduce problems of definition, of calibration, of accuracy, of control, and of comparability."[6] As a result, observation is normally a partial, not a complete, method of evaluation.

An interesting twist to the methodology of direct observation is the simulation of a system and subsequent observation of its activities. This is possible through the imaginative use of the computer and is similar to other "games" used to evaluate everything from economic theory to armies in conflict to management procedures. Simulation has numerous problems, but if carefully constructed, the model gives us "a chance to experiment, to vary inputs, processing times and methods, the allocation of work, and to see the likely effects of these changes on the whole system. . . ."[7]

Even the simple technique of direct observation can have a wide

[5]"Guide to Methods of Library Evaluation," *College & Research Libraries News,* October 1968, pp. 295–297.

[6]Herbert Goldhor, *An Introduction to Scientific Research in Librarianship* (Urbana, Ill.: University of Illinois, 1972), p. 133.

[7]Pauline A. Thomas, "Who Does the Work? Observing Library Activities," *Aslib Proceedings,* July 1975, p. 294–300.

number of variations. For example, there is the so-called participant-observer technique. An observer, who may or may not be identified as such, joins the staff and carries on regular duties. At the end of the study period, the observer submits a report and specific recommendations.

> *Both the strengths and weaknesses of the participant observer method are exemplified in its intimate nature. The observer becomes personally involved in the very settings he seeks to observe, record and understand. It goes without saying that this produces not only understanding but also bias. However, defenders of the method are quick to point out that other methods of studying social institutions are also subject to bias, usually in more subtle, perhaps insidious, ways. A lot depends upon the observer's ability to extend "empathy" without engaging in "sympathy" to the extent of "taking sides. . . . " This method is best suited to the study of a library which is basically sound to start with and which is receptive to suggestions for making further progress toward already established goals. A library needing more radical assistance might be better served by the more usual survey techniques.[8]*

Sampling

This methodology is the type employed for opinion polls, market research, television popularity, and the like. It consists of taking either a random or a specific sample of the population. While subject to error, the method is useful in sampling various aspects of reference service, such as in an analysis of reference questions.

The maintenance of records on questions asked of the service: how many, how answered, who asked, and the like can be useful and should be done periodically by sampling. But if done too regularly, the chances are that the oppressive paper work will get in the way of the service. A better approach is suggested by intensive analyses every few months. For example, some libraries pick two to three days a month every three or four months, and on those days gather complete information on reference queries. This type of sampling indicates, without interfering with the regular conduct of the reference service, basic trends and, if done in an exhaustive fashion, will show user satisfaction or lack of satisfaction.

The sampling technique is employed, too, for questioning users. The usual procedure is to select blocks of time in a day, week, month, or even year and sample user reaction via a questionnaire.

[8]Perry D. Morrison, "Participant Observation as a Method of Studying Libraries," *PNLA Quarterly,* Summer 1978, pp. 8, 10.

Questionnaires

The construction and interpretation of questionnaires is a study in itself; suffice it to say here that the questionnaire is a favored method of gaining both quantitative and qualitative information about libraries and librarians. There are numerous books and studies of the whole process, books any librarian who is considering this method should read.

The double-check questionnaire is a way of ascertaining how well reference service is given and received. One method is to prepare similar questionnaires for both the user and the librarian and then compare results. For example, in one survey the librarians were asked, "During the question-negotiation process, how well did you pinpoint the patron's needs?" The users were asked, "How well did the reference librarian pinpoint your needs?" (The answer in this case: "84 percent of the patrons felt that the librarian had pinpointed their needs 'very well' . . . However, the librarians felt that they had performed 'very well' in only 69 percent of the cases."[9])

Case studies

The case study is an effort to typify a given situation or problem in terms of an individual or a group of individuals. For example, if the researchers want to discover why X group does not use the reference services, they find one or two people typical of X group and then apply various methods for gathering data, methods which may include everything from questionnaires and interviews to observations and checklists. This approach has rarely been used in library science.

Self-evaluation

This technique is often employed because it is relatively simple and certainly less costly than inviting a thorough survey from outside. Employing several of the methods just outlined, one plan began with obtaining "an exhaustive list of all activities performed by the members of the (reference) staff." This was done by interviewing individuals and then compiling a composite list of services. The staff was then asked to evaluate "the ninety-three activities" by rating them

---

[9]Benita J. Howell et al., "Fleeting Encounters—A Role Analysis of Reference Librarian–Patron Interaction," *RQ*, Winter 1976, p. 127. The survey was conducted at the University of Kentucky, and the questionnaire and methodology are quite good models of their kind.

on a scale. Results were analyzed and conclusions drawn—conclusions about both the future and the reference service itself.[10]

THE LIBRARY SURVEY

The first thing a librarian must establish is who is being served or not being served by the library. After that one narrows the field to specific questions about service at the reference desk. The early chapters considered reference-service audiences. It should be recognized that the community study is basic to any long-range evaluation, and while it is not considered here in detail, that is not to discount its importance.[11]

Community analysis is often part of the library user study or survey. Swanson explains:

> It might seem obvious that, to understand how to improve libraries, one should study how people seek and use information. Indeed, much research is so directed. There is, however, a potential circularity in this philosophy. Information-seeking behavior may be severly limited by the way people perceive existing libraries. To observe such behavior without knowing quite what to look for is unlikely to be productive. If, instead, we use a well-chosen problem to guide our observations, we may be led to see new aspects of man's interaction with the body of knowledge he has created—aspects that stimulate us to invent improved solutions to the problem.[12]

In itself community analysis helps the librarian to break out of "potential circularity." Another method is the library survey which, many believe, must come before the community study, or certainly in cooperation with such a broad view.

There are numerous reasons for having a survey, but it usually represents an effort to describe a situation and make recommendations on how that situation might be improved. The type of data and

---

[10]Edward B. Reeves et al., "Before the Looking Glass: A Method to Obtain Self-Evaluation of Roles in a Library Reference Service," *RQ*, Fall 1977, pp. 25–32.

[11]There is an impressive amount of literature on how to determine community needs, e.g., on how to survey the community served by the library. See, for example, chapters in Lancaster's *The Measurement and Evaluation of Library Services*, op. cit.; Chapter 2 in the author's *Collection Development* (New York: Holt, Rinehart and Winston, 1980); and Chapter 4 in G. Edward Evans, *Developing Library Collections* (Littleton, Colo.: Libraries Unlimited, 1979). All of these sources have extensive bibliographies.

[12]Don Swanson, "Libraries and the Growth of Knowledge," *The Library Quarterly*, January 1979, p. 4.

how the data are manipulated and compared are dependent upon the objectives of the survey; however, quantitative evaluations relating to reference service normally concentrate on (1) the size of the collection, as well as such variables as availability of necessary materials from other libraries, subject and form distribution of titles, age of material counted, acquisitions, weeding, etc.; (2) the size of the staff, as well as such variables as staff experience, subject competency, training, etc. (although note here that "clean data" are apt to be muddled after the count of heads—how, for example, does one evaluate subject competency?); (3) the adequacy of physical facilities such as reading space and space for bibliographies, indexes, etc.; and (4) the size of the budget, an integral consideration in the other three elements. Other countable elements may include the number of questions answered compared with the number not answered. There are, to be sure, almost limitless areas for counting this or that and for gathering statistics.

Once the data are gathered, they tend to be evaluated in terms of (1) general standards, which, while not sufficient for judging reference service in particular, do serve as an overview of a given library; (2) comparative data gathered about libraries of similar purpose, scope, and audience in adjoining areas and states, or even about libraries nationally; (3) the competency and the experience of the evaluator, whose knowledge of such things, supported with data, is sometimes enough.

No survey is simply a mass of data, and the heart of most such studies is the conclusions and the recommendations. These will be both quantitative (X library lacks this or that number of books, librarians, dollars in the budget, etc.) and qualitative (owing to this lack, service in R and S areas is bad or poor). In terms of the qualitative, the survey can also point to how service may be improved by doing this or that; that is, the survey results in recommendations.

Most published surveys and studies in library science—in and out of reference work—can often be evaluated in a cursory fashion by the "author." There is obviously some degree of controversy over the work of even the most accepted researcher, as there is over the titles of the most accepted publisher, but when one sees the names of Nelson Associates, Lowell Martin, Arthur Little, Inc., Guy Garrison, Charles Bunge, Anita Schiller and other individuals and firms on a report, one soon learns to have some trust in the findings.

In these days most attacks upon library problems are launched by survey research teams and organizations which have both training in, and an understanding of, the scientific method and its application to surveys. Some say too much faith is put in these "experts," but, except in the small library or isolated situation, the tendency is to depend upon evaluative surveys from either professionals in the field or individuals particularly trained for such work in related fields, such as education, cybernetics, linguistics, and management.

REFERENCE GUIDELINES, GOALS, AND OBJECTIVES

There is no single measure, method, or set of rules which will help to evaluate reference service. There are several approaches which, when identified and employed, do serve to give the librarian at least a fairly accurate idea of the success or failure of the service.

National guidelines

One of the numerous indicators is a set of national guidelines, "A Commitment to Information Services: Developmental Guidelines."[13] Adopted by the Reference and Adult Services Division of the American Library Association in 1976, and amended in later years, the brief guidelines represent a general set of descriptive rather than quantitative standards.

There is nothing in the "Guidelines" to help determine the number of staff members or books or the size of budget needed for adequate reference service in this or that size library. They do give a conceptual notion of reference service, although certainly not a basic philosophy. The "Guidelines" are unquestionably of value to the local library looking for assistance in drawing up goals and objectives, as well as to the librarian or student looking for an overview of what reference librarians think their service entails. They are purposefully general so as neither to mislead nor to offend; e.g., "Staffing patterns and hours open are to reflect directly the needs of the users." The major difference between the current "Guidelines" and past efforts is that this time around, the committee agreed that the institutional structure of information service is less important than the delivery of services of high quality—which is a plug for networks, cooperation, and a dismissal of parochialism. Most significantly, it is a recognition that the user, not the institution, is of primary importance.

As one might suspect, there is a certain amount of criticism of the "Guidelines." The most apparent is their lack of any prescriptive

---

[13]Published with amendments in *RQ*, Spring 1979, pp. 275–278 (earlier version appeared in *RQ* from 1974). The American Library Association's "Standards for Reference Service in Public Libraries" was published in 1969.

advice. There is some merit to this view, although the people who labored over the "Guidelines" time and time again pointed out the difficulty of prescriptive statistical data. Vavrek summarizes this dilemma:

> There are those who stress that you must have standards by which or against which the evaluation is then conducted. . . . Who says what is standard? The difficulty is not in setting standards. Before long, norms of data will be obtainable. . . . It could be then at these times that RASD, or some other such august group, will be willing to call these data standard—and there may be some merit in this. The important question is, What would be the relevance of reference/information service standards compiled on a national level that attempt to accommodate the needs and requirements of tens of thousands of librarians working in so many different types of library situations? We assume, e.g., that there are only so many different types of libraries, i.e., school, college, university, public, special, etc. We forget, however, that frequently the only thing that public librarians share in common is the fact that they work in the type of library that shares a common name. It is really most unimaginative to assume that a volunteer librarian who toils in the public library in a community of 1,000 population really deals with the same kind of institution as, e.g., would librarians at the Carnegie Library of Pittsburgh or the Philadelphia Free Library. This is not to say, however, that the value of service is any different. It's just that institutions are different. Further, what contingencies would have to be developed in a quest for national standards to accommodate the quilt of library networks, which are all competing for the new librarianship? And what about the roles of machine-assisted reference service, and automated data bases. . . .[14]

Local goals and objectives

Beyond the broad national "Guidelines," many libraries have written policies regarding their goals and objectives. This is in keeping with the "Guidelines," which recommend such things as a "published service code with stated objectives" and "a selection policy." After a few generalities, which often incorporate the introduction to the "Guidelines," the local statement tends to ground itself in daily routines—again missing the point about having a broad philosophy of

[14]Bernard Vavrek, "Reference Evaluation—What the Guidelines Don't Indicate," *RQ*, Summer 1979, p. 336. See, too, his article on the same subject, "Bless You Samuel Green," *Library Journal*, April 15, 1976, pp. 971–974. Vavrek is one of the more articulate and certainly one of the fairest critics of the "Guidelines."

service. Ideally, the library should have a written policy statement which would incorporate certain basic considerations

1. There should be a statement of purpose, which includes goals and objectives—not only of the reference process but of the library (and the system) as a whole.
   a. The goals and objectives must be discussed in terms of the reality of budget, political process, staff, space, etc.
   b. More important, the goals must be understood by all; i.e., the librarian should be able to explain the purpose of the proposals, and if the "why" is neither practical nor logical, the goals should be reexamined.
2. There should be a statement defining the broad strategy which will be followed to reach the goals and objectives.
3. There should be a thorough analysis of "time present," i.e., precisely what is going on at the present time in the reference process.
4. There should be a plan, with due consideration of cost, personnel, overall library goals, etc., to change "time present" activities to "time future" activities in keeping with considerations 1 and 2.
5. Finally, there should be periodic evaluation of the movement(s) toward "time future." And in the light of the evaluation, the general and the specific strategies should be modified or even dropped in favor of new approaches.

The statement of purpose includes all the other points, and by now most libraries have developed written statements of goals and objectives. However, few of these statements "are specific in either the language or the levels of the goals . . . the librarians tend to establish goals only for the organization as a whole; few of the institutions had developed objectives for individual departments."[15]

It should not be suggested that libraries are rudderless in the sea of service. Many have effective, realistic, and operational goals, which reflect considerable thought about the philosophy or the purpose of the library in the community. One of the better models (if only in the area of collection development) for an academic library, and suitable in a slightly modified form for other types of libraries, is suggested by

[15]Gail Schlacter and Donna Belli, "Program Evaluation—An Alternative to Divine Guidance," *California Librarian,* October 1976, p. 27. The survey is of 122 California libraries, but findings are similar almost everywhere.

Coleman and Dickinson, who give very specific statements about the basic points just discussed.[16]

Lack of expressed objectives is sometimes counterbalanced by an undue interest in evaluation of service. "Undue" is used advisedly because even here there tends to be more lip service than action, and without goals firmly in mind, it is difficult to evaluate reference service. Evaluation for evaluation's sake takes the form of meaningless statistical records, such as how many reference questions were asked, how many librarians were on duty, how much material from periodicals was photocopied, etc. Each of these questions, if set in the framework of a valid study, has a useful purpose; however, too often the statistics are tabulated and services remain unchanged.

EVALUATION OF REFERENCE SOURCES

How good is the library reference collection? This is a question which librarians must continue to raise and to answer because the collection is in a constant state of change. What may be adequate one year may be less than desirable the next year.

There are several primary questions to be answered: (1) What is the optimum size of the collection for the particular library? (2) What type of materials should it contain, e.g., should there be more emphasis on science than social science? (3) What are the cost considerations?

There are additional factors to be weighed, such as: (1) Who is going to use the collection, and will even the largest (or smallest) collection be suitable? (2) If X type of material is required this year, will the users change and will Y type be necessary the next year? (3) What resources are available from nearby libraries, and how much service can be improved via interlibrary loan and use of data bases? (4) If the budget must be cut, should X or Y be given more consideration?

Then, too, there are related matters: Who is going to make the selection? What is the best physical arrangement? Here, it should be noted, arrangement is not considered. It is assumed that the selection is made by reference librarians, although always in consultation with those served, from the public to faculty to administrators. The question of user satisfaction is taken up later.

[16]Kathleen Coleman and Pauline Dickinson, "Drafting a Reference Collection Policy," *College & Research Libraries,* May 1977, pp. 227–233. For a collection of reference service policies and procedures, including online practices, see the author's *Reference and Online Services Handbook* in the "Suggested Reading" section of this chapter.

Number and type

As answering reference questions may involve the resources of the whole library, and, for that matter, libraries and collections else-where, it is difficult to zero in on the precise type of materials to be evaluated. Normally, one concentrates on reference books per se, those which are dutifully marked as such and are listed in annotated standard guides such as Sheehy's *Guide to Reference Books,* as well as categorized and reviewed by such services as *Library Journal* or *Choice.* Beyond that, the librarian will want to evaluate the serials collections (an obvious and integrated part of the indexes and abstracting services); the governnment documents and how they are treated; and, in more and more cases, the number and type of data bases used directly or indirectly for reference service. One should consider the collection as a whole, as well as its parts, from videocasettes to pamphlets.

Experience indicates some shortcuts. In almost any survey of holdings it has been found that the reference book collection, or, for that matter, tested subject sections in that collection, which meets standards for both retrospective and current holdings, accurately reflects the quality of the library as a whole. That is to say, if the reference book collection, or a representative part of it, is good, the library upon which the reference librarian must draw is likely to be equally good. There are times when this test fails, as in a library where the rest of the staff is not of the caliber of the reference librarians, but this is unusual and unlikely.

The next consideration concerns the number of reference books one should have in a basic collection, the number to be added each year, the number to be weeded, the number of dollars necessary for acquisitions, and so forth. Ideally, one would have the space, money, and time to acquire everything needed, as well as materials on the periphery of need, but this is rarely the case. So some indication of numbers should be useful, some quantitative guide helpful.

Unfortunately—some would say fortunately—no such national or even regional standards or figures exist. Indication of the optimum size of a collection within a library involves so many variables than an attempt to set a standard would be meaningless. When all is said and done, one may give negative answers to some questions: (1) Is there an ideal size for any given type of library? No. (2) Can one work out a ratio between size of the reference collection and of the rest of the collection? No. (3) Can one develop a useful figure by working out a ratio of the number of librarians and the number of potential users? No. (4) Can one determine the size of the collection by applying any other statistical or formulary methods? No. (5) Is there a correlation between the size of the collection and the degree of successful reference performance? Yes and No. It depends who does the study.[17]

It should be emphasized that the negatives apply in national or regional situations. It is apparent that for a single library one or all of the four procedures may be of value; i.e., one may arbitrarily say a collection of 3000 reference books is ideal and, then, via experience and over the years modify up or down depending on other factors.

Size guidelines

There are some rough guidelines to indicate at least the minimum/maximum aspect of size.

Generally the pragmatic test is simplicity itself: Does this library have the right material to answer the reference questions asked here? If the majority of questions are answered, quickly and correctly, by the collection then it is the optimum size. Simple observation and experience give the key to this evaluation exercise. But there are some equally practical modifying considerations.

(1) Where a book[18] or other source must be borrowed, or, more likely, where a librarian must call another library for information from a book not in the library, then consideration should be given to purchase. Where the source is needed more than twice in a single month, the work should be purchased—if, of course, funds are available.

(2) Where the users who do not consult with the reference librarians cannot find what is needed, then consideration should be given to more purchases of single titles or groups of titles in a subject area. Here, of course, one must count upon interviews, questionnaires, and observations to give the answer to the frustration. A simplified technique, which helps at the same time to establish contact

---

[17]Ronald R. Powell, "An Investigation of the Relationships Between Quantifiable Reference Service Variables and Reference Performance in Public Libraries," *The Library Quarterly,* January 1978, pp. 1–19. Powell did find a definite correlation between size and quality, but others have not—and these he nobly cites and quotes. The variables are too numerous to make any definite decision, although Powell does go a long way to show that size of a collection is important. The assumption that the larger the collection (not just in reference works, but all materials in the library), the better the library, is a much debated one. For details and examples of numerous studies in this area of quality/size, see Lancaster, op. cit., pp. 165–172.

[18]Here and throughout this section "book" is used as a keyword for all types of reference materials.

between librarian and user, is to ask people periodically if they are finding what they want.

(3) At one time various standards, now outdated, did at least stab at figures for the ideal size of a collection. One of the more typical, a British standard, but still applicable in a general way, stated that there should be 200 volumes per 1000 population served.[19]

(4) Large research libraries rely on such standard works as *Guide to Reference Books* and/or *Guide to Reference Material*, yet have considerably more than the 10,000 to 15,000 titles described in these titles. Smaller libraries, conversely, may have even fewer reference works than the 1046 carefully chosen for the third edition of *Reference Books for Small and Medium Sized Libraries*. Both large and small libraries keep their collections updated and growing in size by current purchases. Here one may rely on reviews from *Choice* (about 500 reference titles considered each year), *Library Journal* (about 400 titles), and more specialized works. Then, too, there is the *American Reference Books Annual*, which annotates about 1500 to 1800 publications.

(5) Various studies indicate different sized collections are "best" and "better." For example, Powell discovered: "Reference librarians had to have access to collections of at least 800 volumes before they were generally able to answer 50 percent or more of the questions correctly. Similarly, the data indicated that reference collections of at least 1,080 volumes were necessary for 70 percent or more correct answers . . . while the participants needed access to 2,463 volumes to answer 70 percent or more of the questions."[20]

By now it should be apparent that the numbers game with reference titles is more of an educated gamble than a statistically accurate measure. The number of variables make it meaningless and help to explain the reluctance of individuals, committees, or even the American Library Association to assign numbers in the evaluative process.

Instrinsic quality

Throughout the first volume of this text various rules and suggestions have been given as to how to evaluate reference books in general and

---

[19]"Standards for Reference Services in Public Libraries," *Library Association Record*, no. 2, 1970, pp. 53–57. *The Minimum Standards for Public Library Systems* (Chicago: American Library Association, 1967) are not as explicit and simply call for a "broad" range of reference titles.

[20]Powell, op. cit., p. 6.

those categorized by form. In evaluating a reference collection, this type of judgment is most important.

Mechanically the evaluation of a collection by quality may be done in several ways. Three of the more tested procedures include:

(1) Isolating a representative list of *retrospective titles* and checking to see if these are in the library. The list is considered statistically representative of a fair sampling for large libraries when chosen from a random sampling of titles in *Guide to Reference Books,* or for smaller libraries when chosen from titles in *Reference Books for Small and Medium Sized Libraries.* In the former case, a list of about 450 to 500 titles would be available, while in the latter situation, the list would be no more than 100 titles. The library with a majority of these titles is likely to have a good collection.[21]

(2) Isolating two or three *subject areas,* particularly those areas of most interest to people who use the collection, and checking availability of representative titles is a more accurate approach. In this case, a list of titles taken from the same sources cited above would include titles in the subject area. A similar technique is applicable when one turns to even more specialized bibliographies such as *Sources of Information in the Social Sciences.*

Added precision is possible as one draws the subject area into smaller and smaller circles. For example, one may quickly and accurately check the respective quality of travel guides for Asia; whereas the process is more involved, if only in terms of quantity, when one turns to evaluating the reference collection in terms of cultural and social reference works for Asia.

(3) Isolating titles, again using lists, to check the *currency of the collection.* Here one might take representative sampling from (a) *American Reference Books Annual* for the past year; (b) the list of outstanding reference books which appears in *Library Journal,* among other places, in April; (c) a list of titles in the six or seven library journals (or specialized subject journals) for the past six months; and/or (d) a list of titles from almost any source which reviews or

---

[21]Sampling methodology does require a given amount of statistical sophistication, particularly as the method is not always accurate. A representative sampling may be about 5 to 10 percent. Before such a sampling is undertaken the librarian should (1) contact a statistician for advice, and/or (2) read in the field. In the latter situation one may suggest numerous reported studies which are listed in *Library Literature, ERIC,* etc. For a clear explanation of sampling, see Chapter 2 of Ray L. Carpenter and Ellen Vasu, *Statistical Methods for Librarians* (Chicago: American Library Association, 1978). Another useful aid: American Library Association, *Library Data Collection Handbook* (Chicago: American Library Association, 1981) which outlines a system for data collection in all types of libraries.

lists current works. Again, a library having a majority of these, given modifications of subject interest, would be in fairly good condition.

The hidden assumption in using lists is that the list represents the best judgment of reliable experts. This is usually the case, at least in the reference situation, where the librarian can easily become acquainted with the basic guides and bibliographies.

But the list may not represent the particular needs of the community served by the library, and there is the catch. This is obvious and will not be labored here, but one example will suffice. The library may have a fine collection of reference works in philosophy and religion, works dutifully listed in all standard guides. The problem is that no one reads those books in that community and/or (in the case of a school or academic library) neither area is taught. Even where there is demand for such titles, it is possible that everyone in the library circle served is Catholic or atheist, reads only Arabic or Spanish, or has a wild desire for general titles, but not for reference books.

The librarian should at all times consider the fact that the library may have titles not found in standard bibliographies, possibly because the local library collection is superior to, or at least different from, the national average. It may, for example, have numerous retrospective titles no longer in print, valuable works not normally listed in bibliographies.

Where the library does have numerous titles in a subject area not found in retrospective or current lists, then the librarian should examine the titles closely. They may be quite superior—but then again they may be dated, little used, and badly in need of weeding.

Comparison is another often-used technique. One checks to see what other libraries have in the subject area. Where there is a high percentage of relative frequency of the same titles, the chances are good that the holdings are adequate. Comparisons are now easily done via computer.[22]

EVALUATION OF REFERENCE SERVICE

Methods

Once it is determined the collection is adequate in approximate size and quality, the real question becomes: How well does the collection

[22]David A. Kronick and Virginia Bowden, "Management Data for Collection Analysis and Development," *Bulletin of the Medical Library Association,* October 1978, pp. 407–413.

serve the needs of the users? Recalling that the whole library is the "reference collection," but limiting the test to books (if only for purposes of example), there are several methods often employed.

(1) Librarians keep records for a period of two or three days, once a month, or every three or four months, on what questions are asked and where answers are found—or not found. The use sample will soon point out, at least in a rough fashion, any inadequacies in the collection.

(2) A more sophisticated method is, having obtained such records, to interview a random group of people to find out whether the sources (i.e., answers) given were adequate. This sould tell the librarian rather obvious things about the quality and shape of the collection that might not be measured simply by a sampling of questions and answers.

(3) Either of these methods, or a combination, will help considerably in determining what books should be weeded each year, which titles are simply not used. As a guarantee against error, any weeding operation should consider what books, about to be dropped for lack of use, are available in other libraries for the use of the person who inevitably needs them the minute they are removed.

Most of the optimistic findings on reference service are based on little more than the average person's expectations that the library is there and they are at least able to find a book or a magazine they need from time to time. Questioned further, the high praise is likely to diminish. This suggests that one cannot measure the success of reference service by simply counting who comes into the library, how many queries are asked, or how pleased one appears to be with the answer.[23] More is needed. The real questions are "Did the user really receive an accurate and full reply to the question put to the librarian?" and "Why did the user come to the library for assistance?"

Evaluating the librarian

The opinion that some 50 percent or more of reference queries are answered neither well nor correctly is an assumption some librarians hold as a truism. Here, for example, is a too-typical situation: A

---

[23]Unfortunately, this type of statistic (a record of questions asked, sometimes by type, paralleled by a record of answers) is the one most commonly employed. It may be faulted for many reasons, not the least of which is the fact that librarians, being human, claim satisfactory answers for 90 percent or more of the queries. For an objective approach, see Joyce A. Edinger and Steve Falk, "Statistical Sampling of Reference Desk Inquiries," *RQ*, Spring 1981, pp. 265–268.

professional librarian, when asked for books in a certain subject area (and given the reader's needs) cheerfully responded with four titles. The caller was impressed "and asked on what basis his respondent had made her rapid decision." She answered that the four titles were all the library had in the catalog under the appropriate subject entry. The librarian, of course, had won an A-plus for courtesy and response, but flunked totally in the interview.[24]

The correct answer success rate will vary from a low of 15 percent to a high of 85 percent, with most librarians hovering around the 50 percent level. One should quickly add that few of the studies reveal whether or not a reference librarian was asked the test question, or whether it was put to a nonreference librarian, or simply to a clerk on duty at the time. And there are other problems involved which some claim would reduce the number of wrong answers.

Procedures vary, but the method of evaluating personnel and their handling of questions is rather straightforward. The researchers construct a list of "typical" reference questions and then evaluate the reference service on how well the librarians give the answers. There are numerous variables involved, from the type and depth of questions themselves to the education and experience of the librarians who offer the answers. Still, this technique is one of the most useful in that it gets down to the "nitty-gritty" of reference work, and, where used carefully, at least suggests the qualitative level of service given. Some examples of this method will be found in the work of Terrence Crowley and Thomas Childers.[25]

Other examples of this method produced the following results:

(1) In a 1974–75 study of California public libraries of all types and sizes, surveyors asked "a telephone reference question which could be answered by a simple factual response."[26] Of the 20 libraries

[24]John P. Wilkinson and William Miller, "The Step Approach to Reference Services," *RQ*, Summer 1978, p. 293. The problem here, as with other studies is this section, concerns the methodology employed and questions whether professional librarians were always the ones queried. Those who challenge such findings may rightfully claim to be somewhat less than pleased with the methodology of some, but not all, studies.

[25]Thomas Childers, "The Test of Reference," *Library Journal*, April 15, 1980, pp. 924–928. This updates the original study, but the findings are equally dismal. Some 57 librarians were asked (by phone and by visit) several related, relatively easy questions. The results: 56 percent of the time an answer was given, 84 percent of those answers were correct or mostly correct, but "if we were to count nonanswers as wrong . . . about half the time the libraries delivered" the wrong answer. The original study is in Terence Crowley, *Information Service in Public Libraries* (Metuchen, N.J.: Scarecrow Press, 1971).

[26]*California Public Library Systems: A Comprehensive Review with Guidelines for the Next Decade* (Los Angeles, Calif.: Peat, Marwick, Mitchell & Co., June 1975) p. 5.

called, 8 gave a correct aswer, 10 did not answer, and 2 gave a wrong answer.

The same process was tried again, this time with the surveyor actually going to the reference desk and asking "involved questions which could be answered in many different ways, and in almost infinitely varying depth."[27] The result: six of the 19 librarians showed some command of the problem; six others gave a partial but inadequate answer; seven gave a completely inadequate response.

There were many variables—some libraries were members of systems, others were not; some librarians were better trained than others, etc. Nevertheless, the surveyors concluded:

> *Overall, the performance of the libraries was surprisingly poor. . . . The failure of library staff members to perform well was a frequent reason for the poor performance. . . . It would be unrealistic to assume that large numbers of persons will seek to meet their information needs where the expectation of success is no higher than it proved to be in most of the libraries in the test.*[28]

(2) "If you ask the same question of two different reference librarians, do you receive the same answer?" Selecting a question with which most "librarians feel happy," the surveyor found:

> *Twelve libraries out the of the twenty in which the question was put were able to produce no information at all. Six libraries produced some information, and two were able to trace most or all of the information.*

Although this was a study of British public library service in a limited area, the results are familiar to American surveyors. The author concludes with a nod of understanding: "We are conscious of the fact that we have not so far considered the manner and attitude of the enquirer, and the amount of information he gives before the search, which clearly affects the outcome of the encounter."[29]

Much the same success/failure ratio has been found in numer-

---

[27]Ibid., pp. 5–7.

[28]Ibid., pp. 5–12, 14. Various questions were asked over the telephone, but a typical one was "Could you give me the address of the Canadian Chiropractic Association?" (Seven questions are in appendix E-12). The question asked in person was "I am interested in learning about the employment patterns of immigrants in the State of California in relation to their cultural and educational beckgrounds, and their residence. Also, how well have immigrants fared as a whole in relation to the California job market?"

[29]David E. House, "Reference Efficiency or Reference Deficiency," *Library Association Record,* November 1974, pp. 223–224. The question was "Please give me all available information on David Shepherd." The artist is widely known for his African wildlife paintings.

ous library surveys conducted by Lowell Martin, Charles Bunge, and others. Anyone wishing to try the technique at a local level should consult these studies, although the methods, as indicated, are fairly simple.[30]

A good example of such a study is the one of 51 public libraries conducted by Powell. His results fairly well support the findings of others and are worth repeating as a summary: (1) About 60 percent of the reference questions were answered correctly, but the range was from 20 to 96 percent, and the conclusion is that the larger the library budget, the better the reference performance. (2) When tested against materials available in the library, it was found that 78 percent of the questions could have been answered—whereas an average of only 60 percent were answered.[31]

Academic libraries do no better. In a test conducted in the southeastern part of the country, it was found that, in reference situations, "fact type queries asked via telephone were answered correctly about 50 percent of the time." In a follow-up questionnaire it was noted that few librarians were concerned with measuring "the accuracy of response to fact type queries."[32]

Some evaluation of the effectiveness of the answer is done by the librarians themselves. This is a legitimate method of determining not only the value of the service, but of checking on the need for certain types of reference materials. Such continuous efforts as these and periodical samplings, by far the best method of evaluation, contrast sharply with the less effective one-shot-study approaches.

> *For example, in a survey of the telephone reference service at the Madison (Wisconsin) Public Library the librarians answering the questions recorded for each question whether it was answered completely, partially, or not at all. Murfin, in a master's thesis, observed reference service at a university library for a total of 45 hours. In addition to recording verbatim each question and relevant interaction between the librarian and the user, she asked the librarian her assessment of success in answering each question.*[33]

There is an objection raised to a survey such as this: "A number

[30]For a discussion of other surveys and studies in this area, as well as techniques, see Bunge, op. cit., pp. 54–58, and Lancaster, op. cit., pp. 79–109.

[31]Powell, op. cit., p. 7.

[32]Thelma Freides, "Report from Dallas: The RASD Program," *RQ,* Winter 1979, p. 132.

[33]Bunge, op. cit., p. 52. As Bunge observes, "the weaknesses of the librarian as a source of data on reference success are obvious. Unless the librarian can take time for careful followup with the user, it is impossible to know" if the answer was correct.

of librarians feel that it is unfair and misleading to make judgments about the performance levels . . . on the basis of so few transactions. . . . Inevitably, there were those who were unhappy about the content of the particular questions used."[34] The objection may be valid for a single study, but the results are too persistent to make this a serious question. Too many studies find the same thing: too many reference librarians are unable or unwilling to answer questions correctly or fully.

Cost

How much does it cost to answer a reference question, even, one may add, when the answer is incomplete or wrong?

Some discussion of this will be found in relation to data bases. In the daily activity of the average library, however, there is little available material on costs involved.[35] The lack of interest is due as much to the difficulty of compiling and analyzing such transactions as to an unwillingness on the part of many reference librarians to be treated as an item which may be measured in terms of cost effectiveness—some call it accountability. Still, some measure of cost is advisable, particularly when (1) consideration is given to new technologies, and methods must be found to figure the cost of manual and automatic data retrieval; and (2) consideration must be given to local budgetary concerns.

The same problem exists when one considers how much of the library budget should be set aside for the reference collection. This is another exercise in futility, at least at the national level. For example, one might say a minimum of 260 new titles should be purchased each year at an average cost of (what?) per volume. Well, book prices are somewhat ahead of the consumer price index, but by 1980 they averaged close to $30 per volume, with reference books even higher. But at the $30 figure times 260, the budget allocation for reference books alone in a minimum situation is $7800. As there are only about 2300 public libraries with book funds over $10,000 and half of these have less than $25,000, one may readily see that the $7800 figure

---

[34]*Newsletter of Library Research,* no. 17, September 1976, p. 10.

[35]For a discussion of cost models see Lancaster, op. cit., and the *Annual Review of Information and Science Technology* (Washington, D.C.: American Society for Information Science, 1965 to date) which includes one or more articles on the subject in almost every annual volume. *Library Literature,* too, carries countless articles. The problem, as Vavrek notes, is that too much of this material relates either to library costs in general or to computerized services. Though the articles are applicable, they do not describe how to figure specific reference costs.

(even for a single year) is too high, at least for the average medium-sized library. Conversely, it is much too low for a medium-sized to large research library.

In larger libraries where hundreds of thousands or even millions of dollars are available for materials there is another situation. Here the primary concern is with how to allocate the funds. No satisfactory method has been achieved, although there are some excellent guesses and general guidelines.[36] In a general way many libraries use the 60/40 formula; that is, 40 percent of the budget goes to the library for reference and general works, while the other 60 percent is divided among subjects, departments, and area interests.

The introduction of new technologies threatens to upset even the best-constructed reference budgets. Where, for example, is the library to find the money for online services? How much of the budget should be allocated to such services? Should the costs be charged to reference section, to the academic departments, to what part of the budget? Should one charge for the service? And so on.

And . . .

Collection size and development, user studies, and user satisfaction—these are the primary concerns, but they hardly exhaust the possible areas of research and evaluation in reference services. Related areas concern such matters as the relevancy of the material retrieved for the user; the staff (who, after all, makes the best type of reference librarian or administrator?); access, free or closed, to reference titles; types of materials in the reference and in the general collection; titles duplicated for different sections; and the influence of technology in the selection of reference materials.[37]

Still, after all is measured and evaluated, the primary purpose of reference service is always to answer questions. It is extremely

[36]There are numerous articles on budgets for various types of libraries. A good summary, applicable for other types of libraries, is found in Murray Martin, *Budgetary Control in Academic Libraries* (Greenwich, Conn.: JAI Press, 1978). See Gary Sampson, "Allocating the Book Budget: Measuring for Inflation," *College & Research Libraries,* September 1978, pp. 381–383. The allocation problem, deciding even the basic question of allocation by line or by program, continues to bother librarians and there are no absolute solutions in view. There is need for an objective scientific approach, e.g., see Jasper G. Schad, "Allocating Materials Budgets . . . ," *The Journal of Academic Librarianship,* January 1978, pp. 328–332, and various issues of *Collection Management* where this is a constant topic.

[37]These and numerous other related questions (unfortunately not with answers) are raised by Elizabeth Silvester, "Reference Collection Development in Academic Libraries," *Expression,* Autumn 1977, pp. 7–10. See also the Bunge article, op. cit.

important that the purpose never be lost, that no matter what type of evaluative measures are employed the final result will be better service for more people.

SUGGESTED READING

Chen, Ching-Chih (ed.), *Quantitative Measurement and Dynamic Library Service.* Phoenix, Ariz.: Oryx Press, 1980. A compilation of proceedings, but so edited that the reader is given an outline of techniques and tools for the application of statistical analysis to evaluation. Prepared for the nonexpert.

Chwe, Steven, "A Model Instrument for User-Rating of Library Service," *California Librarian,* April 1978, pp. 46–55. A clear study of the use of a model to achieve more exact answers in a questionnaire testing user reaction to library service. The questionnaire is included, and could be modified nicely for reference evaluation.

Childers, Thomas, "Statistics That Describe Libraries and Library Service," in Melvin Voigt (ed.), *Advances in Librarianship.* New York: Academic Press, 1975, pp. 107–122. Virtually a monograph on statistical method and its application in libraries. Note the detailed bibliography. While a bit dated, both the article and the bibliography may serve as an excellent base for any study of statistics and reference evaluation.

Cook, Sybilla, "The Delphi Connection," *Wilson Library Bulletin,* May 1978, pp. 703–706. A clear description of a simplified procedure to test the opinion of the community. Particularly useful as the size of the sample is limited.

DuMont, Rosemary, "A Conceptual Basis for Library Effectiveness," *College & Research Libraries,* March 1980, pp. 103–111. The author summarizes the multiple criteria by which a library may be evaluated. Much of the information may be applied to reference service.

Exon, Andy, "Getting to Know the User Better," *Aslib Proceedings,* October-November 1978, pp. 352–364. A detailed analysis of the user study, a classic method of evaluation of reference service. The author asks the question, "How does one set about doing a user study?" and gives the answer.

Goldhor, Herbert, "Community Analysis for the Public Library," *Illinois Libraries,* April 1980, pp. 296–302. One of the leaders in evaluative methods, and certainly one of the easiest to follow, Goldhor presents basic procedures for community analysis. One of the best articles for a beginning student. See, too: George D'Elia, "The Development and Testing of a Conceptual Model of Public Library User Behavior," *The Library Quarterly,* October 1980, pp. 410–430.

Harter, Stephen, and Mary Fields, "Circulation, Reference, and the Evaluation of Public Library Service," *RQ,* Winter 1978, pp. 147–152. A mathematical model is suggested for the gathering and the use of reference statistics and an obvious example is used. The statistical technique is carefully explained.

Hilton, Robert, "Performance Evaluation of Library Personnel," *Special Libraries,* November 1978, pp. 429–434. The author lists a number of "fairly well accepted principles" used in the evaluation of personnel. If nothing else, the article will give the beginning librarian a notion of how the employer is likely to evaluate work. See too: John Ellison and Deborah Lazeration, "Personnel Accountability

Form for Academic Reference Librarians," *RQ,* Winter 1976, pp. 142–148, which is much more specific and spells out what one might expect from a good reference librarian.

Howard, Edward N., and Darlene M. Norman, "Measuring Public Library Performance," *Library Journal,* February 1, 1981, pp. 305–308. The authors offer an easy-to-understad list of checkpoints for evaluation, many of which are applicable to reference services.

Katz, Bill, and Anne Clifford, *Reference and Online Services Handbook.* New York: Neal Schuman, 1982. A collection of reference and information policy statements of academic, public, and some special libraries. Includes online statements and an introduction which points out the advantages of such policies.

King, Donald W. (ed.), *Key Papers in the Design and Evaluation of Information Systems.* White Plains, N.Y.: Knowledge Industry Publications, 1978. A collection of 26 articles, including the "classics" in the field of evaluation method, e.g., C. W. Cleverdon, F. W. Lancaster, Richard Orr, and Rowena Swanson, to mention only four. The cutoff date is the early 1970s with a few later pieces. The editor also provides a useful bibliography of studies. About one-half of the collection is applicable to reference service evaluation. The remainder tends to be too technical.

Lowrey, Anna, and Robert N. Case, "Measuring Program Effectiveness," *Drexel Library Quarterly,* no. 4, 1979, pp. 12–23. A justification and "how-to" outline for evaluation of school media programs. The clear style of the article makes it a good overall outline of the evaluation process. A related article is Janet Stroud, "Evaluation Tools for Practitioners," *Audiovisual Instruction,* November 1978, pp. 17–18.

Mason, Ellsworth (ed.), "Library Consultants," *Library Trends,* Winter 1980. Nine articles on the role of the consultant in evaluation of various aspects of library service, from buildings to staff development to networks.

Moulton, Bethe "Marketing and Library Cooperation," *Wilson Library Bulletin,* January 1981, pp. 347–352. Practical steps in the approach to planning for library cooperative systems. It presents a clear method of determining such things as who uses the library and how to better meet the needs of these users.

Orna, Elizabeth, and Geoffrey Hall, "Developing an Information Policy," *Aslib Proceedings,* January 1981, pp. 15–22. A well-organized and detailed explanation of why information policies are necessary in libraries. See preceding Katz entry for samples of such policy statements.

Schmidt, Janine, "Reference Performance in College Libraries," *Australian Academic & Research Libraries,* June 1980, pp. 87–95. Childers' experiment (see page 275 of this text) is applied here to three colleges in Sydney, Australia. Only about 50 percent of the 10 questions asked were answered correctly. A useful article for the methodology and the brief examination of evaluative processes, often by American writers.

Strong, Gary, "Evaluating the Reference Product," *RQ,* Summer 1980, pp. 367–372. Various methods of checking user satisfaction with reference service are suggested, primarily from the point of view of the administration. It is based on experience at the Washington State Library.

INDEX